The Vision of Richard Weaver

The Library of Conservative Thought

America's British Culture, by Russell Kirk
Authority and the Liberal Tradition, by Robert Heineman
A Better Guide than Reason, by M.E. Bradford
Burke Street, by George Scott-Moncrieff
The Case for Conservatism, by Francis Graham Wilson
Character and Culture, by Irving Babbitt
*Collected Letters of John Randolph of Roanoke to
John Brockenbrough, 1812-1833*, edited by Kenneth Shorey
A Critical Examination of Socialism, by William Hurrell Mallock
Edmund Burke: Appraisals and Applications,
edited by Daniel E. Ritchie
Edmund Burke: The Enlightenment and Revolution, by Peter J. Stanlis
The Essential Calhoun, by John C. Calhoun
Foundations of Political Science, by John W. Burgess
The God of the Machine, by Isabel Patterson
A Historian and His World, A Life of Christopher Dawson 1889-1970,
by Christina Scott
Historical Consciousness, by John Lukacs
I Chose Freedom, by Victor A. Kravchenko
I Chose Justice, by Victor A. Kravchenko
Irving Babbitt, Literature, and the Democratic Culture, by Milton Hindus
The Jewish East Side, edited by Milton Hindus
The Moral Foundations of Civil Society, by Wilhelm Roepke
Natural Law, by Alexander Passerin d'Entréves
On Divorce, by Louis de Bonald
Orestes Brownson: Selected Political Essays, edited by Russell Kirk
The Phantom Public, by Walter Lippmann
*The Politics of the Center, Juste Milieu in Theory and Practice, France and England,
1815-1848*, by Vincent E. Starzinger
Regionalism and Nationalism in the United States, by Donald Davidson
The Social Crisis of Our Time, by Wilhelm Roepke
Tensions of Order and Freedom, by Béla Menczer
The Vision of Richard Weaver, edited by Joseph Scotchie
We the People, by Forrest McDonald

EDITED BY
Joseph Scotchie

THE VISION OF RICHARD WEAVER

Transaction Publishers
New Brunswick (U.S.A.) and London (U.K.)

Second printing 1996
Copyright © 1995 by Transaction Publishers, New Brunswick, New Jersey 08903

All rights reserved under International and Pan-American Copyright Conventions. No part of this book may be reproduced or transmitted in any form or by any means, electronic or mechanical, including photocopy, recording, or any information storage and retrieval system, without prior permission in writing from the publisher. All inquiries should be addressed to Transaction Publishers, Rutgers—The State University, New Brunswick, New Jersey 08903.

This book is printed on acid-free paper that meets the American National Standard for Permanence of Paper for Printed Library Materials.

Library of Congress Catalog Number: 95-3273
ISBN: 1-56000-212-3
Printed in the United States of America

Library of Congress Cataloging-in-Publication Data

The vision of Richard Weaver / edited by Joseph Scotchie.
    p. cm. — (The Library of conservative thought)
    Includes bibliographical references and index.
    ISBN 1-56000-212-3 (cloth : acid-free paper)
    1. Weaver, Richard M., 1910-1963. 2. American literature—Southern States—History and criticism—Theory, etc. 3. Libertarianism—United States—History—20th century. 4. Conservatism—United States—History—20th century. 5. United States—Intellectual life—20th century. 6. Criticism—United States—History—20th century. 7. Rhetoric—Philosophy. I. Scotchie, Joseph, 1956- . II. Series.
PS29.W43V57 1995
814'.54—dc20   95-3273
                                                                                            CIP

To Anna, with love.

Contents

Acknowledgments	ix
Introduction: From Weaverville to Posterity *Joseph Scotchie*	1
Prologue: Up from Liberalism *Richard M. Weaver*	19
Richard Malcolm Weaver Chronology	37

Part I: Studies of Individual Works

1.	The Vision of Richard Weaver *Donald Davidson*	41
2.	Southern Thought and National Materialism *Calvin S. Brown*	53
3.	Richard M. Weaver and the Metaphysics of Property *Ralph T. Ancil*	61
4.	The Mind of Richard Weaver *Eliseo Vivas*	77
5.	The South Wisely Perceived *Allan C. Brownfeld*	85

Part II: The Rhetor

6.	Richard M. Weaver on the Nature of Rhetoric: An Interpretation *Richard L. Johannesen, Rennard Strickland, and Ralph T. Eubanks*	93
7.	Dialectic Rhetorician *Bruce A. White*	111
8.	Rhetoric and the Tyrannizing Image *John Bliese*	119

Part III: The Southern Conservative

9. The Agrarianism of Richard Weaver: Beginnings and Completions — 133
   M. E. Bradford
10. A Southern Agrarian at the University of Chicago — 145
    Henry Regnery
11. The Conservativism of Affirmation — 163
    John P. East

Part IV: Final Thoughts: Weaver in Our Time

12. Stranger in Paradise — 193
    Chilton Williamson, Jr.
13. Looking Before and After — 197
    Marion Montgomery
14. Is the Battle Over...Or Has It Just Begun? The Southern Tradition Twenty Years After Richard Weaver — 207
    Thomas Landess

    Selected Bibliography — 225
    About the Contributors — 231
    Index — 235

Acknowledgments

The editor wishes to acknowledge the support and encouragement given by the late Russell Kirk during various stages of preparing this manuscript; Polly Weaver Beaton, sister of Richard Weaver, Josephine Osborne, cousin of Richard Weaver, and Wilma R. Ebbitt all for biographical information; Michael Sims of The Jean and Alexander Heard Library at Vanderbilt University, Nashville, Tennessee, for chronological information; and Anna for the typing, research, and extra special encouragement.

* * *

Prologue. Richard M. Weaver, "Up from Liberalism." Originally published in *Modern Age* (Winter 1958–59).

Ch. 1. Donald Davidson, "The Vision of Richard Weaver." Originally published as the Introduction to *The Southern Tradition at Bay*. New Rochelle, N.Y.: Arlington House, 1968.

Ch. 2. Calvin S. Brown, "Southern Thought and American Nationalism." Review of *The Southern Tradition at Bay*. Originally published in *The Southern Literary Quarterly*, Volume 1, Number 2 (Spring 1969).

Ch. 3. Ralph T. Ancil, "Richard Weaver and the Metaphysics of Property." Essay on *Ideas Have Consequences*. Originally published in *Intercollegiate Review* (Spring 1992), pp. 33–45.

Ch. 4. Eliseo Vivas, "The Mind of Richard Weaver." Essay on *Visions of Order*. Originally published in *Modern Age* (Winter 1964).

Ch. 5. Allan Brownfeld, "The South Wisely Perceived." Review of *The Southern Essays of Richard Weaver*. Originally published in *The University Bookman* (Winter 1989).

Ch. 6. Richard L. Johannesen, Rennard Strickland, and Ralph T. Eubanks, "Richard M. Weaver on the Nature of Rhetoric: An Interpretation." From *Language is Sermonic: Richard M. Weaver on the Nature of Rhetoric,* edited by Richard L. Johannesen, Rennard Strickland, and Ralph T. Eubanks. Copyright © 1970 by Louisiana State University Press. Reprinted with permission of Louisiana State University Press.

Ch. 7. Bruce A. White, "Dialectic Rhetorician." Originally published in *Modern Age* (Summer/Fall 1982), pp. 256-59.

Ch. 8. John Bliese, "Rhetoric and the Tyrannizing Image." Originally published in *Modern Age* (Spring/Summer 1984), pp. 208-14.

Ch. 9. M. E. Bradford, "The Agrarianism of Richard Weaver: Beginnings and Completions." Originally published in *Modern Age*, Volume 14 (Summer/Fall 1970), pp. 249-55.

Ch. 10. Henry Regnery, "A Southern Agrarian at the University of Chicago." Originally published in *Modern Age* (Spring 1988), pp. 102-12.

Ch. 11. John P. East, "The Conservatism of Affirmation." Originally published in *Modern Age* (Fall 1975), pp. 338-54.

Ch. 12. Chilton Williamson, Jr., "Stranger in Paradise," © 1985 by *National Review*, Inc., 150 East 35th Street, New York, NY 10016. Reprinted by permission.

Ch. 13. Marion Montgomery, "Looking Before and After." Reprinted from *The Men I Have Chosen for Fathers: Literary and Philosophical Passages* by Marion Montgomery, by permission of the University of Missouri Press. Copyright © 1990 by the Curators of the University of Missouri.

Ch. 14. Thomas Landess, "Is the Battle Over...Or Has It Just Begun? The Southern Tradition Twenty Years After Richard Weaver." Originally published in *The Southern Partisan* (Spring 1983).

Introduction: From Weaverville to Posterity

Joseph Scotchie

A brilliant defender of the Old South's "aristocracy of achievement," Richard Weaver was not descended from the landed gentry. Still he was heir to a prominent Western North Carolina family, one that exemplified the agrarian culture that Weaver fiercely defended as a cornerstone to any civilized community.

Richard Malcolm Weaver was born in 1910 in Asheville, North Carolina, the eldest son of Richard Malcolm and Carrie Embry Weaver. Richard, Sr., was the great grandson of John and Elizabeth Weaver, the young couple who, in 1787, became the first permanent white settlers in the Dry Ridge area of Western North Carolina. John Weaver emigrated to North Carolina from northeastern Tennessee and came to own hundreds of acres of land throughout the area. His sons continued settling the land and establishing a community. In 1811, John Weaver's eldest son, Jacob, built the first homestead in Dry Ridge. His youngest son, Montraville, settled the village that eventually became Weaverville and later donated land to Weaver College, the town's first institution of higher learning. For these achievements, the town was named in honor of Montraville Weaver.[1]

Richard Weaver only spent a small portion of his early years in Weaverville. His father died when Weaver was only six years old. Immediately afterwards, the family moved to Lexington, Kentucky, where Weaver's mother's family, the Embrys, operated a millinery business. The Embrys were a well-known family in an Old South town where name and place still counted. The millinery business enabled Mrs. Weaver to have some economic security for her young family. Summers were spent in Weaverville among the large Weaver tribe. There the young Weaver enjoyed the usual pleasures of country living. Along with his brother and two sisters, the young Weaver swam, hiked, and played in the foothills of the Carolina mountains. Later, when his career took him to Chicago, Weaver took up target practice as a form of leisure. Polly remembers her brother as having an interest in reading from an early age. When I interviewed her, she insisted that as a child, Weaver would crawl to the bookshelf in the family living room to pull out a volume. At any rate, Weaver's bookish nature had worried his father who apparently thought his oldest son lacked typical boyhood interests.²

Recognizing the young Weaver's intellectual interests, Mrs. Weaver, in 1924, sent him to The Academy of Lincoln Memorial, a college preparatory high school in Harrogate, Tennessee. Students at Harrogate were generally not wealthy youths privileged enough to receive a prep school education. While at Harrogate, Weaver worked the entire three years in the school's cafeteria to help pay tuition. He also found time to form, along with two other classmates, a philosophy club. In his tribute to Weaver, brother-in-law Kendall Beaton described the club as evidence of the young Weaver's seriousness and devotion to deep thinking:

> The course Dick chose for himself was deliberate and mapped out early. Among his papers was found the constitution of a philosophical society which he and two other young men organized when Dick was fifteen. The document, in his handwriting, indicates a remarkable seriousness of purpose in one so young. The purpose of their society was, to quote the Preamble, "to promote the exchange of ideas, investigate theories, propagate principles, follow an argument wherever it goes, and develop ourselves.... Article I (obviously the most important) states: "No member shall cherish society above solitude or engage promiscuously in social activities." They met in their dormitory every Sunday afternoon, required attendance, forbade levity of conduct, and obliged each member to present something serious and significant at each meeting. Here, certainly, is a blueprint for the life of high purpose that Dick adhered to steadfastly, despite hardship and difficulty, for the remainder of his days.³

Thus, we have the beginnings of Weaver's dedication to a life of scholarship and philosophical inquiries. Weaver continued his intellectual odyssey at the University of Kentucky, matriculating as a freshman in 1928. The conditions there suggested a less than rigorous approach to liberal education. By the time Weaver entered Kentucky, it along with many southern universities, had become enthusiastic boosters of a "New South" which championed industry, commercialism, and sought to emulate the economic prosperity of the northeast corridor. In a move that observers of our current educational scene might appreciate, the university, as Weaver recalled, was "given to the 'elective' system, whereby seventeen-year-old students, often of poor previous training and narrow background, tell the faculty (in effect) what they ought to be taught." Weaver's professors were progressive minded and the young student soon signed up for the socialist cause, a move not uncommon among college students during the Depression.[4]

Clifford Amyx, in his engaging essay "Weaver the Liberal: A Memoir," gives us the finest insights into the young Weaver's progress at the University of Kentucky. Weaver was a good student. As an upperclassman, he was elected to the Phi Beta Kappa honor society and he performed well enough to earn a teaching fellowship at Vanderbilt University. He was also an excellent debater. Amyx recalls a debate between Kentucky undergraduates and three young English women from Oxford, Cambridge, and the University of London. Although the English ladies, armed with superior debating skills, easily prevailed (Amyx doesn't say what subject they debated), the ladies did acknowledge that Weaver was the best debater they had yet encountered in America.[5]

Weaver benefited from his time on the debate team. Amyx recalls the debate coach, William R. Sutherland, a native of Michigan, as a "man of good size and enormous prescience, a sometimes actor, and a consummate player of roles in class." Sutherland, Amyx writes, had a great influence on Weaver. According to Amyx, "much of the incisive scorn in Weaver's *Ideas Have Consequences* derives from Sutherland's love of flagging contemporary fallacies...it was Eliseo Vivas who said the chapters, 'The Great Stereopticon' and 'The Spoiled Child Psychology' were the key to much of Weaver's writing then. I read those with a sense of almost total familiarity with the attitude and the subject matter. Many of the parts of these chapters derive, perhaps at some distance, from Sutherland."[6]

Life at Kentucky was not all spent pursuing a determined socialist vision for a Depression-racked America. Amyx has fun debunking Weaver's description of himself in those days—borrowed from the French writer Peguy—as completely "gloomy, ardent, stupid." As his colleagues at the University of Chicago also remembered, Weaver enjoyed a good song, a drink, a joke, and the company of friends. Amyx recalls he was "anything but gloomy, especially on our long night's carousings, when he was utterly human and joyful."[7]

Although a socialist, Weaver hardly abandoned his southern sympathies. One hilarious account has the young Weaver—in, according to

Amyx, a "dangerous ploy"—rooting for the University of Tennessee football team to whip the Kentucky squad in a home game played at Lexington, the reasoning apparently being that while Kentucky remained in the Union during the war (although many of her sons fought for the South), Tennessee had voted to join the Confederacy and, as such, the game represented a new battle in an old war. Amyx wryly noted that Weaver had "misplaced the Mason-Dixon line" that day.[8]

With such strong southern proclivities as still part of his makeup, it is easy to see the young Weaver gradually shedding his socialist sympathies. In "Up from Liberalism" he recalled that he never liked his fellow socialists as persons. They "seemed dry, insistent people, of shallow objectives; seeing them often and sharing common endeavors, moreover, did nothing to remove the disliking."[9] But there were other intellectuals working in America that Weaver would eventually find much in common with. At the same time that Weaver was working on his undergraduate degree, a group of young English professors and students at Vanderbilt University, among them John Crowe Ransom, Allen Tate, Donald Davidson, Andrew Lytle, and Robert Penn Warren, were writing and publishing a collection of essays entitled *I'll Take My Stand*. The book, which has never gone out of print during its sixty-five-year history, was a spirited defense of the South's agrarian culture and a withering assault on the specter of industrialism already imposing its way on the South. *I'll Take My Stand* was published in 1930 to great controversy. Despite getting many negative reviews, the attention the book received pleased its authors; and the defense of the South's—and really the nation's—agrarian tradition cut the same raw nerve in the nation's consciousness that Weaver's *Ideas Have Consequences* would do nearly two decades later. The agrarian movement never evolved into the strong political force some of its authors hoped it might become. The authors themselves—some of whom were still struggling to earn an living as assistant professors of English or as free-lance writers—were soon dispersed to universities across the country when the Vanderbilt hierarchy saw agrarianism as a threat to their own progressive aims.

While Weaver would soon see himself as a kindred spirit to those gentlemen—and in the view of some, an even more radical defender of agrarianism—the younger scholar had temporarily committed himself to a progressive South and embraced socialism as the best way to ensure a more prosperous society. But after receiving his B.A. from Kentucky in 1932, fate intervened and Weaver matriculated at Vanderbilt to study for his master's degree. At Vanderbilt, Weaver was reintroduced to his agrarian roots. Like Warren, Davidson, Tate, Lytle, Peter Taylor, Robert Lowell, Randall Jarrell, and countless others, Weaver was greatly nurtured by the subtle teaching talents of John Crowe Ransom. Weaver was especially influenced by Ransom's 1930 book, *God without Thunder,* the "unorthodox defense of orthodoxy" which helped convince the young Weaver that traditionalism could be defended even in a time of rampant materialism. As opposed to his socialist cohorts at Kentucky, Weaver found he liked the Agrarians as persons. He also found their rejections of science and rationalism and their defense of regional cultures and social classes as unsettling to his socialist sympathies. Yet while at Vanderbilt, Weaver did not come around completely to agrarianism. He continued his solitary pursuit of literature and philosophy. As part of his fellowship, he taught in the English department. In 1934, he earned an M.A. in English and began work on a Ph.D.[10]

Weaver left Vanderbilt in 1936 without his doctoral to earn a living teaching full-time. He spent a year at Alabama Polytechnic Institute (now Auburn University) and three years at Texas A & M in Lubbock. If Weaver had not come over to the agrarian side while at Vanderbilt, the years at Texas A & M completed the conversion. His years on the Texas plains exposed him to the dehumanizing world of naturalism and, as he later termed it, a "juggernaut technology." The "lion of applied science," it seemed to Weaver, was set to "devour the lamb of humanities." Life in Texas was the complete opposite of the humane tradition the Agrarians struggled to uphold. Texas A & M had swallowed the philosophy of materialism, plus a "rampant philistinism, abetted by technology, large-scale organization and a complacent acceptance of success as the goal in life." Finally, in 1939, the young instructor decided to give up his unhappy existence at Texas A & M. Weaver quit his job and enrolled at Louisiana State University to complete his Ph.D.[11]

When Weaver enrolled at LSU, two Vanderbilt Agrarians—Robert Penn Warren and Cleanth Brooks—were established at the university's English department and were editing the *Southern Review,* a journal already recognized as one of the premier literary quarterlies in the English-speaking world. Weaver found the atmosphere congenial and while Europe and Asia were engulfed in World War II, he immersed himself in an extensive study of the literature of the postbellum South.

Weaver was appalled by the total warfare of World War II. Years later, in *Visions of Order,* he remarked on the tragedy of seeing innocent farm boys from Texas and Kansas carpetbombing European cities. The chivalry of the Confederate soldier offered a compelling contrast to indiscriminate warfare waged against men, women, and children. The dissertation, "The Confederate South, 1865-1910: A Study in the Survival of a Mind and Culture," examined novels, diaries, and reminiscences of soldiers, politicians, lawyers, journalists, and feisty southern women. Almost all were southern apologists. Weaver found that the unifying theme of the apologists was a defense of the South as the Western world's "last non-materialistic society." All aspects of the heritage—the feudal order, the education of the gentleman, the code of chivalry, and the older religiousness—were non-materialistic. They emphasized honor, courage, responsibility, compassion, and a proper code of conduct over any drive for material gain. As such, a return to the ethos of the Old South and the Middle Ages, which must be shaped with the rhetoric of progress, will only come when men learn to live strenuously or romantically, allowing them to reject the cradle to grave social security of the welfare state set up by the masters of the new twentieth-century "global dictatorship." William Havard adds that Weaver benefited from the literary culture at LSU. "The Confederate South" was "an unusual dissertation to come out of an English department and probably could not have been approved as a proper topic anyplace other than at LSU, with its interesting combination of social and cultural traditionalism and openness to literary criticism and creative writing."[12]

The dissertation was completed in 1943. Weaver submitted the manuscript to the University of North Carolina Press, but it was turned down and the young scholar never pursued the project with other publishing companies. In 1968, the dissertation, with an introduction and epilogue added by Weaver, was finally published as *The Southern Tradition at Bay.* According to M. E. Bradford, who along with George Core edited the published version of the dissertation, Weaver had never lost faith in the rightness of the manuscript and at the time of his death was preparing it for publication. In Weaver's lifetime, the manuscript did make the academic grapevines as a work of first-class scholarship. More importantly, it helped him land a position in the English department at the University of Chicago.

II.

Weaver joined the faculty at the University of Chicago in 1944. He would remain there until his untimely death nearly twenty years later. Wilma Ebbitt, a colleague in the English department, described Weaver's life in Chicago as "a regimen." His closest friend during his early years, Albert Duhmeal, wrote that Weaver's life "was as methodical in his daily regimen as he was in his thinking; thereby affording another illustration of one of his favorite principles—that style reflects substance."[13]

Upon accepting the 1988 Richard M. Weaver Award for Scholarly Letters from the Rockford Institute, Edward Shils also recalled his former colleague:

> I never exchanged a word with Richard Weaver. I knew him because he was a figure at the University of Chicago. I heard that he was a teacher who expected his students to meet a high standard of intellectual probity and rigor: I think that he expected the same of his colleagues. I was told, with a mixture of admiration and resentment, that he was not a member of any of the ruling parties at the college in the years in which he taught there. To me, when I occasionally passed him on the campus...he looked the part. He looked quietly and concentratedly independent; not bellicose, but determined to follow the path that he thought was right. The path he thought right was not one that was plucked out of the air; it was one that had been taken deliberately and adhered to with purposeful tenacity. It was not easy. At that time there was a certain enthusiastic mateyness among the teachers of the humanities in the college at the University of Chicago. They were ebulliently confident that they had the protection of Robert Hutchins and Richard McKeon. There was much optimism in the United States at that time and they shared it. Although they knew nothing of economics and little of politics, I think that they were generally devotees of the New Deal. Those who did not agree with them were ostracized as "reactionaries." That was Richard Weaver's position.[14]

Weaver taught two morning classes, and then had an early lunch on campus. He then retired to his rented room to write two pages and take a short nap before heading back to campus, teaching a 2:30 P.M. class, meeting with students and eating a 5:30 P.M. dinner. Evenings were spent writing until 9:30 P.M. Mrs. Ebbitt relates that weekends were filled with the same rigorous writing schedule. On Saturday, Weaver worked in his campus office. He spent afternoons rummaging through second-hand bookstores before having dinner in a German restaurant. Saturday evenings were spent at a local pub, waiting for an early edition of the *Chicago Tribune*. Sundays were reserved for more writing.[15] Russell Kirk tells us that Weaver only attended church services once a year. An Episcopal high mass at Christmas time provided Weaver with enough emotional satisfaction to last the rest of the year.

Weaver disliked city life, but enjoyed the challenge of being a southern traditionalist at a citadel of New Deal optimism. He did not need to be exposed to urban life to attack modernism. The bulk of *The Southern Tradition at Bay*, for instance, was written in Baton Rouge. However, Weaver's life in Chicago certainly hardened his view that agrarian culture was superior on both a spiritual and economic level to the culture of megalopolis. Life in Chicago exposed Weaver to the chaos of urban culture. Now he had seen the industrial man (whom he recognized as the spoiled child) that he had heard about while a young socialist at Kentucky. Had Weaver not lived in Chicago, it seems unlikely he could have written his first published book, *Ideas Have Consequences*. His dislike of modern life might have produced a book similar to it, but such an effort would have lacked the brilliant contrasts between urban and rural living that added to the urgency of his first book.

Weaver's life in Chicago was not spent as a total recluse. Mrs. Ebbitt points out that Weaver enjoyed the company of friends, even acting as an "after hours bon vivant of sorts." At faculty parties, he enjoyed a bourbon and branch water, folks songs, and a good story. "Nobody relished a felicitous phrase more than he; nobody was more given to aphorisms," Mrs. Ebbitt recalls. Weaver, she added, was "tough, in the sense that he would fight and die for a principle, but he was also romantic and sentimental. He remembered Mexico City in the 30's the way others remembered Paris in the 20s...he enjoyed the company of attractive women."[16]

Weaver's Chicago years were productive. He was one of the many southern writers—Warren, Ransom, Tate, and Brooks all come to mind—who were forced to find employment in the North, but who also flourished in foreign parts. In 1944, Weaver's first essay "Lee the Philosopher," a piece praising Robert E. Lee as not only a leader of men but also a student of human nature, was published, followed by "The Older Religiousness of the South," an essay adapted from *The Southern Tradition at Bay*. In 1948, *Ideas Have Consequences* was published, establishing Weaver as a thinker to be reckoned with. The history behind the book is illustrative of the hostile elements that Weaver occasionally encountered in Chicago. The director of the University of Chicago Press was W. T. Couch, a man who had previously served in the same capacity at the University of North Carolina where he published, among other books,

Donald Davidson's *The Attack on Leviathan*. Couch liked Weaver's manuscript, agreed to publish it, and also put some effort into promoting the book. The only disagreement came over the title. The manuscript was originally called *The Fearful Descent*. Couch, however, insisted on publishing it under the title *Ideas Have Consequences*, which Weaver intensely disliked. The reaction to the book, both pro and con, was strong and the University of Chicago never published another Weaver volume. In 1949, when Weaver was awarded the Quantrell Prize for outstanding teaching, the dean of the English department said, "Weaver, I hope you take the money and go elsewhere."

The 1950s saw *The Ethics of Rhetoric*, a textbook, *Composition* (revised in 1967), and the publication of dozens of reviews and essays in various scholarly journals. Weaver established himself further as a contributing editor to two nascent conservative publications, *Modern Age* and *National Review*, where his traditionalist/libertarian philosophy was articulated in essays later published in *Life without Prejudice*.

Essays and lectures on rhetoric also occupied his time, establishing him as one of the nation's premiere scholars in that field. The 1970 publication of *Language is Sermonic* made additional Weaver essays on rhetoric available to the public. With *The Southern Tradition at Bay* mostly behind him, Weaver developed his own philosophical defense of the South in such essays as "The Southern Tradition," "The South and the American Union," and "The Aspects of Southern Philosophy," all published in his last book, *The Southern Essays of Richard M. Weaver*.[17]

Eliseo Vivas, in his introduction to *Life without Prejudice*, noted that there have been different portraits of Weaver by Kirk, Kendall, and E. Victor Milione. One thing is certain. Weaver lived modestly in Chicago, preferring, in Fred Hobson's words, a "life of plain living and high thinking." A fierce opponent of modernism, Weaver only flew on an airplane once in his life. While on his way to California for a speaking engagement, Weaver enjoyed the scenery over the Grand Canyon, but he later wrote in *Visions of Order* that the invention of the airplane had added great and unnecessary anxiety to an already stressed-filled world. With money received from winning the Quantrell Prize, he bought an automobile and nervously battled the Chicago traffic before giving up on the machine. Every spring, as soon as the last term paper was graded, he traveled by train to Weaverville, where he spent summers writing essays and books and plowing his patch of land with only the help of a mule-driven harness. Tractors, airplanes, automobiles, radios (and certainly television)—none of these gadgets of modern life were for Richard Weaver. His essays and books were written by hand and later typed into a final draft. He battled the Chicago winters by wearing two overcoats, but spent his time there in a rented room at a modest hotel near the university campus. Vivas recalls that Weaver, while friendly enough, also had a private, impenetrable side. Through the course of a productive and important career, Richard Weaver never strayed from the life of solitary scholarship to which he dedicated himself while still a young man.

III.

The theme that runs through these essays is Richard Weaver's importance to us in an age when the entire idea of Western culture is under assault not only inside the academy, but in the culture at large. Many of these authors also acknowledge Weaver's importance to their own thought and careers. Marion Montgomery writes that in "a confused moment of history, Weaver steadies us. He knew, early enough to help us, that violence of language and to language speaks a person or a people dislocated from the surest grounds of ideas, from an old faith in being that is necessary to community vision and vitality." He is referring to Weaver's view of man and society. Every civilized society must seek to answer the ancient question: What is man? For Weaver, it meant acknowledging man's dual nature, namely, his capacity for evil and heroism. It meant accepting original sin as an explanation for man's propensity to do the wrong thing when he knows he should do the right thing. It also means accepting man as an intelligible being who is capable of saving his civilization from barbarism. Henry Regnery begins his essay "A Southern Agrarian at the University of Chicago" by quoting Weaver: a "man saves himself, if at all, by bringing his community around to right reason."

These essays celebrate Weaver's worth to us as a rhetor, a political philosopher, a social critic, and a southern agrarian. Weaver's fame rests primarily as one of the founders of the modern conservative intellectual movement. His conservatism was rooted in the agrarian culture of western North Carolina and bluegrass Kentucky that nourished him. M. E.

Bradford tells us in "The Agrarianism of Richard M. Weaver: Beginnings and Completions" that Weaver came to share the basic agrarian concerns of his Vanderbilt mentors. He was skeptical about the wisdom of unlimited progress. Weaver opposed the "depersonalization" of industrialism, applied science, and "dehabilitating materialism." He rejected the idea of "atomistic" or specialized man, the "cowardly dream of uniformity," and the utopian "impulse to fix everything."

Weaver also shared with the Agrarians a spiritual rather than a materialistic view of man. Weaver placed an emphasis on roots, memory, cultural pluralism, human differences, and "submissive[ness] before the frame of creation." By making the case for the South's "humane social order" through its literature, its sense of *pietas,* its respect for high and honest rhetoric and resistance to modernism, Weaver carried on the crusade waged by both the Agrarians and postbellum southern apologists that the region would serve as the "flywheel" of the republic, slowing down progress when it needed slowing down, and picking it up when progress was needed. From Bradford, Davidson, Brown, East, Landess, and Brownfeld the theme is the same: A revival of the Old Republic can began with an understanding of the southern tradition.

Solely on the importance of his first published book, *Ideas Have Consequences,* Weaver, along with Russell Kirk, was recognized as the founder of the traditionalist wing of modern conservatism. Frank Meyer's praise is representative of the way the Old Right felt about Weaver. *Ideas Have Consequences* was the *font et origin* (source and origin) of the post World War II conservative movement. Before *Ideas Have Consequences* (and Kirk's *The Conservative Mind,* William F. Buckley's *God and Man at Yale,* and the founding of *National Review* and *Modern Age*), conservatism, according to Meyer, was a scattered remnant of "supporters of free enterprise, and the market system...traditionalist humanists and individualist philosophers."[18] There was opposition to the New Deal in the 1930s. Numerous Republican party lawmakers opposed, for instance, regulations placed on small businessmen and the rapid expansion and power of a centralized state. There was enough opposition to defeat President Roosevelt's plan to expand membership to a Supreme Court that had struck down much New Deal legislation. However, anti-New Deal forces never captured control of the Republican party. In 1940, the GOP nominated Wendell Wilkee—who later achieved greater fame as the author of the internationalist manifesto *One World*—as its presidential nominee. FDR's own successful prosecution of World War II seemed to end all domestic opposition to the New Deal. Conservatives such as Henry Regnery remembered the postwar era as a moment of unquestioned liberal dominance:

> Liberalism [new style] reigned supreme and without question; the Liberal could believe, in fact, that no other position was conceivable. The war, which represented the triumph of good over evil, had been won. Fascism, militarian and colonialism had been banished from the earth; the Peace-Loving Nations, joined together in San Francisco in a perpetual bond, would preserve peace, protect the weak, and guarantee the rule of democracy—the future seemed assured. It was a beautiful picture and questions about conformity to the facts of life were not welcome.[19]

The publication of Frederich Hayek's *The Road to Serfdom* and works by Ludwig von Mises, Albert Jay Nock, and Frank Chodorov signaled the rebellion by libertarians against the triumph of socialism in Great Britain and the United States. Then came *Ideas Have Consequences* to mount a defense of chivalry, private property, and piety against the cult of the masses. Meyer credited Weaver as the inspiration for the former's own traditionalist/libertarian "fusionist" strategy for uniting different strains of conservatism. Weaver did not seek conservative approval; he even acknowledged that the book generated a response far greater than he ever expected. But he did not shy from the task of being a new conservative spokesman, spending a fair amount of time writing and lecturing on behalf of this new cause.

Regnery points out that traditionalists were drawn to Weaver because *Ideas Have Consequences,* written at the height of post-World War II optimism, represented a brilliant counterattack to the reigning collectivist spirit of the day. Here, written "in words as hard as cannonballs," Weaver brought forth a memorable assault on the cult of masses, including the "Great Stereopticon," or what we would call the mass media; the turn to rampant egotism in art and the idea of work; and the general leveling of distinctions and hierarchy. The consequence of radical egalitarianism was wide-scale resentment among the masses, which, citing Richard Hertz, "may well prove the dynamite which will finally wreck Western society."[20]

Modern man in Megalopolis was given a false view of life and history. He had become a spoiled child told by his demagogic leaders that a life of ease and comfort were birthrights. When those conditions were not realized, modern man was given a plethora of scapegoats to blame for his lack of material goods. In *Ideas Have Consequences,* Weaver wrote that a citizen in Megalopolis did not understand what it meant to be a man; he did not realize that life is a struggle and a matter of discipline and forging. Modern man also suffered under the illusion of unlimited progress. A theme hammered through again and again throughout Weaver's works is that the present point in history—whether it be 1948 or 1995—represents the highest point of progress ever reached by mankind. By this reckoning, modern man was free to look at his past as one large error. Cut off from that past, important lessons of history, including those of tragedy and man's limitations, were now considered heresy. Traditionalists were also drawn to Weaver's defense of a society that grows organically as opposed to one built by state power. All of us start out the same in life, but in the course of events, some of us will achieve more than others and show greater talents and aptitudes than the rest. From this free society, distinctions and a hierarchy develop. That hierarchy was not exclusive; it drew from other classes for support and it adapted to societal evolutions, but it was made up wholly of men with superior gifts, which in turn provided a somber leadership class. In American history, Weaver most often cites George Washington as a man from the Old Republic's aristocracy of achievement. A wealthy landowner, he was willing to lose his life's possession to fight a long, bitter, and very uncertain struggle for what he maintained was the right cause.

In the final three chapters of *Ideas Have Consequences,* Weaver's libertarian/traditionalist philosophy evolved. He called for freedom from state despotisms through a rousing defense of private property, asking "is it not...quite comforting to feel that we can enjoy one right which does not have to answer the sophistries of the world or rise and fall with the tide of public opinion?" Private property was the rock from which modern-day conservatives could mount offensive operations against the forces of planned disintegration. Private property was a character-building institution and Weaver's defense of it was made in near-religious terms.[21]

Freedom from the whims of the state did not a mean a strange libertarianism where rampant relativism would also reign supreme. In the final chapter of *Ideas Have Consequences,* Weaver quotes Plato: "Let parents, then, bequeath to their children, not riches, but a reverence for the past." Piety also entailed respect for God's nature. Secular religions of science and technology promised to create a new man and a prosperity so great that lessons of history—to quote Henry Ford—were now all "bunk." The age of science and technology only served to sever the pieties and institutions that bound generations. "In our own contemporary setting, the young man stands for science and technology and the father for the order of nature," wrote Weaver in *Ideas Have Consequences*, adding that "for centuries now we have been told that our happiness requires an unrelenting assault upon this order." That being so, modern man felt free to destroy the institutions of his ancestors and rationalize it with "talk of emancipation."[22]

In the tradition of the ancient Greeks and Romans, Weaver saw the landowner as the man fit for the responsibilities of freedom. As a man of the soil, the agrarian knew the cultural worth of private property. Far from the distractions of urban life, the agrarian was a well-integrated man; he was a man who had time for reflection; he had a sense of piety; and he was reliable in times of crisis. If urban man was cut off from his past, rural man was firmly attached to it. The life of his grandparents, for instance, was important to him. The past taught him life's hard lessons of man's fragility, lessons forgotten in an age of unlimited progress and "hysterical optimism."

Traditionalists were attracted to this favorable comparison of rural man to urban man. Many of them had little use for the distractions of urban America; in Weaver's time at least, many preferred the early America of landowners and frontiersmen to the twentieth-century superstate. Even East Coast conservatives (and conservatism soon became a Manhattan/Washington phenomenon) such as Meyer and James Burnham championed the virtues of Middle America, a region which, in Meyer's words, was the "last heir to Western civilization."

How goes the struggle today? To be sure, Richard Weaver is not every conservative's favorite philosopher. Some conservatives, most notably neoconservative intellectuals, have urban roots: They would dispute Weaver's contention that urban culture is by nature decadent. Similarly, many conservatives believe that America's transformation from an agrarian to an industrial society has, on the whole, been a positive development resulting in a more prosperous and powerful nation. Many conservatives believe that the economic prosperity an industrialized (or "developed") economy brings is the first step to political freedom. Those conservatives hardly share Weaver's suspicions toward mass democracy or economic capitalism.

Introduction: From Weaverville to Posterity   15

Also, much has changed politically since Weaver's death over thirty years ago. Conservatives tasted unexpected political triumph when Barry Goldwater captured the Republican party nomination in 1964. When Goldwater suffered a landslide defeat to President Lyndon Johnson, conservative ideas seemed discredited, but starting in 1968, the GOP began a long string of presidential victories that lasted for a quarter of a century. Conservatives were generally satisfied with Ronald Reagan's performance and tolerant of Richard Nixon, but the administrations of both Gerald Ford and George Bush were occasions for outright mutiny in some conservative quarters. In *The Conservative Movement,* Thomas Fleming and Paul Gottfried argue that following 1964, conservatism became more pragmatic, worrying more about public opinion polls and finding electable candidates than fighting to preserve the permanent things. American conservatism, which began as a spirited opposition to the New Deal, has long made its peace with the modern welfare state.[23] In addition, during the 1980s, Old Right followers of Weaver and Russell Kirk increasingly found themselves at odds with the ascendant neoconservative movement. The tensions that developed during the 1980s were further exacerbated by Reagan's retirement and the end of the cold war. Now disputes broke out over the Persian Gulf War (and the general role of American foreign policy), immigration, trade, and the challenge by Patrick J. Buchanan to President Bush in the 1992 presidential primaries. The 1993 debate over the North American Free Trade Agreement only served to explain that sharp differences among conservatives will continue throughout this decade and beyond. Since the 1992 election also highlighted the viability of a third party candidacy, it is very possible that the conservative splits of the 1980s and 1990s may end up in the formation of a new political party. Indeed, since the mid-1970s, conservatives have, off and on, openly discussed the desire to bolt from their uneasy marriage with the Republican party.

So Chilton Williamson is correct when he notes that Weaver's stern philosophy is mostly out of favor with today's Washington conservatives. As Williamson notes in "Stranger in Paradise," utopian creeds of unlimited economic wealth and social progress, originally provinces of the left, have been adopted by the conservative establishment as well. There has also emerged a "big government conservatism," which only seems to believe that if card-carrying conservatives man large bureaucracies, then a centralized government can work in their favor. Writes

Williamson, "According to new 'conservative' (and particularly 'neoconservative') creeds, the sky is the clear, clear limit, with no cloud to be seen threatening disaster from resource depletion, environmental depredation, crowd culture, uncontrolled immigration from Third World countries, the dehumanizing effects of technology, or metaphysical materialism—so long, of course, as all the proper prescriptions, as handed down by Republican politicians and 'conservative' think tanks are conscientiously applied."

Weaver's influence does remain strong among certain factions of the right. His traditionalist/libertarian philosophy is echoed on the pages of *Chronicles, Modern Age, Intercollegiate Review, Southern Partisan*, and *National Review*. The Rockford Institute annually awards the Richard M. Weaver Award for Scholarly Letters. This award is given alongside the T.S. Eliot Award for Creative Writing, thus elevating Weaver as an equal to one of the heroic figures of twentieth-century literature. Past winners have included Kirk, Burnham, Andrew Lytle, John Luckas, Forrest McDonald, Edward Shils, and Eugene Genovese. The Intercollegiate Studies Institute has for several decades awarded scholarships in Weaver's name to worthy undergraduates. E. Victor Milone, Weaver's old friend from his days at *Modern Age* and *Intercollegiate Review*, recently notes that Weaver fellows "have gone into teaching or writing careers, creating a formidable conservative block in the academy, as well as in politics and public policy institutes."[24] None of this means we have turned the corner in the current cultural wars. It does mean, however, that a stubborn, independent force bears Weaver's influence and has not fallen victim to the whims of popular culture.

Finally, Donald Davidson is correct when he writes that Richard Weaver is one of those "brave, rigorous, courageous" thinkers who has the power to change the way the reader looks at the world, at his own assumptions, that indeed Weaver is a writer powerful enough to change one's life. There remains also the permanence of Weaver's philosophy. The final paragraph of *Ideas Have Consequences* reminds us, even in a dark age, of man's capacity for heroism:

> It may be that we are awaiting a great change, that the sins of the fathers are going to be visited upon the generations until the reality of evil is again brought home and there comes some passionate reaction, like that which flowered in the chivalry and spirituality of the Middle Ages. If such is the most we can hope for, something

toward that revival may be prepared by acts of thought and volition in this waning day of the West.[25]

Notes

1. Conversation with Josephine Osborne, cousin of Richard M. Weaver, May 1994.
2. Conversation with Polly Weaver Beaton, sister of Richard M. Weaver, August 1993.
3. Kendall Beaton, "Richard M. Weaver: A Clear Voice in an Addled World" (unpublished essay), 1964, p. 1.
4. Richard M. Weaver, "Up from Liberalism," *Modern Age* (Winter 1958-59): 22.
5. Clifford Amyx, "Weaver the Liberal: A Memoir," *Modern Age* (Spring 1988): 102.
6. Ibid., 102-103.
7. Ibid., 103.
8. Ibid., 105-106.
9. Weaver, "Up from Liberalism," 22.
10. Ibid., 23.
11. Ibid., 24.
12. William Havard, "Richard M. Weaver: Rhetor as Philosopher," in *The Vanderbilt Tradition: Essays in Honor of Thomas Daniel Young*, ed. Mark Royden Winchell (Baton Rouge: Louisiana State University Press, 1991), 167.
13. Wilma Ebbitt, "Richard M. Weaver: Friend and Colleague" (unpublished essay), 1988, pp. 1-5.
14. Edward Shils, "Liberalism: Collectivist and Conservative," *Chronicles* (July 1989): 12.
15. Ebbitt, "Richard M. Weaver: Friend and Colleague," 3.
16. Ibid., 4-5.
17. For a discussion of Weaver's thoughts on one-worldism and "emperor worship," see the epilogue to Richard Weaver, *The Southern Tradition at Bay* (Washington, DC: Regnery Gateway, 1989), 372-80.
18. Frank Meyer, "Richard M. Weaver: An Appreciation," *Modern Age* (Fall 1970): 243.
19. Henry Regnery, "A Conservative Publisher in a Liberal World," *The Alternative 5* (October 1971): 15.
20. Richard M. Weaver, *Ideas Have Consequences* (Chicago: University of Chicago Press, 1948), 43.
21. Ibid., 132.
22. Ibid., 171.
23. Thomas Fleming and Paul Gottfried, *The Conservative Movement* (New York: Twayne Publishers, 1988), 42.
24. E. Victor Milione, "Ideas in Action: Forty Years of Educating for Liberty," *The Intercollegiate Review* (Fall 1993): 53.
25. Weaver, *Ideas Have Consequences*, 187.

Prologue: Up from Liberalism

Richard M. Weaver

There is a saying by William Butler Yeats that a man begins to understand the world by studying the cobwebs in his own corner. My experience has brought home to me the wisdom in this; and since the contemporary ideal seems to run the other way, confronting the youth first with the abstractions of universalism, collectivism, and internationalism, I propose to say something on behalf of the historic and the concrete as elements of an education.

The discovery did not come to me as a free gift, for practically every conviction I now hold I had to win against the propositional sense and general impetus of most of my formal education. This was owing partly to special circumstances, but mainly, I now believe, to the fact that the United States tends to institutionalize the chaotic and superficial type of education and to impose it with an air of business efficiency. This is not to imply that I was wiser than my generation, for I was filled with the formless aspirations which make such an education look like a good thing, and I fell into most of the pitfalls that were left open. But I hope that a retrospect of twenty-five years, involving much change of opinion, gives some right to pass judgment; and furthermore I wish in this testament, to discuss education as one of the proven means of doing something about the condition of man.

I was born in the Southern section of the United States, and at the age of seventeen I entered the University of Kentucky. I have more than once recalled how well Charles Peguy's description of himself at the beginning of his career at the *Ecole Normale* fitted me at this time: "gloomy, ardent, stupid." The University of Kentucky was what would be called in Europe a "provincial university," but I have since come to believe that if it had been more provincial in the right way and less sedulously imitative of the dominant American model, it would have offered better fare. Like most of our state-supported universities during the period, it was growing up in enrollment and physical plant and losing in character; moreover, it was given to the "elective" system, whereby seventeen-year-old students, often of poor previous training and narrow background, tell the faculty (in effect) what they ought to be taught. After many wayward choices I managed to emerge, at the end of my undergraduate course, with a fair introduction to the history but not the substance of literature and philosophy.

The professors who staffed this institution were mostly earnest souls from the Middle Western universities, and many of them—especially those in economics, political science, and philosophy—were, with or without knowing it, social democrats. They read and circulated *The Nation*, the foremost liberal journal of the time; they made sporadic efforts toward organizing liberal or progressive clubs; and of course they reflected their position in their teaching very largely. I had no defenses whatever against their doctrine, and by the time I was in my third year I had been persuaded entirely that the future was with science, liberalism, and equalitarianism, and that all opposed to these trends were people of ignorance or malevolence.

That persuasion was not weakened, I must add, by the fact that my class graduated in May, 1932, at almost precisely the time that the Great Depression reached its lowest point on the economic charts. College graduates were taking any sort of job they could get, however menial or unrelated to their preparation, and many, of course, were not getting jobs at all. It seemed then that some sort of political reconstruction was inevitable, and in that year I joined the American Socialist Party. My disillusionment with the Left began with this first practical step.

The composition of our small unit of the Socialist Party was fairly typical, I have since learned, of socialist organizations throughout the world. There was on the one side a group of academic people teachers and students who were intellectually trained and fairly clear in their objectives, but politically inexperienced and temperamentally not adapted to politics. On the other side was about an equal number of town people who cannot be described for the good reason that they were nondescript. They were eccentrics, novelty-seekers, victims of restlessness; and most of them were hopelessly confused about the nature and purpose of socialism. I remember how shocked I was when a member of this group suggested that we provide at our public rallies one of the "hillbilly bands" which are often used to draw crowds and provide entertainment in Southern political campaigns. This seemed to me entirely out of tone with what we were trying to do. I have since had to realize that the member was far more astute practically than I; the hillbilly music would undoubtedly have fetched more auditors and made more votes than the austere exposition of the country's ills which I thought it the duty of a socialist to make. But I am sure that the net result would not have been socialism. The two groups did not understand one another, and it is a wonder to me that they worked together as long as they did.

In the course of a membership of about two years, during which I served as secretary of the "local," as it was called, I discovered that although the socialist program had a certain intellectual appeal for me, I could not like the members of the movement as *persons*. They seemed dry, insistent people, of shallow objectives; seeing them often and sharing a common endeavor, moreover, did nothing to remove the disliking. I am afraid that I performed my duties with decreasing enthusiasm, and at the end of the period I had intentions, which I did not then face, that this was not the kind of thing in which I could find permanent satisfaction.

Meanwhile another experience had occurred which was to turn my thoughts in the same direction. I had gone as a graduate student to Vanderbilt University to pursue an advanced degree in literature. Vanderbilt was another provincial university, but it had developed in the hands of men intelligent enough to see the possibilities that exist in a reflective provincialism. It was at that time the chief seat of the Southern Agrarian school of philosophy and criticism. This was one of the most brilliant groups in the United States, but its members held a position antithetical in almost every point to socialism and other purely economic remedies. By some their program was regarded as mere antiquarianism; by others it was attacked as fascist, since it rejected science and rationalism as the supreme sanctions, accepted large parts of the regional tradition, and even found some justification for social classes. But here, to my great surprise and growing confusion, I found that although I disagreed with these men on matters of social and political doctrine, I liked them all as persons. They seemed to me more humane, more generous, and considerably less dogmatic than those with whom I had been associated under the opposing banner. It began to dawn upon me uneasily that perhaps the right way to judge a movement was by the persons who made it up rather than by its rationalistic perfection and by the promises it held out. Perhaps, after all, the proof of social schemes was meant to be *a posteriori* rather than *a priori*. It would be a poor trade to give up a non-rational world in which you liked everybody for a rational world in which you liked nobody. I did not then see it as quite so sharp an issue; but the intellectual maturity and personal charm of the Agrarians were very unsettling to my then-professed allegiance.

Moreover, during my residence at Vanderbilt University I had the great good fortune to study under John Crowe Ransom, a rare teacher of literature and, apart from this and in his own right, a profound psychologist. Of the large number of students who have felt his influence, I doubt whether any could tell how he worked his effects. If one judged solely by outward motions and immediate results, he seemed neither to work very hard at teaching nor to achieve much success. But he had the gift of dropping living seeds into minds. Long after the date of a lecture—a week, a month, a year—you would find some remark of his troubling you with its pregnancy, and you would set about your own reflections upon it, often wishing that you had the master at hand to give another piece of insight. The idea of Ransom's which chiefly took possession of me at this time was that of the "unorthodox defense of orthodoxy," which he had developed in his brilliant book *God without Thunder*. I began to perceive that many traditional positions in our world had suffered not so much because of inherent defect as because of the stupidity, ineptness, and intellectual sloth of those who for one reason or another were presumed to have their defense in charge.

This was a troubling perception, because the 1930s were a time when nearly all of the traditional American ideologies were in retreat, and I had never suspected that this retreat might be owing to a kind of default. If there was something to be said for them, if their eclipse was due to the failure of their proponents to speak a modern idiom or even to acquire essential knowledge, this constituted at least a challenge to intellectual curiosity. I had tried some of the Leftist solution and had found it not to my taste; it was possible that I had been turned away from the older, more traditional solutions because they wore an antiquarian aspect and insisted upon positions which seemed irrelevancies in the modern context. Actually the passage was not an easy one for me, and I left Vanderbilt University poised between the two alternatives. I had seen virtually nothing of socialism and centralism in practice, and the mass man I had never met; there was also reluctance over giving up a position once publicly espoused, made somewhat greater by a young man's vanity. Nevertheless, I had felt a powerful pull in the direction of the Agrarian ideal of the individual in contact with the rhythms of nature, of the small-property holding, and of the society of pluralistic organization.

I had left the University to take a teaching post in a large technical college in Texas. It has been remarked that in the United States California is the embodiment of materialism and Texas of naturalism. I found the observation true with regard to my part of Texas, where I encountered a rampant philistinism, abetted by technology, large-scale organization, and a complacent acceptance of success as the goal of life. Moreover, I was here forced to see that the lion of applied science and the lamb of the humanities were not going to lie down together in peace, but that the lion was going to devour the lamb unless there was a very stern keeper of order. I feel that my conversion to the poetic and ethical vision of life dates from this contact with its sterile opposite.

I recall very sharply how, in the Autumn of 1939, as I was driving one afternoon across the monotonous prairies of Texas to begin my third year in this post, it came to me like a revelation that I did not *have* to go back to this job, which had become distasteful, and that I did not *have* to go on professing the cliches of liberalism, which were becoming meaningless to me. I saw that my opinions had become formed out of a timorous regard for what was supposed to be intellectually respectable, and that I had always been looking over my shoulder to find out what certain others, whose concern with truth I was beginning to believe to be not very intense, were doing or thinking. It is a great experience to wake up at a critical juncture to the fact that one does have a free will, and that giving up the worship of false idols is a quite practicable proceeding.

Anyhow, at the end of that year I chucked the uncongenial job and went off to start my education over, being now arrived at the age of thirty.

In the meantime I had started to study the cobwebs in my own corner, and I began to realize that the type of education which enables one to see into the life of things had been almost entirely omitted from my program. More specifically, I had been reading extensively in the history of the American Civil War, preferring first-hand accounts by those who had actually borne the brunt of it as soldiers and civilians; and I had become especially interested in those who had reached some level of reflectiveness and had tried to offer explanations of what they did or the manner in which they did it. Allen Tate has in one of his poems the line

"There is more in killing than commentary." The wisdom of this will be seen also by those who study the killings in which whole nations are the killers and the killed, namely, wars. To put this in a prose statement: the mere commentary of an historian will never get you inside the feeling of a war or any great revolutionary process. For that, one has to read the testimonials of those who participated in it on both sides and in all connections; and often the best insight will appear in the casual remark of an obscure warrior or field nurse or in the effort of some ill-educated person to articulate a feeling.

I once heard of a man who made it a lifetime hobby to study the reasons that people in various circumstances give as to why they felt it necessary to tell a lie. I believe that it is equally worthwhile and perhaps more interesting to study the reasons that people have given for passing from the use of reason to the use of force. At what point does reason tell us that reason is of no more avail? The American Civil War, because it was a civil struggle, with an elaborate ideology on both sides, left a rich store of material on this subject.

From the viewpoint of my general purpose, I had come to believe that one way to achieve the education which leads to understanding and compassion is to take some period of the past and to immerse oneself in it so thoroughly that one could think its thoughts and speak its language. The object would be to take this chapter of vanished experience and learn to know it in three if not four dimensions. That would mean coming to understand why certain actions which in the light of retrospect appear madly irrational appeared at that time the indisputable mandate of reason; why things which had been created with pain and care were cast quickly on the gaming table of war; why men who had sat in the senate chamber and debated with syllogism and enthymeme stepped out of it to buckle on the sword against one another. Almost any book of history will give you the form of such a time, but what will give you the *pressure* of it? That is what I particularly wished to discover.

I am now further convinced that there is something to be said in general for studying the history of a lost cause. Perhaps our education would be more humane in result if everyone were required to gain an intimate acquaintance with some coherent ideal that failed in effort to maintain itself. It need not be a cause which was settled by war; there are causes in the social, political, and ecclesiastical worlds which would serve very well. But it is good for everyone to ally himself at one time with the defeated and to look at the "progress" of history through the eyes of those who were left behind. I cannot think of a better way to counteract the stultifying "Whig" theory of history, with its bland assumption that every cause which has won has deserved to win, a kind of pragmatic debasement of the older providential theory. The study and appreciation of a lost cause have some effect of turning history into philosophy. In sufficient number of causes to make us humble, we discover good points in the cause which time has erased, just as one often learns more from the slain hero of a tragedy than from some brassy Fortinbras who comes in at the end to announce the victory and proclaim the future disposition of affairs. It would be perverse to say that this is so of every historical defeat, but there is enough analogy to make it a somber consideration. Not only Oxford, therefore, but every university ought to be to some extent "the home of lost causes and impossible loyalties." It ought to preserve the memory of these with a certain discriminating measure of honor, trying to keep alive what was good in them and opposing the pragmatic verdict of the world.

For my part, I spent three years reading history and literature of the Civil War, with special attention to that of the losing side. The people who emerged were human, all-too-human, but there was still the mystery of the encompassing passion which held them together, and this I have not yet penetrated. But in a dozen various ways I came to recognize myself in the past, which is at least an important piece of self-knowledge.

Toward the end of this inquiry, I published my first article, "The Older Religiousness in the South." It was an attempt to explain why the South, although it was engaged in defending institutions which much of the world was condemning on moral grounds, seemed to exhibit a more intense religiosity than its opponents. It was a first effort toward an unorthodox explanation of orthodoxy, and it showed me how much more was to be done in historical revision of the kind before the shallow liberal interpretation could be exposed in its inadequacy.

Looking back over this discipline, I feel confident enough of its principle. The aim is to strip aside the cliches of generalization, the slogans which are preserved only because they render service to contemporary institutions, and of course to avoid the drug of economic interpretation. Henry Adams felt an impulse to do something like this amid the hullabaloo of his America, and his inquiry led him this bloodless, self-questioning descendant of New England Puritans to ponder the mystery of the Virgin. It seems to me that in some corresponding way the process will compel any honest seeker to see that the lines of social and political force are far more secret than the modern world has any mind to recognize, and that if it does not lead him to some kind of faith, it will lead him safely away from the easy constructions of those who do not wish to understand, beyond grasping what can be turned to serve a practical purpose. Whereas conventional schoolbook history leaves men cocksure and ignorant, this multidimensional kind ought to leave them filled with wonder. Long before, I had been impressed by Schopenhauer's statement that no one can be a philosopher who is not capable at times of looking upon the world as if it were a pageant. This kind of detachment, produced by a suppression of the instinct to be arbitrary, seems to me a requirement for understanding the human condition.

The attempt to contemplate history in all its dimensions and in the fullness of its detail led directly to the conviction that this world of substantial things and substantial events is the very world which the Leftist of our time wishes to see abolished; and such a policy now began to appear egotistical and presumptuous. I am disinclined to the view that whatever exists necessarily is a commission to go on existing. On the contrary, I have a strong tendency to side with the bottom dog, or to champion the potential against the actual if the former seems to have some reason behind it; and I am mindful of the saying that God takes delight in bringing great things out of small ones. To this extent I am a reformer or even a subverter. But I feel that situations almost never present themselves in terms so simple. They usually appear in terms like these: we have before us a tremendous creation which is largely inscrutable. Some of the intermediate relationships of cause and effect we can grasp and manipulate, though with these our audacity often outruns good sense and we discover that in trying to achieve one balance we have upset two others. There are, accordingly, two propositions which are hard to deny: we live in a universe which was given to us, in the sense that we did not create it; and, we don't understand very much of it. In the figure once used by a philosopher, we are inhabitants of a fruitful and well-ordered island surrounded by an ocean of ontological mystery. It does not behoove us to presume very far in this situation. It is not a matter of affirming that whatever is, is right; it is a recognition that whatever is there is there with considerable force (inertia even being a respectable form of force) and in a network of relationships which we have only deciphered.

Therefore, make haste slowly. It is very easy to rush into conceit in thinking about man's relationship to the created universe. Science paved the way for presumption, whether wittingly or not; and those political movements which appeal to science to vindicate their break with the past have often made the presumptuous attitude one of their tenets. I found myself in decreasing sympathy with those social and political doctrines erected upon the concept of a man-dominated universe and more and more inclined to believe with Walt Whitman that "a mouse is miracle enough to stagger sextillions of infidels."

As a further consequence of reflecting upon this problem, I began to see it in theological terms. As I have suggested, "the authority of fact" is a phrase that I am a little uncomfortable with, because it is readily turned, unless one is vigilant, into an idolatry of circumstance, and this is the most unspiritual of all conditions. Nevertheless, there is a way in which "the authority of fact" carries a meaning that we can accept. It merely requires that we see "fact" as signifying what the theological philosophers mean by the word "substance." Now the denial of substance is one of the greatest heresies, and this is where much contemporary radicalism appears in an essentially sinful aspect. The constant warfare which it wages against anything that has *status* in the world, or against all the individual, particular, unique existences of the world which do not fit into a rationalistic pattern, is but a mask for the denial of substance. If one benighted class of men begins by assuming that whatever is, is right they begin by assuming that whatever is, is wrong. Had we to decide between these two—and I hope to make it clear that I do not think we have to decide thus—the latter would appear more blasphemous than the former because it makes a wholesale condemnation of a creation which is not ours and which exhibits the marks of a creative power that we do not begin to possess. The intent of the radical to defy all substance, or to press it into forms conceived in his mind alone, is thus theologically wrong; it is an aggression by the self which outrages a deep-laid order of things. And it has seeped into every department of our life. In the reports of the successful ascent of Mt. Everest, the British members of the expedition talked of "conquering" the mountain, but the Nepalese guide who was one of the two to reach the summit spoke of a desire to visit the Buddha who lives at the top. The difference between these attitudes is a terrible example of the modern western mentality, with its metaphysics of progress through aggression.

Here again was an invitation to ponder one of the oldest and deepest of human attitudes, which is generally expressed by the word "piety." The war of the radicals against substance is a direct repudiation of this quality. It is true that a great many instances of sham, in both word and deed, have been associated with this term, so that one runs a danger by bringing it into any modern discussion of ethics and religion. Nevertheless, it seems to me that it signifies an attitude toward things which are immeasurably larger and greater than oneself without which man is an insufferably brash, conceited, and frivolous animal. I do not in truth see how societies are able to hold together without some measure of this ancient but now derided feeling. The high seriousness of this life expresses itself as a kind of *pietas,* or a respect for the tragedy of existence, if nothing else. Piety is another one of those orthodoxies which have broken down because the defenders have not been able to show what is necessary in them. They have erected their defenses on positions quite easily overrun, and the places they could easily have defended they have left unmanned. As long as the term is associated exclusively with avoidance of foibles and minor vices, there seems no hope of restoring the vital idea for which it stands. But when one shows that the habit of veneration supplies the whole force of social and political cohesion, one hits at its enemies where the blow cannot be ignored.

The realization that piety is a proper and constructive attitude toward certain things helped me to develop what Russell Kirk calls "affection for the proliferating variety and mystery of traditional life." I feel now, in looking over the course of things, that such an attitude has always been in my nature, but that it has been repressed by dogmatic, utilitarian, essentially contumacious doctrines of liberalism and scientism, so that it was for me a kind of recovery of lost power or lost capacity for wonder and enchantment: The recovery has brought a satisfaction which cannot be matched, as far as my experience goes, by anything that liberalism and scientism have to offer.

It is what I feel when I return to the South, as I do each summer. There are numberless ways in which the South disappoints me; but there is something in its sultry languor and in the stubborn humanism of its people, now battling against the encroachments of industrialism and with so little knowledge of how to battle which tells me that for better or worse this is my native land. It is often said today that the hope of the world lies in internationalism. That may be true, but it is also true, and true with a prior truth, that there can be no internationalism without a solid intelligent provincialism. That is so because there is nothing else for internationalism to rest on. And if philosophical sanction for this is wanted, there is the wise and beautiful saying of Thoreau: "I think nothing is to be hoped for from you, if this bit of mould under your feet is not sweeter to you to eat than any other in the world, or in any world."

Nevertheless, it is most important, as I have tried to suggest earlier, to draw a line between respect for tradition because it is tradition and respect for it because it expresses a spreading mystery too great for our knowledge to compass. The first is merely an idolatry, or a tribute to circumstance, which has engendered some of the most primitive, narrow, and harmful attitudes which the human race has shown. There is a worship of tradition and circumstance which is all fear, distrust, and feebleness of imagination, and to this the name "reaction" is rightly applied. There can be no hope for good things from an attitude as negative as this. But the other attitude is reverential and creative at the same time; it worships the spirit rather than the graven image; and it allows man to contribute his mite toward helping Providence. Obviously free will would be meaningless if the world were to be left entirely untouched by us. Some things we have to change, but we must avoid changing out of *hubris* and senseless presumption. And always we have to keep in mind what man is supposed to be.

At the same time that the radical is engaged in denying the substance, he is engaged in denying the existence of evil, which is another great heresy. This takes the form today, as we all recognize, of assuming the perfectibility of man, the adequacy of social and political measures for the salvation of the individual person, and all the means of state engineering which are supposed to take the place of the old idea of redemption. Apart from the dilemma that the denial of evil involves us in, it brings into our moral, intellectual, and cultural life a number of destructive fallacies. It brings in, for example, the flattery of the popular will, the idealization of the mediocre, and along with these a spirit of rebellion toward anything that involves self discipline, sustained effort, and service to autonomous ideals. There is abroad in democracies today an idea that to criticize anybody for anything is treasonable, that the weak, the self-indulgent, and the vicious have the same claims toward respect and reward as anybody else, and that if a man chooses to be a beast, he has a sort of natural, inviolable right to be one. As far as I can see, there is no possible way of opposing this idea until we admit the existence of evil and the duty of combatting it. Here modern radicalism has failed again to interpret the issue.

It has been said that a disillusionment with human nature most often turns the mind toward Christianity. I know that in my period of jejune optimism the concept of original sin seemed something archaically funny. Now, twenty years later, and after the experience of a world war, there is no concept that I regard as expressing a deeper insight into the enigma that is man. Original sin is a parabolical expression of the immemorial tendency of man to do the wrong thing when he knows the right thing. The fact of this tendency everyone should be able to testify to, not only from his observation but also from his personal history. And it is the rock upon which nine tenths of the socialist formula for universal happiness splits. The socialists propose to offer man peace and plenty; and they seem not to realize that he may reject both for crime and aggrandizement. He has done so before in both the individual and the national units. It would be more realistic for the reformers to start with the old assumption that the heart of man is desperately wicked and that he needs external help in the form of grace. At least, we cannot build on the quicksand that he is by nature good, for he is not. Whether he has inherited his sin from Adam is perhaps a question for another level of discussion; the plain situation is that he has inherited it, and that it will sink any scheme which is founded on a complacent faith in man's desire always to do the good thing. Nothing can be done if the will is wrong, and the correction of the will is precisely the task which modern radicalism fails to recognize.

It is only realistic to point out that the concept of original sin, if not anti-democratic, is at least a severe restraint upon democracy. Democracy finds it difficult ever to say that man is wrong if he does things in large majorities. Yet even politically this notion has to be rejected; and that is why constitutions and organic laws are created in nearly all representative governments and are indeed regarded as the prime unifiers of such governments. A constitution is a government's better self, able to rebuke and restrain the baser self when it starts off on a vagary: If the mass of every electorate were wholly right at every period, constitutions would be only curious encumbrances. This means of distinguishing what is right deeply and naturally from what is wrong needs to be carried over also into our individual lives, where it sets a limit on indulgences of the self.

For all these reasons, those who say that evil is but a bad dream or an accident of history or the creation of a new antisocial men are only preparing us for worse disillusionments and disasters. It is necessary to recognize evil as a subtle, pervasive, protean force, capable of undoing plans that promise the fairest success, but also capable of being checked by proper spiritual insight and energy. This makes the problem of improving the individual and society continuous with known human history and not different according to different phases of economic and technological development.

The persistence of the fact of evil was then being underlined for me by the dreadful events of the Second World War. A question was posed in sharp form when the claims of modern and "advanced" civilization were being refuted by the presence of this greatest creator of misery. Wars not only were becoming more frequent, they were also becoming more absolute or more undiscriminating in their ends and means.

The prosecution of the war by the Western allies was to me a progressive disillusionment. My study of the American Civil War had made me acquainted with the principle that as a war continues, the basis of the war changes, but I had not been prepared to see the extent to which the moral aim may deteriorate. My faith in the honesty of our case was shaken by an incident that occurred about the middle of the conflict. The incident is not very well remembered because it concerned chiefly a small country, and what does a small country count for in a world where everything is decided by a Big Four or Big Three or a Big Something? This was the abandonment of Finland by Britain and the United States, who had previously bucked up her morale and to some extent her strength against the Russian foe. I felt that if Finland could be cheerfully thrown to the wolves in the taste for victory and vengeance, much worse things must be anticipated and so it has proved. And the Yalta Conference seemed to me at the very time when the newspapers were crowded with the most fantastic tributes and eulogies a piece of political insanity.

In sum, I felt that, thanks to our wonderful press and our Office of War Information and our political leaders, almost nobody in the United States knew what the war was really about. I recall sitting in my office in Ingleside Hall at the University of Chicago one Fall morning in 1945 and wondering whether it would not be possible to deduce, from fundamental causes, the fallacies of modern life and thinking that had produced this holocaust and would insure others. In about twenty minutes I jotted down a series of chapter headings, and this was the inception of a book entitled *Ideas Have Consequences*. At first it seemed destined to have only a *succes de scandale,* since it was so out of line with most current thinking on the subject. But many letters I later received from readers convinced me that other minds were tormented by the same questions, and that I had only gone to the point of saying what numerous people were thinking. The kind of opposition it aroused too seemed a confirmation.

It may sound odd, but it is true that the thesis of this book was first suggested by the bygone ideal of chivalry. My reading of history had encouraged the belief that at one time this had been an ideal of considerable restraining power, and that it contained one conception that seems to be absent from all the contemporary remedies for curing war—the conception of something spiritual which stood above war itself and included the two sides in any conflict. I have never had any faith in the notion of ending wars by fighting one war to a victorious and sweeping conclusion. The idea of a "war to end all wars" is worthy only of a mountebank. What such an attempt does in actuality is to scatter the seeds of war more widely, and possibly plant them more deeply. It does not take into account the intransigence of human nature.

The profoundly interesting feature of chivalry was that it offered a plan whereby civilization might contain a war and go on existing as civilization. It did not premise itself upon simplifications which are soon rejected, such as the proposition that "all war is murder." On the contrary, it tried to treat war or human combat as one of the activities of civilization, a dangerous one, to be sure, but one that could be kept under control. War under the code of chivalry might be likened to what the insurance companies call "a friendly fire." It is a useful thing to man as long as it is kept in a furnace or whatever place is intended for it. But a fire which gets out of the place created for it ceases to be friendly; it is a foe and can spread quick and terrible devastation. Thus the warfare controlled, or the war of limited objectives, is the friendly fire; but a war which has unlimited objectives has broken out of control and may, with the weapons now available, be capable of consuming civilization in a holocaust. Hence the problem is: what kind of thing is capable of controlling war, or of keeping it *within* civilization? It would be absurd to claim that chivalry accomplished all that the ideal pointed toward; there were episodes in the age of chivalry which make unpleasant reading.

Nevertheless, it was a moderating influence; and it did one thing which makes it appear realistic in comparison with the solutions which are being proposed today. It insisted that even in war, when maximum strain is placed upon the passions, man may not become an absolute killer. In war there are some considerations which must not be crowded out by hatred and fear. This is true because even your foe has some rights, and these rights you must respect although your present course has his destruction in view. This may seem to some too paradoxical, but let us consider it in terms of an analogy. Modern wars have tended increasingly to resemble lynching parties. A lynching party acts in the belief that the guilt of the victim is absolute and unqualified, and that the only thing that matters is to put him to death immediately. Any means will do: beating, pistol fire, a tree and a rope. Of course this idea is contrary to that of judicial procedure. The law never takes the view that a man's guilt is so absolute and so completely known that he is not allowed to say a word in his defense. On the contrary, the most atrocious murderer is given police protection and a trial according to forms of law, with a chance to state his side of the affair.

The law is in such instances upholding an idea similar to that of chivalry, inasmuch as it takes the position that no one—not even an "enemy of society"—can be denied rights entirely. In modern international warfare, however, the idea of a binding agreement such as this is being abandoned rapidly. The object now is to pulverize the enemy completely, men, women, and children being lumped into one common target; it is to reduce a country to "atomic ashes," to recall a frightful phrase which I saw recently in a newspaper. And then, if anything remains, the next step is the unethical one of demanding unconditional surrender. No further analysis should be needed to show that this moves in a direction opposite to that of the chivalric ideal, in that it pulls everything into the madness and destruction of war and leaves nothing, as far as I can see, to help pull even the victor out again.

There are those who maintain that modern technology, when applied to war, makes all such concepts as the one upheld by chivalry simply fantastic. There is no way of restraining a technology, they say, which is so developed that it cannot produce anything short of annihilation once it is turned to destructive ends. Perhaps this cannot be disputed as a fact. Yet if it is a fact, it seems one more proof that we have allowed science to reach a point at which it no longer allows us to be human beings. If we have got ourselves into a position where our only choice is to blow up or be blown up, this circumstance refutes the idea that we have increased the mastery of our lives.

There cannot be any improvement in the world's condition until the human spirit has counterbalanced and more than counterbalanced the hectic brilliance of technological invention. The deadly trap into which the pride of the modern world in technology and invention has led us is not often described in its real nature. It has produced a world condition of unheard-of-instability. The only way in which this instability can be overcome even temporarily is through rigid, centralized control of the national life. And the only way that a rigid, centralized control can be maintained is to keep the people living in a mentality of war. One can do this by filling them with desire of conquest, or one can do it by keeping them fearful of a real or imaginary enemy. Then one has a trump card to play on every occasion. If there is any relaxing or any resentment of controls, one has only to invoke "the national security" to silence opposition and even render it disreputable. We in the United States are living under the second of these policies now. The choice appears to lie between chaos and perpetual preparation for war, and the trouble with preparation for war is that it always issues in war. Here again technology steps in to make the dilemma more cruel, since it causes warfare to be increasingly total and nihilistic, and increasingly beyond the power of civilizing influences to absorb. From now on, as Maurice Samuel has pointed out, humanity will be living in the shadow of its own demonic omnipotence, and this is a calamity so great that almost nobody is able to face it. The chance that the world will not use atomic bombs if it goes on making them is infinitesimal.

How this tide is flowing even into the small interstices of our lives may be shown by a small incident. A few years ago there stood on the edge of the campus of the University of Chicago a small cafe. It was a poor affair, without style or pretensions; but here in the afternoons members of the liberal-arts faculties were wont to go for a cup of coffee, to get out of their professional grooves for an hour, to broach ideas and opinions, to be practicing humanists, you might say. Today a monstrous gray structure given to atomic research covers the site; the little cafe is no more; and the amiable *Kaffeeklatsche* no longer takes place.

The chief result of what I now think of as my re-education has been a complete disenchantment with the liberalism that was the first stage of my reflective life. Liberalism is the refuge favored by intellectual cowardice, because the essence of the liberal's position is that he has no position. It may be true, with due qualifications, that in certain transitional phases, where the outline of issues is none too clear, the liberal or uncommitted attitude has its expediency. But as something to construct with, never! It is that state of mind before we have made up our mind. The explanation of why liberalism has been erected into a kind of philosophy in our time is perhaps to be sought in the fact that our world is disintegrating rapidly. It is thereby creating the impression that nothing is permanent but change, and that the very concept of truth is a stumbling block to adaption as the disintegration goes on.

But even after this concession to the state of affairs, it is easy to see how the liberal's lack of position involves him in contradictions that destroy confidence. He is a defender of individualism and local rights, but let some strong man appear, who promises salvation through "leadership," and the liberal becomes indistinguishable from the totalitarian liberal of our times, a contradiction in terms, but an embodiment in the flesh, and a dire menace to government based upon rights. In times of peace, the liberal is often a shouter for pacificism, but let something he dislikes appear upon the horizon and he is the first to invoke the use of armed force. In education, he believes in the natural goodness of the child and abhors the idea of corporal discipline, but he believes in spanking nations with atomic bombs until their will is broken.

It is frequently said that while our knowledge of the natural world is increasing rapidly, our knowledge of the nature and spirit of man shows no gain, and that most of our troubles arise out of this disproportion. I think that our situation is considerably worse than this figure represents it, for I am of the opinion that our knowledge of the nature and spirit of man is decreasing, and this is not relatively but absolutely. No one can study Greek philosophy or medieval Christianity or the other great religions of the world without realizing that these saw man as a creature fearfully and wonderfully made, and that each tried to lead him with appropriate imagination and subtlety. Today, living under the shadow of this demonic technological omnipotence, we are trying to get along by supposing such crudities as economic man, "naturally good" man, and so on. Of course they do not work, and the more they are tried in our context, the nearer we are to catastrophe.

Somehow our education will have to recover the lost vision of the person as a creature of both intellect and will. It will have to bring together into one through its training the thinker and the doer, the dialectician and the rhetorician. Cognition, including the scientific, alone is powerless, and will without cognition is blind and destructive. The work of the future, then, is to overcome the shallow rationalism and scientificisms of the past two centuries and to work toward the reunion of man into a being who will both know and desire what he knows.

Richard Malcolm Weaver Chronology

March 3, 1910	Born in Asheville, N.C. Lived in Weaverville, North Carolina.
1916	Family moved to Lexington, Kentucky.
1927-1932	Attended University of Kentucky. Member of Phi Beta Kappa. Received A.B. degree.
1933-1936	Attended Vanderbilt University. Studied under John Crowe Ransom. Was a teaching fellow. Received masters in English.
1936-1937	Instructor in English at Alabama Polytechnic Institute.
1937-1940	Acting assistant professor at Texas A & M.
1940-1943	Student at Louisiana State University where he worked with Cleanth Brooks and Robert Penn Warren. Summer sessions at the Sorbonne, Harvard University, and the University of Virginia.
May 1943	Received Ph.d from Louisiana State University.
1944-1963	Professor of English at the University of Chicago.
1948	*Ideas Have Consequences.*
1949	Won University of Chicago Quantrell Award for excellence in undergraduate teaching.
1953	*The Ethics of Rhetoric.*
1957	*Composition: A Course in Writing and Rhetoric.*
1958	Participant in Vanderbilt University Literary Symposium.
1962	Received Young Americans for Freedom award for "service to education and the philosophy of a free society."
April 9, 1963	Died in Chicago, Illinois.
1964	*Visions Of Order.*
1965	*Life without Prejudice.*
1968	*The Southern Tradition at Bay.*

1970   *Language is Sermonic.*
1983   The Rockford Institute, Rockford, Ill., establishes the annual Richard M. Weaver Award for Scholarly Letters.
1987   *The Southern Essays of Richard M. Weaver.*

I
Studies of Individual Works

1

The Vision of Richard Weaver

Donald Davidson

From every book written by the late Richard Weaver surges a tide of intellectual force that critics, even the friendliest, have had difficulty in describing. No wonder—the force is light. And it is never easy to describe light, especially when it shines in times and places where it is disturbing and where darkness, or only a shadowed light, is preferred. To an unaccustomed reader Weaver's light may at first seem only exploratory and instructive. He may be tempted to think that it is merely picking out a devious way among heaps of ancient rubbish. But that reader may not realize how deeply his own thought is being engaged—how he is being persuaded to look and look again at what he may have taken for granted or ignored or assumed, in some vain way, that he understood. Presently, he is "seeing" (in the sense of understanding or knowing) as never before. He may also feel that he is in the company of a vision that is high and generous and very brave, and that this vision—the vision of Richard Weaver—is making irresistible claims upon his attention, indeed upon his life. So was it with the poet Rilke when he gazed upon the mutilated "Archaic Torso" of Apollo in the Louvre:

> ...da ist kein Stelle
> die dich nichdt sieht. Du musst dein Leben...andern.
> [...here is no place
> That does not see you. You must change your life.]

The present book, the work of Weaver at age thirty-three, is in scope and theme very far-reaching, as its title and subtitle suggest. But *The Southern Tradition at Bay,* covering both the Reconstruction and the

New South through an exploration of persons and ideas rather than events, is in the end about a good deal more than the South or the Southern tradition or the hundred or more writers, speakers, generals, politicians, nurses, diarists whom Weaver examines in his study of the half-century after Appomattox. As in indirect fire by artillery, his "aiming point" is indeed the South, but the "target," just over the hump, is the modern regime, both North and South, that has emerged in the mid-twentieth century and brought the Republic of the United States of America into its time of troubles. It is a book whose substance fills out the summary statements of the remarkable last paragraph of an article, "Aspects of the Southern Philosophy," that Weaver wrote for the *Hopkins Review* in the summer of 1952:

> If the world continues its present drift toward tension and violence, it is probable that the characteristic Southern qualities will command an increasing premium. While this country was amassing its great wealth, those qualities were in comparative eclipse; but virtues needed to amass wealth are not the virtues needed to defend it.... Belief in tragedy is essentially un-American; it is in fact one of the heresies against Americanism; but in the world as a whole this heresy is more widely received than the dogma and is more regularly taught by experience. Just as certainly as the United States grows older, it will have to find accommodation for this ineluctable notion; it is even now embarked upon policies with tremendous possibilities if not promises of tragedy. If we are in for a time of darkness and trouble, the Southern philosophy, because it is not based upon optimism, will have better power to console than the national dogmas.
>
> > It will do good to heart and head
> > When your soul is in my soul's stead.[1]

"A rhetor doing the work of a philosopher, he tackled problems for which he was not equipped," said his good friend and admirer, Eliseo Vivas, in reviewing Weaver's posthumous *Visions of Order*. "But," Vivas adds, "he was nearly always returned from his adventures with something worthwhile to show for them."[2] Elsewhere Vivas describes Weaver as "an intellectually bold man, capable of audacity behind or above the deliberate reflective thinker."[3] I do not think Weaver would have fretted against these honest and realistic observations.

But no philosopher, no philosophical-minded historian even, had tackled his subject. To be sure, there was the psychologist Dollard's appalling naive *Caste and Class in a Southern Town*, and W. J. Cash's piece of Menckensque journalism, *The Mind of the South*, and Howard Odum's laboriously statistical, facing-many-ways *Southern Regions*, and Vann Woodward's exclusively political-economic historical *Origins of the New South,* 1877-1913 (which discreetly passed over Reconstruction), and other books of these types. None filled the gap that Weaver saw.

If Weaver had waited to add, to his equipment as a teacher of literature and rhetoric, the perfected equipment of a philosopher, of a historian, a sociologist, a psychologist, and economist, a jurist, a journalist, and so on, he would never have written the present book or any of the books we have from his hand. *Time would not have waited on him.* If challenged as to his competence, he might have had to say that the teaching of literature had already required him to be a "generalist" rather than a "specialist." He did not care to escape the battle by enlisting in philology. The times needed men who could and would think as well as annotate. There were larger subjects that could not be handled as pure literature, pure philosophy, pure history, or by any symposium of specialists in those and other fields. *And the times would not wait!* Then Richard Weaver, after long tribulation of heart and mind, saw a task must be undertaken that called for one hand. And the hand might be his. And in the darkness of the modern night he said like Samuel of old, "Lord here I am...Thy servant heareth."

Such was the nature of Richard Weaver's audacity.

Another word for it might be devotion, taken in its oldest, most literal sense. Surely Richard Weaver made a vow—whether or not in a formal religious way, a vow that could not have been a merely secular resolve. It came from a certain experience not altogether different from that of Bunyan's Pilgrim when he decided to turn his face away from the City of Destruction. To his dying day Richard Weaver would study, as he long had studied, to better his imperfect equipment. But the experience in part made up for the inevitable equipment. But the experience in part made up for the inevitable lack of the special training for which his life allowed no time. It was the experience of a change of heart, of mind, of life. With it came a period of intense study and thought—above all, of self-searching. One immediate result was the present book.

In its first form it was the dissertation that he presented for the degree of Doctor of Philosophy in English, at Louisiana State University, 1943. His "Major Professor and Chairman of the Examining Committee" was Cleanth Brooks, not long back from Oxford, Professor of English and, with Robert Penn Warren, an editor of *The Southern Review.* In his acknowledgements, Weaver expresses his thanks to John Crowe Ransom and to Arlin Turner, as well as to Brooks and Warren.[4]

In his revision of his manuscript for publication Weaver substituted the present title for his cumbrous original one—*The Confederate South, 1865-1910: A Study in the Survival of a Mind and a Culture*. He added an introduction and an epilogue, but otherwise did little more than tighten the prose where he found it loose. It was already a book to begin with— a work in a genuinely literary and historical vein, though it had had to conform to the regular graduate school pattern. He offered it for publication. It was rejected. He laid it aside. One chapter, "The Older Religiousness in the South," appeared in a periodical—his first published article. By this time Weaver was in Northern surroundings, a teacher of English in the College of the University of Chicago, among new friends, busy on a new project. In 1948 it appeared, from the University of Chicago Press, his first published book, *Ideas Have Consequences*. The other one, unpublished, he obviously did not forget. It was found among his papers after his death in 1963. That Weaver kept it for twenty years, all the while virtually ready for the printer, suggests that he may have intended, at some opportune moment, to resurrect it for publication.

Well might he cherish it and wish to have it close at hand. For it marks the turning point of his career—the moment when he renounced the facile radicalism of the Roosevelt period for something more truly radical—the kind of "radicalism" that the current term "conservative" does not always suggest. John Crowe Ransom, commenting on *Ideas Have Consequences*, spoke of Weaver's radical-conservatism as "thoroughgoing, and philosophically articulate." *The Southern Tradition at Bay* can be considered a groundwork for *Ideas Have Consequences* and much of Weaver's subsequent work. For though the South-North issue does not arise in *Ideas Have Consequences*, and even the words "South" and "North" hardly appear, the book could well be entitled "The Northern Tradition at Bay" or "The Tradition of Western Civilization at Bay." For to "Northern" or "American" society in general Weaver puts the same fundamental questions and applies the same searching tests that he had used for the defeated but not reconciled South of 1865 to 1910. In *Ideas Have Consequences* and in later books and essays Weaver gives a broader development of views that had a preliminary exposition and illustration in *The Southern Tradition at Bay*. The chapters entitled "Distinction and Hierarchy" and "Piety and Justice," for example, in *Ideas*

Have Consequences, owe much to the analysis that Weaver makes in his earlier work of postbellum Southern society under such headings as "The Code of Chivalry," "The Attack upon Secular Democracy," "The Christian Warrior," "The Class System." In his posthumous book, *Visions of Order* (1964), the remarkable chapters on "Status and Function," "The Attack upon Memory," and "A Dialectic on Total War," bring into a broad, contemporary setting problems that he had already treated briefly in his survey of the South's long effort, during the sequel of Appomattox, to declare what it had been fighting for and what it had been fighting against—what it still was reluctant to accept as right and proper, however materially rewarding or pleasantly idealistic the victor's program might be.

To understand fully the unique quality of Weaver's first book and the momentum that it imparted to his later enterprises, one must go back to the experience that came to him at the crossing of the ways. The story is told by Weaver himself in his autobiographical essay that he called "Up from Liberalism," first published in *Modern Age* (Winter, 1958-1959).[5] Nowhere in that essay, however, does he mention the unpublished manuscript that was at the heart of his experience and that lay close at hand.

Weaver was born in North Carolina, but brought up in Lexington, in the fine "bluegrass" country of Kentucky, and he got his undergraduate education at the University of Kentucky. His professors, he relates, "were mostly earnest souls from the Middle Western universities, and many of them...were, without knowing it, social democrats...I had no defenses whatever against their doctrines." By his junior year Weaver was a young socialist in thought. Socialism had for him, he said, "an intellectual attraction." In 1932, after his graduation, he formally joined the American Socialist Party. "My disillusionment with the Left," he writes, "began with this first practical step." The academic people of the group were wildly, comically innocent of politics. Others were nondescripts, eccentrics. Most were "hopelessly confused about the nature and purpose of socialism." Despite the boredom he felt and his rising doubt about socialism, Weaver kept his membership for two years and even served as secretary of the "local."

His discontent with socialism was greatly increased by the years that he spent in graduate work at Vanderbilt University, where he studied under John Crowe Ransom and came in touch with the lively intellectual and literary activity that he found in the company of the "Agrarians."⁶ Weaver was particularly taken with the idea that "an unorthodox defense of orthodoxy" was feasible. Ransom, indeed, had demonstrated as much by the defense of religion against science and modernism that he developed in his *God without Thunder*. Weaver was suddenly troubled by his realization that "many traditional positions in our world had suffered not so much because of inherent defect as because of the stupidity, ineptness, and intellectual sloth of those who...are presumed to have their defense in charge."

When Weaver left Vanderbilt he had still not decided which road to take. At this stage, when he had not met the "mass man" face to face or seen the actual workings of socialism and centralism, he did not find it easy to reverse his course, although he felt the strong pull upon him of "the Agrarian ideal." What Weaver calls "my conversion to the poetic and ethical vision of life" did not come until he had taught for some time in Texas in close contact with "its sterile opposite," the rampant an complacent Philistinism that he met around him. One afternoon when he was driving across the prairies of Texas to begin his third year of teaching, the moment came, abruptly: "It came to me like a revelation that I did not *have* to go back to this job, which had become distasteful, and that I did not *have* to go on professing the cliches of liberalism, which were becoming meaningless to me.... It is a great experience to wake up...to the fact that one does have a free will, and that giving up the worship of false idols is quite a practicable procedure." At the end of the year he gave up his Texas job "and went off to start my education over at the age of thirty."

Officially, he recommenced his education at the Graduate School of the Louisiana State University, and in summers at the Sorbonne, Harvard, and the University of Virginia. Unofficially, he had already begun it by giving himself a course in extensive reading in the history of the American Civil War, "preferring first-hand accounts by those who had actually borne the brunt of it as soldiers and civilians." It was a kind of education that "had been almost entirely omitted from my program." Among other things, he could perhaps learn from it the point at which reason tells men that "reason is of no more avail." They must resort to force. The Civil War, which had "an elaborate ideology on both sides," was a fruitful field for this kind of inquiry. He soon discovered that it had other values—for example, the value of studying "a lost cause":

> I cannot think [writes Weaver] of a better way to counteract the stultifying "Whig" theory of history, with its bland assumption that every cause which has won deserved to win, a kind of pragmatic debasement of the older providential theory. The study and appreciation of a lost cause have some effect of turning history into philosophy. In sufficient number of cases to make us humble, we discover good points in the cause which time has erased, just as one often learns more from the slain hero of a tragedy than from some brassy Fortinbras who comes in at the end to announce the victory and proclaim the future disposition of affairs.

With such thoughts stirring in his mind, Weaver spent three years, he says, in reading "the history and literature of the Civil War, with special attention to that of the losing side." He could not claim to have grasped the whole mystery of "the encompassing passion which held them [the Southern people, 1861-1865, and later] together. But...I came to recognize myself in the past." This recognition was something more definite than the so-called "search for identity" on which many frustrated moderns are said to be engaged. Weaver did not need to ask: "Who am I?" He knew that. But it braced him in that self-knowledge and enabled him more consciously to relate himself to those all-too-human Southerners—and unquestionably many Northerners too—whose history and memoirs he had been studying. He knew now what path to take. Instead of the tortured, egocentric question "Who am I?" he could proceed to the larger, more philosophical questions "Who are we?" and "What are we doing?" and "What ought we to do?" in the books and articles that soon followed this first-written but last-printed of his works. In somewhat the same way Henry Adams fled the contemporary American scene to study the meaning of Chartres Cathedral and the Virgin. Weaver not fleeing, but dwelling in the very center of the modern American tumult at Chicago, thought that a devoted and rigorous study of some past experience of disaster—the fall of Rome, the overthrow of Napoleon, the destruction of the Old South—"will compel any honest seeker to see that the lines of social and political force are far more secret than the modern world has any mind to recognize, and that if it does not lead him to some kind of faith, it will lead him away from the easy constructions of those who do not wish to understand, beyond grasping what can be seized for a practical purpose."

That is it! Richard Weaver's book leads away from "easy constructions" and toward faith. It is not about the events of Civil War—Reconstruction, and the long aftermath of Populism, farm and labor trouble, the new industrialism. "Things reveal themselves passing away," Weaver writes, quoting Yeats. He is intent to discover what the postbellum Southerners, defeated, all but ruined, yet not really convinced, may consciously or unconsciously reveal about the great American experiment, from Jamestown and Plymouth to date. Events are "the text of a lesson, but not the lesson itself." The lesson must go beyond "the waywardness of events."

> In this research, therefore [he writes], I have attempted to find those things in the struggle of the South which speak for something more than a particular people in a special situation. The result, it may be allowed, is not pure history, but picture of values and sentiments coping with the forces of a revolutionary age, and though failing, hardly expiring.

The last four words—*though failing, hardly expiring*—declare the center of Richard Weaver's historical and philosophical interest in the amazingly varied material that he explores. What deep-lying beliefs and principles enabled the South so long to be "conspicuous for its resistance of the spiritual disintegration of the modern world?" From what sources of strength did the South derive its immunity to the subversive romanticism of Rousseau and the French Revolution and so hold out to become, as Weaver expresses it, *"the last non-materialistic civilization in the Western world"*?

It is a subject that in one way or another has recently attracted other serious writers. I believe it is particularly useful to think of Weaver's book in comparison with William R. Taylor's *Cavalier and Yankee: The Old South and American National Character* (1961), a book that has drawn praise from Edmund Wilson and Vann Woodward. Mr. Taylor's book also started its career as a doctoral dissertation, but at a Northern institution—Harvard. For his academic guides and directors Mr. Taylor had Oscar Handlin, Kenneth Murdock, and the later Perry Miller. Furthermore, he says, "A stimulating discussion of Southern thought in Louis Hartz's seminar in the Fall of 1951 probably determined me to write about the South." Although Mr. Taylor's Ph.D. degree was in history (and he is now a Professor of History), the sources on which he focuses are, as he says, "chiefly literary."

> There are many things [writes Mr. Taylor], about the history of an era that cannot be learned from literature, but historians, it seems to me, have been too timid about searching out the things that can. Stories and novels, even bad and unskillful ones, possess an element of fantasy which is sometimes very revealing.

Now Mr. Taylor, in his highly interesting and often instructive book, seems to take the position that the sectional differences between North and South, so far as they represent divergent ideas are pretty much "historical rationalization." His book aims to show how the idea of two different "civilizations" developed in the first half of the nineteenth century: "what social problems produced the need for this kind of historical rationalization, what kind of men and women contributed to its growth and dissemination—what sort of mentality, in other words, created this legendary past and this fictional sociology, and what sort of needs it satisfied."

Mr. Taylor then dwells on a relatively few figures, whom he places in a historical context and subjects to extensive critical analysis—mainly William Wirt's biography of Patrick Henry; Cooper's *The Spy;* the writings of Sarah Josepha Hale, the Northern "Lady Editor" of *Godey's Lady's Book,* especially her didactic novel, *Norwood,* which is largely about the South; Daniel Hundley's *The Valley of the Shenandoah;* John Pendleton Kennedy's *Swallow Barn* and *Horseshoe Robinson;* the novels of William A. Caruthers; the writings of James Kirke Paulding ("The Northern Man of Southern Principles"); and the writings, especially the seven Revolutionary War novels, of William Gilmore Simms.

Many other figures are touched in passing, but Mr. Taylor's large and highly speculative thesis rests upon this quite narrow base. And though it is attractively presented, the upshot of his study is that "myth" and "legend" have dominated over reality; the idea of "Southern nationality," based on the notion that "Southerners and Northerners were distinct and different peoples" was just "popular supposition," which was exploited by fiction writers and used by politicians. The line drawn by the English astronomers Mason and Dixon to settle a boundary dispute "possessed no geographical definition. It was a psychological, not a physical division, which often cut like a cleaver though the mentality of individual men and women everywhere in the country." With the collapse of the Confederacy "the Old South as a concrete entity passed beyond history and into legend." Accordingly, in Mr. Taylor's view there is no "lesson" to draw. But he admits that the vitality of the "legend" continues "to startle those unfamiliar with our culture, with our collective anxieties about the kind of civilization we have created, and with our reservations concerning the kind of social conformity which, it appears, it has been our destiny to exemplify before the world."

Richard Weaver's book, surveying the half-century after Appomattox, but not excluding the conditioning features of the half-century or more that preceded it, presents evidence for a *philosophical,* not merely a *psychological,* division. He, too, deals with fiction writers and their "myths," all the way from Cooke's highly romantic *Surry of Eagle's-Nest* (1866) to Thomas Nelson Page, Walter Hines Page, flamboyant Thomas Dixon, and "realist" Ellen Glasgow of the later Southern generation; and like Taylor he believes that the works of fiction should be viewed in the context of intellectual history. But Weaver's treatment of Southern fiction is only a part—and not the major part—of his broad-based study. Where Taylor finds "myth" Weaver finds "the older religiousness" and with it a tradition of "piety" that pervades everyday manners, in fact the entire secular life, and deeply affects the conduct of war itself. He is no sentimentalist. His eyes are open to Southern failings, and in castigation of Southern sins he is a Jeremiah. The numerous works that Weaver examines are, in fact, a long procession of witnesses that testify, each after his own fashion, to the reality beneath and within the "myth" or "legend" that Mr. Taylor hypostasizes. Weaver deals, for example, in "The Case at Law," with the writings of that hard-headed, stubborn advocate, Albert Taylor Bledsoe, who, before the War, practiced law in Springfield, Illinois, and knew Lincoln, and coached Lincoln on the use of broadswords for the duel with Shields that never came off. Bledsoe's *Is Davis a Traitor?* would have been the brief for Jefferson Davis' defense in court if Davis had been tried for treason, as was planned, in the Federal court at Richmond. There is nothing mythical or legendary about Bledsoe, or about the arguments of the various generals—Early, Hood, Longstreet, for example—that sought to vindicate their strategy; or in that remarkable book, *Destruction and Reconstruction,* by Richard Taylor, son of Zachary Taylor and brother-in-law of Jefferson Davis. Of the Confederate political leaders at the beginning of the war Richard Taylor remarked that they seemed "as unconscious as scene-shifters in some awful tragedy."

In these and many other writers, striving earnestly in one way or another to review their past and deal with their present, Weaver found evidence enough for the existence of a tradition that differentiated the South from the North. Its greatest fault in the end was its failure, after all, to give its latent "philosophy" an articulate form. "It [the South] is in the curious position," he concludes, "of having been right without realizing the grounds of its rightness. I am conscious that this reverses the common judgment; but it may yet appear that the North, by its ready embrace of science and rationalism, impoverished itself, and that the South, by clinging more or less unashamedly to the primitive way of life prepared itself for the longer run."

But the South failed "to study its position until it arrived at metaphysical foundations." This book, with much of Weaver's subsequent writing, is a large step toward supplying foundations.

It comes late. But the accidents of time evade our understanding. There seems after all to be a symbolic, even a practical rightness that Weaver's "Study in the Survival of a Mind and a Culture" should appear in the 1960s rather than in the 1940s as he once hoped. A book like this would hardly have been noticed in the uproar that followed the explosion over Hiroshima and that attended other noisy events in our recent history. It was not quite the appropriate book, either, for the centenary of the Civil War, which we observed a little awkwardly in some few ceremonial occasions but with a great show of expertness in our vast lavishment of ink upon book and periodical paper.

Now the centenary of the Reconstruction is upon us, but where are the celebrations? Where are the books and magazine articles? June 13, 1966, was the centenary of the adoption by Congress of the Fourteenth Amendment. With averted faces we seem to have tiptoed past that and other anniversaries akin to it. All the same, the Fourteenth Amendment, which immediately preceded a decade of non-legendary military rule over the Southern States, is grimly there. Still there, as the song says our flag is. Raised up by a virtual *coup d'etat,* a century ago, the Fourteenth Amendment has become "a proud tower," like Edgar Allen Poe's, from which the Supreme Court "gigantically looks down" upon our frantic little scurrying. And the South, yes, is still there. The North too, disguised as the nation. And the Freedmen—or the descendants of the Freedman—of a century past, having been freed over and over, are still there, still querulous. With suitable modern variations, history is being repeated.

If, in such time, questions about the nature of American society are to be bruited about or forced upon our attention, ceremoniously or not, it is exactly the right time to take counsel with Richard Weaver in his wise, good-tempered book.

Notes

1. Reprinted in Louis D. Rubin, Jr, and Robert D. Jacobs, eds., *Southern Renascence* (Baltimore: Johns Hopkins University Press, 1953), 29-30.
2. Eliseo Vivas, review, *Modern Age* 7 (1964): 309.
3. Richard Weaver, *Life without Prejudice and Other Essays*, with an introduction by Eliseo Vivas (Chicago: Regnery/Gateway, Inc., 1965), xii-xiii.
4. The names of the examining committee who accepted this most unusual thesis should also be recorded. They are, with Brooks, William O. Scroggs, Dean of the Graduate School, Earl L. Bradshaw, T. A. Kirby, W.J. Oliver, Robert B. Heilman.
5. Reprinted in Weaver, *Life without Prejudice*, 129-55. The quoted passages are from this source.
6. He entered Vanderbilt in September 1933 and in the spring of 1934 received his M.A. degree in English. His thesis subject was "The Revolt against Humanism." He continued graduate studies at Vanderbilt for two more years as a candidate for the Ph.D., and also taught in the English department, but left in 1936 without completing requirements for his doctor's degree.

2

Southern Thought and National Materialism

Calvin S. Brown

This is too good a book to satisfy many people.[1] By refusing to take sides violently and irrationally, it will necessarily alienate all the bigots on both sides, and their number is legion. The doctrinaire conservative worshipper of the Old South and the doctrinaire liberal hater of it will give equally short shrift to a man who has the balance and sanity to see that "Thomas Nelson Page and Harriet Beecher Stowe are ridiculous by the same test," for it is the nature of bigotry to refuse to apply the same test to both sides. But many who can scarcely be called bigots will be equally offended. It is fine strategy to be informed, objective and judicious, provided (of course) one arrives at the orthodox goal; but for a man who obviously has all these qualities to arrive at the conclusion that though the Old South was far from perfect, it stood for values whose loss endangers our civilization—this will seem intolerable to many who like to consider themselves fair-minded. The proper way to deal with the Old South is obviously the old vigilante way—"give him a fair trial and then hang the son of a bitch."

Weaver has not done this. In fact, he did not really set out to try the Old South at all. What he set out to do was to write a doctoral dissertation in English at Louisiana State University, under the direction of Cleanth Brooks. This work, completed and accepted in 1943, was a study of Southern thought in the half-century following the Civil War. Though it was not published, it came to be widely known and quoted by students of the subject and its author not only revised it for publication, but apparently kept it more or less up to date until his untimely death in 1963. When its publication was finally arranged, Donald Davidson was asked to supply an introduction, which he fortunately finished not long before his own death. Now both Weaver's and Davidson's work have been meticulously checked and seen through the press by George Core and M. E. Bradford, and the work is at last available to the public. It is a pity that the publishers have burdened such an attractive and intelligent book with a smarty and misleading jacket design—a Confederate flag at half mast—but *non ragioniam di lor, ma guarda e passa.*

Weaver's work defies classification under any of the usual categories. One might expect a dissertation in English to be devoted primarily to *belles lettres,* with a sprinkling of other material as background; but the discussion of post-bellum fiction, admirable though it is, comes late in the book and is not its central argument. Weaver begins with the Southern tradition as it developed before the Civil War, and then moves on to the legal, political, sociological and racial defenses of the Confederacy written after its military collapse. Since he shows that the primary intellectual energy of the Old South went into political thought rather than science or literature, it is proper that this discussion should be the first order of business. Then he moves on to the testimony of the Confederate veterans as to their side's motives, valor, and religion, as well as their appraisal of the character of the enemy. The accounts of Reconstruction—"The Second American Revolution"—come next. In this section Weaver is not primarily concerned with retelling the sorry story of what happened. Instead, he draws on contemporary testimony to show what took place in the minds of the vanquished, and to point out that along with the inevitable helpless frustration and sense of oppression there was often a clear, impersonal, philosophical awareness of the deliberate destruction of an irreplaceable set of values. Only after these matters have been explored does Weaver consider the world created in the fiction of the post-bellum South. This was at first the world of an impossibly perfect and splendid old regime, but vague criticism soon began to appear. This was followed by humorous satire, and then, early in the present century, by a full-blown realism. "It was no accident that Southern literature became mature when it first became capable of irony, for the road to maturity lies through the ironic understanding of life. Because irony proceeds from critical awareness, it opens up alternatives and leaves one confronted with the multiplicity of the actual world." Next Weaver traces the gradual weakening of the South's will to resist its critics, a weakening that seems to have been compounded of about equal parts of acceptance of valid criticism, sheer weariness, and creeping commercialism. An epilogue unsparingly traces the failure of the South to its refusal to cultivate the intellect, and its consequent lack of a metaphysic or of adequate spokesmen. "It needed a Burke or Hegel; it produced lawyers and journalists." Nevertheless, if the Old South's values as *"the last non-materialistic civilization in the Western World"* (Weaver's italics) can be grasped and projected forward without nostalgia, they may offer some hope for a world writhing in the noose of its own materialism.

In this work, Weaver approaches his subject from various points of view which are now usually considered the private domains of different intellectual unions, of historians, literary critics, political scientists, sociologists, and philosophers. It is a work on the history of ideas, in the best sense of that much abused term. The inherent danger of superficial knowledge has been countered by a tremendous amount of study, and though experts in the various disciplines involved can and doubtless will pick flaws here and there as they do in the work of fellow experts they can hardly accuse Weaver of either ignorance or incompetence. In addition to his information and ability to organize it, he has that broad human intelligence which readers of his later works, such as *Ideas Have Consequences* and *The Ethics of Rhetoric,* have come to expect of him. If no one but a technical expert could get a hearing, we could never have broad syntheses like this, and it is only by such syntheses that human values can be extracted from technical information.

These values turn out to be Weaver's real subject. The history of Southern thought from Appomattox to the *Lusitania* is not a mere pretext for him, but it is a test-case rather than an end in itself. Assuming, then, that Weaver's information is accurate (and this seems to be about as safe as any assumption can be) and that his analysis of the significance of this information is sound, what of his insistence that the ideas found in the Southern tradition are basically valid and are relevant to the modern world?

This tradition, Weaver finds, "has a fourfold root." It is based on a feudal theory of society, a code of chivalry, the "ancient concept of the gentleman," and a generally religious view of the world. It should not be necessary to explain that "feudal" is not here intended as the popular journalistic term of abuse, but is used as an accurate historical designation for an agricultural society based on large, centrally managed estates worked by laborers fixed in their position. The code of chivalry is, of course, inseparably linked with the ideal of the gentleman. Weaver does not pretend that chivalry and the gentleman were perfectly realized in every thought and act of the plantation owner. No ideal is ever attained in practice, but the stars that men steer by govern their courses, even though the stars remain out of reach. The point is not that Lee was a gentleman and Sherman was not, but rather that Lee strove to be a gentleman in a way that the Chevalier Bayard or Sir Philip Sidney would have understood, and that Sherman did not understand. Nor was the concept confined to the plantation-owners. The idea of a binding code of honor permeated the whole society, and continued long after the society itself had gone to ruin. Finally, there was a religiousness which had little to do with formal creeds or theology (again the distrust of metaphysical speculation), but was more an attitude towards life than a formal faith, "a sense of the inscrutable, which leaves man convinced of the existence of supernatural intelligence and power, and leads him to the acceptance of life as a mystery." This is the fourfold root that Weaver finds at the base of the Southern tradition.

No one today would call for a return to either medieval feudalism or modern slavery. But the fact remains that a classless society is an impossibility. It takes a great deal of regulation of everyone's life to homogenize society (as Robert Frost said) so that the cream can never again rise to the top. And where there is this much regulation, the society cannot be classless, for the bureaucracy itself becomes a ruling class. (In a melting-pot, of course, it is the scum that rises to the top.) In an absolutely egalitarian society there can be neither incentives to effort nor rewards for achievement. And if there are incentives and rewards, society becomes a melee in which the great object is to claw one's way to the top of the heap by the most efficient means, and every man's hand is against every other man's.

Probably the ideal is a society in which classes exist and are generally accepted, but there is sufficient mobility for an individual to be able to ascend (or descend) to his proper class. Certainly we are now reaping the fruits of immoral visionary promises of prestigious jobs for people who are neither able nor willing to do the work they require. The fruit of the rejection of social classes is a loss of that self-respect which a decent workman can have in any job, if only he has not been taught that it is beneath him. My father once remarked that the University of Mississippi (where he taught for forty years) had produced some fine scholars and professional men, but had also ruined a lot of good blacksmiths.

If there is to be mobility, what shall the criteria be? Here is where both the concept of chivalry and the ideal of the gentleman are necessary. Where these exist, they set standards and direct aspirations. Where they do not exist, as in our present society, something else takes over. It may be a purely material worship of money, no matter how acquired or how used, by which essential values are so muddled that "How much is he worth?" comes to mean the same thing as "How much has he got?" A gentleman is aware that a man may have two million dollars and not be worth two cents. Worse still, the standard may not even rest on acquisition, but on sheer puffery. We now have, for instance, popular singers who admittedly cannot sing, and whose fans love them all the more for the publicity which has made the fraud successful. Any society will look up to some models, and a corrupt society will look up to models of corruption. As Carlyle put it, when Bobus goes to the polls, he will elect Bobissimus.

Religion may seem a trickier root than the others, but only if we forget Weaver's definition and confuse it with dogma, church-going and slum-clearance. The sense of human life as a mystery ultimately insoluble by modern "problem-solving techniques" has been replaced by the notion that everything will be made manifest if only enough sociologists tabulate enough questionnaires. We pour billions into such activities, and produce snappy new models of human aspirations every year as regularly as Detroit produces snappy new models of cars. But the fundamental questions remain unanswered, and it has now become bad manners even to ask them. They will doubtless remain forever unanswered, but a habit of recognizing the mystery and reiterating the question would do much to restore that humility and sober, long-range view which are crying needs of our shallow and frenetic civilization.

Weaver's analysis of post-bellum thought stops short of the First World War, but he argues that by this time the essential character of the modern South was established. If he is correct, the Southern view of life should still spring from the same fourfold root. A good way to test his analysis, then, is to see whether the same qualities dominate the work of recent Southern writers. To make a brief test of this sort, it seems reasonable to choose Faulkner, whom the whole world accepts as the interpreter of the South. The choice is particularly appropriate because Weaver seems not to have considered him at all when formulating his analysis, for though he does refer to Wolfe and some other recent writers, he does not even mention Faulkner in *The Southern Tradition at Bay*.

The religious sense is certainly an essential part of Faulkner's world and in this expression I include both the world of Faulkner's own mind and the one in which his characters move. This sense is seen as good only when it operates privately as an impulse of the heart rather than through institutions and creeds. Faulkner is always hard on the Baptists as an excessively vocal and self-righteous group. His overtly religious characters are likely to be fanatics of one sort or another, like McEachern, Doc Hines, and Hightower, or at the very best to be hard prigs like Cora Tull. But such unpretentious, humble characters as Dilsey and Byron Bunch are caught up in religion in an admirable way. Faulkner finds no religion that he can respect in the organized activities of the respectable town churches, but there is powerful religious feeling in the incoherent poetry of the Eastern sermon in *The Sound and the Fury* and in the no-nonsense marine-sergeant faith of Goodyhay. Mink Snopes is profoundly suspicious of churches, but he trusts "Old Moster" to play fair with him. By the time this occurs, Mink has become an admirable character, in his way. It seems a fair generalization that Faulkner's worst characters are either religious bigots or utterly unreligious (like Popeye and Jason Compson), whereas his best ones usually have exactly that nonsectarian, undogmatic religious sense which Weaver describes as one branch of his fourfold root. Faulkner's overall view of humanity and his overt statements in his "Stockholm Address" show that he personally had it too.

In the world of Yoknapatawpha County, the concept of a feudal society, of the gentleman, and of chivalry as a personal sense of honor are so organically related that it is impossible to separate them or to see them as the badge of any single class or race.

Weaver's analysis is finally verified by the presence of the Snopes clan. At their worst, as in Flem Snopes, they illustrate the extirpation of the fourfold root. The only mystery in human life as Flem lives it is how to find out the weaknesses of others so that he can manipulate them for his own profit. As the embodiment of realistic commercialism, he will do anything for a profit and suffer anything to avoid a loss. He not only does not practice chivalry or gentility; he does not even know that they exist, for there is no money to be made from them. Faulkner was not writing a crude allegory, of course, but was showing universal human nature through the situation of his own particular time and place. Nevertheless, Flem Snopes is the perfect incarnation of that soulless rational commercialism which is opposed to the old tradition, and Flem's rise in Jefferson shows precisely how this spirit is taking over, and with what consequences.

There is something of Flem Snopes in everyone, and the gentleman makes it his job to keep this part of his nature under strict control. It is also his job to fight it in society as a whole, just as Stevens and Ratliff make it their business to fight Shopesism in Yoknapatawpha County. Weaver shows, with great learning and humanity, that the South is the only place where this battle goes on, for the simple reason that it is behind the times. Everywhere else the victory of the Snopeses is already decisive.

Note

1. *The Southern Tradition at Bay: A History of Postbellum Thought* (New Rochelle, N.Y.: Arlington House, 1968).

3

Richard M. Weaver and the Metaphysics of Property

Ralph T. Ancil

Property is traditionally a matter of importance and pride to the middle class of any industrial or commercial society. Respect for private property is often linked to political freedom as well as to financial and commercial success and to the ideology of modern liberalism. It was thus with some apprehension that Richard Weaver, in a work dedicated to the criticism of modern liberalism, undertook to praise property. He knew how dear to the heart of modern man this topic is. And yet Weaver's treatment is significantly different from most discussions of property, for it is precisely the modern justification of property that Weaver rejects in favor of an older, philosophical view of the matter. In what follows, I shall try to explain Weaver's viewpoint and how it is distinguished from the modern version, focusing especially on one fundamental example that illustrates the issues and consequences of accepting one view or the other.

Intuitively we understand property to involve ownership or possession, that is, to exercise some level of authority over objects, and in an older view, even over persons. In discussions defending private property it is not unusual to catalogue its social usefulness. Richard Weaver is not unaware of the social utility of property, yet the uses he cites are perhaps not common. In his book *Ideas Have Consequences* he gives four major uses of property under the curious chapter title, "The Last Metaphysical Right."

First and foremost, he argues, private property gives a measure of political freedom such that not everything is dependent upon the state, upon government: "Nothing is more certain than that whatever has to court public favor for its support will sooner or later be prostituted to utilitarian ends."

An example in this connection is the freedom and quality that those liberal education institutions enjoy that maintain a private income, and so have been able to insist that education be not entirely a means of breadwinning. State-run institutions, on the other hand, tend increasingly toward specialism and vocationalism. They cannot direct the use of their resources because their own is not private: "It seems fair to say that the opposite of the private is the prostitute" (p.127).[1]

Second, for Weaver, private property provides a training in virtue. Virtue involves choice and flourishes only where there is at least some range of volition. As Weaver writes, "It is...important to keep substance in life, for a man's character emerges in the building and ordering of his house.... Substance has a part in bringing out that distinction which we have admitted to be good; it is somehow instrumental in man's probation" (p. 146). But the attack against volition as manifested in the attack against property is perhaps another attack on reason. For if it is no longer believed that there is a restraining reason to which men may conform their volitional acts, it is not surprising that government will not permit individual centers of control. It cannot see how anyone would be guided by something other than itself. "For liberty and right reason go hand in hand, and it is impossible to impugn one without casting reflection on the other" (p. 138). Property is the training ground linking the liberty of volition with right reason.

Third, on a more pedestrian level of virtue, property cultivates foresight and providence, an awareness of the past and the future. It requires us to take into account the non-present, and hence exercise reason and imagination, a "play of the mind," to go beyond mere sense experience. Bearing the responsibility today of past effort, industry or sloth helps develop character; it "is an opportunity to develop personal worth" (p. 138). Otherwise, if a majority's begging from a present need to override rewards earned by past efforts is allowed, manipulation will be seen as the source of reward and not production. This, Weaver reminds us, is the essence of corruption (p. 139).

Fourth, property in Weaver's sense also protects against the dishonor of adulteration. When your personal *name* goes on a product, your reputation is at stake, so you try harder to deliver a good or honorable product or service. Weaver relates this to the value of money and national honor, where nations renege on their economic promises in the name of some present urgency, "values determined politically by governments under shortsighted popular control tend to depreciate" (p. 140). Rather, Weaver argues, an individual getting his sustenance from property which bears his imprint and assimilation has a more real measure of value.

These arguments, though very important, show primarily the usefulness of private property; in addition to suggesting that our idea of property, as in other important areas, will have profound social, political, and economic consequences. But still, in what way is private property *metaphysical?*

Weaver sees property as an affirmation of transcendence, and it is this affirmation which makes it of special significance for our own age. Weaver is concerned to show that the idea of property has moved away from its metaphysical basis from values, giving it an independence which distorts our view of the world: "The idea of metaphysical right subsumes property, and it is this idea that was lost to view in man's orientation away from transcendence" (p. 144).

The problem of affirming the transcendent by means of property as a metaphysical right, is dealt within the context of his treatment of the rise of nominalism and the consequent decline of the West. As a metaphysical realist, Weaver believes things have a knowable, enduring inner structure or nature. Human reason can discern this substance, or "quiddity," and, in fact, in order to lead the good life it is necessary to discover and understand these natures.

Yet to understand fully Weaver's view of the nature of property as a metaphysical right, we need first to understand his view of the nature of human personality, since these are inseparably connected. In studying this connection, three constituent ideas are discovered common to both: transcendence, distinction, and piety.

His fundamental view of personality is that it carries with it the imprint of the divine or the universal. Man's personality is "theomorphic" in that he participates with the divine (universal) by means of his reason (p. 181). This is consonant with the Christian view that man is created in the image of God.

Also for Weaver, "personality is the beginning of distinction." By this he means that rationalism and mechanism, the breeders of uniformity, cannot mix with personality. They contribute to the formation or sustenance of modern dictatorships and bureaucracies which reject the distinction of personality, this "last citadel of privacy." According to Weaver, "Deviation from the proletarian norm bids fair to become the heresy of the future, and from this heresy there will be not court of appeal" (pp. 181–82). Distinction of each particular personality means deviation or differing from others in a way that needs to be respected as private right.

Here Weaver brings in his other major element, piety, which asks that "we admit the right to self-ordering of the substance [property] of other beings" (p. 182). Piety means respecting the distinction of others, and this means allowing some degree of freedom to make independent choices, especially control over one's own "substance" or property.

As above, piety also means understanding that personality is something given to us: "personality, like nature, has an origin that we cannot account for..." (p. 176). Again, piety is needed to respect that which is given, and so is pre-rational. Personality is the substance of other selves. It is that property by which all other properties are possessed.

It is because of his metaphysical realism that Weaver is able to achieve a balanced view of the individual. He does not advocate "individualism" in the sense of selfish eccentricity, which is so much a part of the very modernism he criticizes. Nor does he lose the distinction of the individual in a collective entity. There is a balance which affirms both separateness and continuity, distinction and sameness, rooted in the reality of the universal expressed in the particular. As Weaver states:

> But personality is that little private area of selfhood in which the person is at once conscious of his relationship to the transcendental and the living community. He is a particular vessel, but he carries some part of the universal mind.... There is piety in the belief that personality, like the earth we tread on, is something given us. (p. 181)

With this understanding of personality we can understand Weaver's view of property. As personality has the imprint of the divine, of the universal, bespeaking man's relationship with God, so a man's property bears his imprint: "By some mystery of imprint and assimilation man becomes identified with his things, so that a forcible separation of the two seems like a breach in nature" (p. 134).

It is the *Eigentum* of man, as the German word goes; it asserts the domain of (what is) mine. It is the hisness of his, *proprietas*. "[T]he very words," writes Weaver, "assert an identification of owner and owned" (p. 132). Putting Weaver's thoughts on personality and property together:

if property bears man's imprint, and man's personality bears the imprint of the divine, then man stands in relation to God in a manner similar to the relation a man's things stand to him, i.e., man is God's property, an expression of God's "personality."

This sort of person-property relationship, however, cannot be the "property" of abstract, impersonal ownership of stocks and bonds and other creatures of "finance capitalism." Rather, it is one which keeps its identity with the individual by maintaining a close, personal relationship between owner and property (pp. 132–33).[2]

From this, it follows that property involves distinction, as does personality, and is not conducive to mechanical uniformity, or the abstract rationalism of modern economics, bureaucracies, or dictatorships. Weaver's use of distinction here implies freedom of the personality to determine its own course, at least within some range. This is what Weaver means when he insists upon "the right to self-ordering of the substance of other beings" (p. 182).

Like personality, property or substance is something given. It, too, is a pre-rational concept, not logically derived from something prior: "Therefore we are bound to maintain that some rights begin with the beginning and that some sort of private connection with substance is one of them" (p. 134). Property is the starting point in terms of which other action may be justified, though it itself lies beyond justification in terms of social utility. It transcends utility and provides the framework within which such utility makes sense.

"Now the great value of this," explains Weaver, "is that the fact of something's being private removes it from the area of contention. In the hisness of property we have dogma.... The right to use property as something private is...a sanctuary. It is a self justifying right..." (p. 132). In fact, Weaver indicates that this pre-rational nature of property includes a moral aspect which is a logical necessity:

> Therefore one inviolable right there must be to validate all other rights. Unless something exists from which we can start with moral certitude, we cannot depend on those deductions which are the framework of coherent behavior.... And I think it true that the sort of metaphysical moral right we have outlined bears comparison with the *a priori* principles which we cannot doubt when we do our thinking.... Moral certitude gives the prior assurance of right sentiment. (pp. 146–47)

The moral certitude begins with the recognition, "That the thing is not true and the act is not just unless these conform to a conceptual ideal..." (p. 130). It is private property which expresses this idea, the idea of the rightness of right, of inviolable right, and this is what makes it "metaphysical."

We see the implication of property as a morally certain right guiding proper sentiment when Weaver later speaks of piety, of that respect and reverence for things received such as nature, the past, and especially other people. Recognizing one's own right to a private connection with substance also requires recognizing the same right in others. It involves crediting "the reality of other selves" (p. 175) and the "substance of other beings." It follows, then, that if these other beings are to be respected, one must respect the property with which these other real beings, selves, or personalities identify. This is in fact foundational of community for "being has a right qua being" (p. 175), just as personality and property do.

Property is, in other words, self-limiting in that it concedes something to the nonself. By recognizing substance in the world we recognize limits and credit the extramental world with a reality whose ultimate origin we cannot fully comprehend, but which we acknowledge must have a transcendent source. Such limits suggest an enduring and fixed creation rather than the total evolutionism that is a denial of substance, of limits, and of fixity and distinctions (especially as these relate to human personality and property), and which instead deifies or absolutizes indefinite change. Here we see that property is real and limited; it is genuine but not absolute (in the sense of being inexhaustible, or unlimited).

Given the position of metaphysical realism Weaver takes, it is not surprising to find him linking language and property together, and it is through this connection that we may better understand his meaning of property as metaphysical substance.

From his treatment of the rhetorical nature of grammatical categories, Weaver identifies the noun with substance, with an enduring nature or underlying reality. Nouns involve a respectful "naming" of what *is*, recognizing the prior existence of substance, a given reality of a distinct thing or being in the extramental world. As Weaver describes:

> The noun derives its special dignity from being a name word, and names persist, in spite of all the cautions of modern semantics, in being thought of as words for substances. We apprehend the significance of that when we realize that in the ancient philosophical regimen to which the West is heir...substances are assigned a higher degree of being than actions or qualities. Substance is that which primordially is.... Nouns then express things whose being is completed, not whose being is in process.[3]

Thus, when one is using a noun or naming, "one is manipulating the symbols of a self-subsistent reality." This gives the noun a superior status in the sentence; it is the *Hauptwort* which other words are about.[4]

However, not only does "naming" identify a "self-subsistent reality," but it implies that the identifier or giver of names exercises authority over that which is named. "I am certain," writes Weaver, "that this is why Plato in the *Cratylus* calls the giver of names a lawgiver...for a name, to employ his conception, is 'an instrument of teaching and of distinguishing natures'" (p. 168). Elsewhere he explains: "To discover what a thing is 'called' according to some system is the essential step in knowing, and to say that all education is learning to name rightly, as Adam named the animals, would assert an underlying truth" (p. 149).

The method by which this naming or lawgiving occurs is not one of nominalistically imposing any label on a creature or thing for the sake of convenience. In general, Weaver argues language is "a bridge to the noumenal," not "a body of fictions convenient for grappling with transitory phenomena" (p. 150). In order to name rightly, one must discover via dialectics what the true nature of a thing is. Only then can we be said to "put our house in order" (p. 168).

It is this linguistic ability of dialectical naming, the vehicle of reason, and the theomorphic part of man's personality, that allows him to partake of the universal mind, to participate, in a way, with God in creation. Naming is a form of authority expressing dominion and property right. Hence, Weaver writes, "man's overlordship begins with the naming of the word. Having named the animals, he [Adam] has in a sense ordered them" (p. 149).

Weaver views the creation as a hierarchy of given distinctions or things rooted in a or pointing toward the transcendent. Naming, and thus the exercise of man's overlordship or authority, requires respect for this given creation as a real world of (material) things and a "respect for words as [noumenal] things" (p. 169). This implies the acceptance of an epistemology claiming a reliable fit between thing and thought, one rooted in metaphysical realism.

The relationship between language ("naming") and property as an exercise of proprietary authority or overlordship becomes especially crucial and relevant when we recognize that Adam not only named the animals, but also named Eve. These two gave names to their children and yet God the Creator gave Adam or man his name. This implies a primordial hierarchy of proprietary authority rooted in what Weaver constantly refers to as the Logos. In short, there is implicit in Weaver's argument for property an argument for a particular form of property, namely, patriarchy, or the patriarchal family. This is an especially good example separating Weaver's view of property, as something akin to philosophic substance, from the modern view.

With the rise of nominalism and the rejection of substance, modern man has become preoccupied with process and change, and not with fixity and things. Modern man harbors a distrust of the extramental world, for it is something not of his own making; he cannot accept the substance of other selves and the right a being has qua being. In the pragmatic and utilitarian frame of mind characteristic of the age, property too must serve only social utility; it must be useful as an instrument of reform or progress. Property, then, has become increasingly abstract and subjective.

Modern man, following in what philosopher Thomas Molnar argues is the Heremetic tradition, views creation with its distinctions, limits, and finiteness, as an ontological flaw, as sinful, and devoid of true being; fragmented and alienated.[5] Because of his nominalism, modern man holds that one cannot know truly unless one knows exhaustively, and yet this cannot be done unless man sheds his limits and distinction, his creatureliness, and becomes god. He thus equates a growth of knowledge with a growth of being.

The distrust of reason, which is the basis of rejecting the reality of universals, leads to an Ockhamist stress on inner experience, intuition, and the subjective in order to grasp knowledge directly (immediately) and immanently without the mediation of concepts. True knowledge and being are achieved by an "ontological promotion" (Molnar's phrase), which overcomes the fragmented multiplicity of non-being by achieving an exhaustive monistic unity, i.e., the knowing self fuses with the knowable object, abolishing the distinction between self and non-self. The thinking self may then turn entropically inward to focus on thought itself, the only object now worthy of its attention. Thus, Maritain could say such individuals do not begin their speculation by an act of knowing *things,* but by an act of knowing knowledge.[6]

This epistemology affects our idea of property. If knowledge of things and being is not genuine unless it is exhaustive, then surely ownership of things is also not real unless it is absolute or exhaustive, and this occurs only with God. Hence, we do not really own things, we own only our subjective interests, rights, or privileges in things; in short, we own our ownership.[7]

More technically, property is said to exist only if there are competitors needing exclusion, and a sovereign power who grants and protects these rights. Neither Robinson Crusoe, nor Adam could hold property in this sense. Property is thus wholly functional, a useful positivistic fiction of the state, a creature of human will and power alone. It is to be continuously changed and adapted to human or social needs. There is no necessary connection with personality in Weaver's sense and certainly no connection with metaphysical substance or transcendence. As Barlowe writes:

> ...one may argue that society is the true fount of property rights. Society allows individuals...to acquire, exercise, and maintain property rights and thereby maximize their personal satisfactions because this procedure usually enhances the prevailing concept of "Social welfare." In an ultimate sense, however, society always retains its right to regulate the allocating and distribution of property rights; and as the interests and goals of society change, the institution of property also changes.[8]

Thus, there is nothing to transcend society which changes property rights according to its subjective notions of the good and subjects property rights to the economic and political process, and thus absolutizing them (eliminating any limits that property rights had previously placed on them). Barlowe favors the modern belief that property is merely the interest acquired in objects or things, but not the things themselves. Instead it is a part of an evolutionary flux, an abstract process of changing social utility. Ultimately, in this view property can be reduced to a "euphonious collocation of letters," a convenience which names no reality, the familiar *flatus vocis* of the nominalist.[9]

Marx himself senses the importance of property, which he holds to be a "prolongation of the body." He sees the close connection between the division of labor and property which in turn results in trade and a market economy. However, for him this is a form of alienation, since property and the division of labor imply personal differences or inequalities which require mediation with or dependence on others. Such a limit represents a non-human, or alienated form of existence since he wishes to grasp life directly in its fullness and absoluteness. Marx is not content that man has mediation with the divine; he wants to become divinity itself. Man has no nature until he has this "ontological promotion," unmediated total knowledge and total being. Property involves distinctions, and these imply limits, and limits are obstacles on the road to divinity.

Among those many obstacles Marx recognizes the patriarchal family to be the "nucleus" or first form of private property where, as he describes it, the wife and children are "slaves" of the husband.[10] Marx sees the connection between property and patriarchy so that when he elsewhere states that the transformation of man into God will occur with the abolition of private property, we may infer this includes the abolition of patriarchy and thus the family.[11]

The attack against patriarchy as a basic form of private property, however, is not limited to self-conscious Marxists. The nominalistic impiety at the root of this opposition partakes of a much broader rejection of creation as something fixed and given. In the traditional view the received order in creation is that woman was made for man, out of his flesh, brought to him to become some flesh, and named by him. Adam held authority over Eve. Yet to the modernist this story and its implications are anathema. To accept that Adam held private property rights in Eve, in a sense owned her, as well as their children, is completely unacceptable to modern ears.[12]

The rejection of this property form of the family is rooted in the rejection of the family as a collective reality in favor of mere "individuals" who are "equals." The "prerogatives of sex" which Weaver mentions as another metaphysical right (p. 131) are banished and the family, with its authority anchored in the husband/father, is seen as a mere human institution, and male dominance as mere exploitation. Commenting on the erosion of the woman's traditional role, Weaver records the following lament:

> I put forward here an instance which not only is typical of contempt for natural order but which also is of transcendent importance. This is the foolish and destructive notion of the "equality" of the sexes. What but a profound blacking-out of our conception of nature and purpose could have borne this fantasy? Here is a distinction of so basic a character that one might suppose the most frenetic modern would regard it as part of the *donnee* to be respected. What God hath made distinct, let not man confuse! But no, profound differences of this kind seem only a challenge to the busy renovators of nature. (pp. 177–79)

Since things have no substance, no enduring nature, only unfortunate limitations, we may reform or renovate them. The limits implied in nature, a created order with giveness, are to be changed. Thus, woman's natural role as preserver of life, as biological, nurturant and natural is rejected. That the woman's role was intended to be ceremonial and emblematic must also be rejected and replaced with a hollow functionalism (p. 180).[13]

With the rejection of the natural order in the woman's role comes an undermining of the man's role, as his job is no longer to provide for or protect wife and children, but merely to satisfy his own selfish interests, and often to compete with his wife and other women. There is certainly no room for chivalry here. The ceremonial nature of the husband's role is likewise undermined. It is normally a small-scale enactment of Christ's sacrifice for the church. The man is expendable and the woman and child are not. As the woman is of the man's body and so under his authority, i.e., his property, so also the Church is the body of Christ and is His property. In both cases it is the property-owner who sacrifices himself on behalf of his property. But with the modernist attack on property, especially as it relates to the family, its ceremonial and transcendent character is lost in the mire of egalitarian individualism and egotistical "self-fulfillment."

The principle of patriarchy as a fundamental form of private property thus illustrates the difference, serves as a watershed, between traditional and modern views, between property that serves mere social utility. Christian faith, property, and patriarchy are not trivially related. More broadly, this case illustrates what Weaver describes as man's orientation away from transcendence.

In conclusion, we may say that Richard Weaver provides us with a metaphysical basis for private property. Instead of justifying it merely in terms of social utility, he argues that it belongs to those basic things which we cannot doubt if we are to be properly oriented in the world, morally and intellectually.

Contrary to the Faustian subjectivism of the modernist who seeks monistic unity, Weaver gives us a balanced, reality-oriented view of the individual and of property. He sees the creation as a hierarchy of distinct beings and things pointing to a transcendent source of origin which commands reverence, not renovation. Property is a part of the original divine order, an extension of the theomorphic human personality. It is akin to philosophic substance or dogma or the noun in that it is something received, given to us from beginning. It is the essence which subsequent thought and action are about, a starting point or right which justifies other rights, but which itself must stand beyond utilitarian justifications. Indeed, unless social utility has some fixed substance as its point of reference, it loses all meaning and becomes the target of mere caprice or of those in political power. Thus, in the arena of ordered liberty, reason demands that there be one right establishing the freedom of the will, which is itself not subject to human will but remains inviolable. The moral importance of this fixity or limit is as relevant today as it was when Weaver first penned these thoughts. As he describes the problem:

> The issue involves, finally, the question of freedom of the will, for private property is essential in any scheme which assumes that man has choice between better and worse. It is given him like the Garden of Eden...there is for us in this critical battle against chaos the concept of inviolable right. We prize this instance because it is the opening for other transcendental conceptions. So long as there is a single breach in monism or pragmatism the case of values is not lost...(p. 146)

Weaver's argument is worthy of consideration by economist and Christians alike, and by all men who recognize the reality of eternal values.

Notes

1. Richard Weaver, *Ideas Have Consequences* (Chicago, 1958). Unless otherwise indicated references to Weaver will be from this book, and the page number will be designated in the text by parentheses.
2. The property brought into existence by "finance capitalism" is wrong: "Such property is, on the contrary, a violation of the very notion of *proprietas*. This amendment of the institution to suit the uses of commerce and technology has done more to threaten property than anything else yet conceived." Furthermore such legal ownerships "destroy the connection between man and his substance without which metaphysical right becomes meaningless. Property in this sense becomes a fiction useful for exploitation and makes impossible the sanctification of work. The property which we defend as an anchorage keeps its identity with the individual." And finally he writes that "corporate organization and monopoly are the very means whereby property is casting aside its privacy." It tends to narrow the owner's responsibility to mere specialism. The property Weaver defines would provide "one ultimate protection for what is done in the name of the private person."

  We may begin to explain these views by investigating what Weaver means by the "sanctification of work." Work is sanctified insofar as it incarnates or appropriates the ideal in one's task. Honor in work means loyalty to this ideal and since honor is individual and personal, it requires private property. This allows the worker to identify with his product in a way which gives public testimony to his honor and so to acquire a good reputation or "name" (i.e., by putting his name on his work he assumes full responsibility for its quality). This is why Weaver insists that true property always retain its identity with its owner; it is never distant, abstract or anonymous. This also gives work its ceremonial and transcendent character, elevating it above mere utilitarianism. (Implicit here is the notion that

the worker has a kind of property right in the ideal to which he owes some allegiance. His employer may hire him, but having done so, the worker's duty is to this ideal. This places a limit on the authority of the employer. See Weaver's chapter on "Egotism in Work and Art.")
3. Richard M. Weaver, *The Ethics of Rhetoric* (Chicago: Henry Regnery, 1963), 127-28. Compare this with Garret Hardin's modernist view of language:

> It is language that deceives us. Our language breeds gods: it is admirably suited to dealing with substances and persons, but poorly adapted to dealing with processes, which it constantly tends to degrade to things or beings. Perhaps no single ability is so characteristic of the true scientist as the ability to think in terms of process in spite of language.

See his *Nature and Man's Fate* (New York: Mentor Books), 60. On the relation between property and language see also Gottfried Dietze's *In Defense of Property* (Baltimore and London: John Hopkins Press, 1971), as well as on the importance of property generally.
4. Ibid., 128 and fn. 7.
5. Thomas Molnar, *God and the Knowledge of Reality* (New York: Basic Books, 1973), see especially pp. 125-42.
6. Ibid., 113.
7. The precise significance of creation, writes Molnar, is that man's being and its modalities are given him by God. As Creator God is in everything (pp. 208-9) and this at once is a limit of man's being and knowledge, and a guarantee of their validity. This reality of ultimate origins is likewise a limit of man's proprietary authority. As a part of the creation his dominion is derived and contingent; its origin lies outside its present functioning and so is not explained by it. This, too, at once limits and guarantees its validity. So any attempt to render it autonomous, for example, by impious acts against nature, the past or people, invalidates it. To be valid man's authority must be both real, in that he genuinely owns real, extramental things, and limited, in that the divine origin of both nature and man places limits on his dominion and demands respect. Weaver similarly argues that the denial of substance is a denial of the rightfulness of creation (p. 171). This also implies limits on man. The Author of creation is the one authority man cannot challenge. So when Weaver speaks of the right to private property as "self-justifying," he does not mean it is autonomous in some secular sense but precisely because of its divine "giveness" it requires simultaneously piety toward creation (hence limit) but real authority which, within its legitimate sphere, is inviolable.

But this is exactly what modern man cannot accept. By reversing the Mediaeval dictum that the order of knowing follows that of being, he is driven to a kind of hubristic activism. The activity of knowing becomes energetic doing aimed at the renovation of nature and the creation, as a hierarchy of being, is replaced by an evolution of functional changes supposedly leading to the desired "ontological promotion." (Cf., for example, Eugene M. Klaaren's *Religious Origins of Modern Science* [Grand Rapids, Mich.: William B. Eerdmans Publishing Co., 1977], see esp. pp. 123-24.)
8. Raleigh Barlowe, *Land Resource Economics*, 3d ed. (Englewood Cliffs, N.J.: Prentice-Hall, 1978), 400, fn. 14.
9. Ibid., 395.
10. Bertell Ollman, *Alienation*, 2d ed. (Cambridge: Cambridge University Press, 1976), 161.

74   The Vision of Richard Weaver

11. Molnar, *God and the Knowledge of Reality,* 135.
12. Alexis de Tocqueville comments on the property-person relation between masters and servants in Europe:

    Amongst an aristocratic people the master gets to look upon his servants as an inferior and secondary part of himself, and he often takes an interest in their lot by a last stretch of egotism.

    Servants on their part, are not averse to regard themselves in the same light; and they sometimes identify themselves with the person of the master, so that they become an appendage to him in their own eyes as well as in his.

    (See his *Democracy in America* and the chapter on "How Democracy Affects the Relation of Masters and Servants.") In the New World, however, with its egalitarian view and contract basis, the "warm and deep-seated affections" which can sometimes arise under the old system of status cannot occur, nor will the new type of relation allow master and servant to "exhibit strong instances of self-sacrifice." Neither could a modernist understand how an Israelite could voluntarily become a slave for life.

    James W. Wiggins similarly argues for a person-property continuum. He points out man's tendency to identify himself with objects, people, and ideas as an extension of self. He notes the reflection of this tendency in language. He specifically cites the Bible account of creation as well as the Ten Commandments as evidence of the primordial treatment of woman as private property and, more generally, the relation between private property and the person. Three of the commandments, Wiggins argues, even identify God with His property. He writes: "The person who is private property seems to identify reciprocally with, and find personal extension in, attachment to the owner." This is illustrated when one becomes a child (i.e., property) of God, in the slave whose person expands to include his owner (and here he cites both Hebrew and Southern slavery) and in the wife who "flowers" as a "part" of her husband. See his paper, "The Decline of Private Property and the Diminished Person," in Samuel L. Blumenfeld, ed., *Property in a Humane Economy* (LaSalle, Ill.: Open Court, 1974), 71-84.

    Similarly, see Blackstone's *Commentaries* on the laws of England on the relations between man and wife. Here is a beautiful example of the incorporation of the Biblical and universal principle of patriarchy into the law. Man and wife are considered as one person, and the wife, under the husband's authority, is said to be in her "coverture" and he is her "lord."
13. Weaver argues that the woman's true role can be restored to her only when "she finds privacy in the home and becomes, as it were, a priestess radiating the power of property sentiment. Her life at its best is a ceremony" (p. 180). But again the nominalistic dictum that being follows doing allows no escape from its voracious appetite for the reconstruction of nature, and womanhood in its ordained role is replaced by a functional hermaphroditism. It is interesting that Weaver links such a restoration of woman's natural role to the restoration of true property, comfortable to man's theomorphic personality. This relationship is underscored when we understand that woman *is* property, a situation which enhances her privacy as well as her husband's. Or, as Weaver states, whatever is not private is prostituted to utilitarian ends (cf. p. 136).

    The great tragedy here is that many people, including women, who use the name of Christ eagerly compromise on the principle of patriarchy. (Thus, it is almost embarrassing to assert the authority of husband over wife.) The spirit of accommodation to the anti-Christian views observed from nominalism constitutes the great bane of what passes today for the Christian Church. Until this relationship between man and wife within a biblical metaphysical context is reaffirmed intellectually and implemented in public policy, there is little hope of salvaging the family from its present troubles and degenerate condition.

4

The Mind of Richard Weaver

Eliseo Vivas

Richard Weaver's posthumous book exhibits, as one would expect from the concentrated personality he was, the weaknesses no less than the excellences that distinguished him as a writer.[1] He left it in manuscript and had no opportunity to make final revisions. In this review I shall dwell on both its virtues and its defects, in the conviction that to praise him by selective emphasis would be to insult the responsible writer. A thinker, particularly a thinker of Weaver's rare integrity, wants his due need of recognition and acclaim, of course. But one does not flatter him who accepts the product of mind uncritically. I know of no other way to take a writer seriously than to hold him fully responsible for what he chooses to publish.

Before turning to what I take to be the qualities, negative and positive, of his last book, I must sketch, hastily, its content. Although its title suggests a positive standpoint, its subtitle is a more accurate indication of Weaver's interests. "Visions of order" enter into the book as criteria which enable us to examine our disorder. It is true that the first two chapters, "The Image of Culture," and "Status and Function," and to some measure the third, "The Attack Upon Memory," furnish us with a general conceptual scheme by means of which to perform the diagnosis. But it is the disorder that Weaver found in his world that prompted him to undertake theoretical considerations of the nature of culture, of stasis and flux, and of the indispensable role of memory in humane living. This is to say that Weaver was not a man interested in theoretical questions as specialists in these matters are. He was forced to think in abstract terms because this was an indispensable condition in order to come to terms with the malformations of the world in which he lived.

"The Image of Culture" sketches an "organic" view (a term Weaver does not use) of culture. It is asserted early in this chapter that the controversy as to whether a given culture is flourishing or declining cannot be settled unless "one is willing to contemplate the order of human values" and consider "the nature and proper end of man." But while this conviction is repeated throughout the book, the very difficult problems to which it gives rise are not elucidated. Weaver prefers to turn from these to the discussion of a principle of culture he deems of great importance in our present crisis, namely the principle of integration and exclusiveness. Culture integrates the individual by imposing on him a "tyrannizing image " which "is an ideal of excellence," thus giving its members a sense of the value of their lives.

But because integration entails exclusiveness, the notion of a "democratic" culture is inadmissible. Culture is not open to everybody at all times on equal terms. And for that reason, in turn, the task of the conservative today is to defend the discriminations and exclusions of culture. There is nothing new in this view. Weaver learnt it initially from Ralph Linton and other social scientists, by way of a friend. What is new and important is the courageous and bold manner in which he applies it, drawing from it consequences that the social scientists who originated the view would be horrified to draw. For with rare exceptions, these gentlemen are part of the well-disciplined liberal academic herd. And that means that while they would think it unforgivable to meddle with the cultures of primitive peoples, they choose to serve in the front lines of the struggle to destroy their own culture, by prescribing for it all sorts of scientific nostrums.

Emphasis on integration and exclusiveness might have led Weaver to a kind of Realpolitik attitude towards culture. But in chapter 5, "Forms and Social Cruelty," Weaver acknowledges that a culture sometimes tends to levy an excessive tribute upon the human beings for whom it exists. Obviously Weaver was not an apologist for the status quo. He could recognize that a culture was capable of iniquity.

The second chapter is a difficult one to digest. Entitled, as indicated, "Status and Function," it seems to collapse the topics social scientists would normally consider under these rubrics and the more pervasive and general problem of stasis and flux. But exactly what Weaver takes to be the relation between status (in its usual sociological acceptation) and social and cosmic stasis, I am afraid I could not make out clearly. In any case, the problem of the "terrible mobility" of our day is one that is close to Weaver's heart, as it must be to the heart of any conservative. But I must report that Weaver has no more viable solution of this problem than any of us has. For it is one thing to propose measures to control the drift of our world toward socialism and quite a different thing to prescribe how to slow down the erosion of the basic values of our civilization. It is the latter that concerned Weaver, but against it he had no possible practical advice to offer.

The third chapter, "The Attack Upon Memory," analyzes a disorder called by Weaver "presentism." This is the belief that only the present can confer significance upon things. It is easy to see how such a shallow delusion would cut our roots and would end by denying our organic relationship to one another and to our traditions. But Weaver goes farther in his analysis of presentism. He contrasts history with positive science, and shows with great ingenuity that presentism is the result of the scientism we so uncritically accept. Chapter 4, "The Cultural Role of Rhetoric," is one of the two most original and best thought out of the eight. The relationship of rhetoric to dialectic is a subject on which Weaver thought deeply and fruitfully, as *The Ethics of Rhetoric* amply shows. What this chapter establishes may perhaps be suggested by the reference to Pascal's famous pensée: The heart has reasons that reason knows not of.

On the fifth chapter I have already touched. The sixth is the second of the two best and to the reviewer it comes as a pleasant and complete surprise. On the subject of "The Dialectic of Total War" Weaver, though not a pacifist, contributes wisdom, clear thinking, and as realistic and sober a discussion of the problem as we can expect from any of our contemporaries. The penultimate chapter has the Voegelinian title of "Gnostics of Education." If we leave out of account the unconvincing, because utterly factitious, parallelism between the gnostic heresy and the precious errors of the contemporary liberal ethos, what Weaver has to say about the so-called "philosophy" of progressive education is something with which educated men today are, by and large, fairly well acquainted.

Regarding the last chapter, "The Reconsideration of Man," the less said the better. To at least one of his admirers it constitutes an embarrassing performance. For reasons I was never able to fathom, Weaver wasted a good deal of time and energy seeking what he took to be damaging arguments against the evolutionary hypothesis. But it would have taken far more science and philosophy than he had at his command to begin to undermine successfully the work of Darwin and his heirs.

These eight chapters do not constitute a complete examination of our contemporary disorders, but those aspects of our plight that they do examine are important, and all that Weaver has to tell us about our illness in specific terms—something the preceding account could not convey— deserves careful attention. Because I want to leave my reader a sense of my own high regard for the book—a regard that remains untarnished even after the unsparing consideration of its weaknesses—I am going to examine some of these first, closing the review with a sketch of what I take to be the positive virtues of the thinker.

Some of the weaknesses of Weaver's work are serious, but among the most serious is one that, given the audience he sought to reach, is not altogether a fault: the audacity of his mind. His was an audacity that contrasted sharply with his external appearance and the superficial aspects of his personality. This courteous academic man, who in so many ways was the prototype of the square professor with his two-bit can of pipe tobacco and his bargain-counter pipe, spent the major part of his working day (seven days a week, I understand) swimming far from the safe shores of his own competence towards high seas that were beyond his depth. A rhetor doing the work of a philosopher, he tackled problems for which he was not equipped. But—and this is no less important—he nearly always returned from his adventures with something worthwhile to show for them.

His disregard of his limitations can be illustrated by his treatment of the nature of culture. Infecting it with incoherence is a defect that runs like a geological fault throughout the whole of the book's length. Early in chapter 1, the reader becomes aware that Weaver oscillates between the sociological and the honorific meaning of the term "culture." We know, of course, that the term is far from having a univocal acceptation among social scientists.

But its diverse meanings all aim to refer to the fact that human groups pursue values and accept meanings that enable them not only to survive but to give some worth to their lives. In this sense, any group that holds together at all has culture, even though its values may be so incompatible that their pursuit may lead to basic frustrations. In the honorific sense—although here "culture" is no more of a univocal term than it is in the sociological sense—not all groups can be said to have culture. By and large culture in this sense seems to be only attainable by sub-groups in a society. Greek cultures or the Italian culture of the Renaissance was the possession of a minority, and was possible because the minority used for its own ends a less cultivated majority. Since the two meanings refer to totally different things, one cannot achieve coherence if one fails to reckon with the required distinctions.

We are not confronted here with a nice but sterile academic question. Weaver wanted to criticize the crisis of our world. But which of the two cultures was open to criticism? Shuttling freely between the two meanings, Weaver avoids trouble with the social scientists, who claim that the fact of culture in their sense is the valid ground for their espousal of cultural relativism. But Weaver—who at times sounds like Melville Herskovits—informs us that he is no cultural relativist. However, merely to deny it is not enough. If he is no relativist, what in Weaver's view gives superior cultures their pride of place? It cannot be their successful integration and their exclusiveness, for on these criteria most primitive cultures would be ranked as superior to contemporary civilization. A defender of Weaver might argue that he intended the term in its honorific sense. But the defense is inadmissible, for the fact is that he often uses "culture" in its sociological sense, and sometimes it is not possible to decide in which of the two senses he is using it.

No, it is not their integration and exclusiveness that are the criteria of excellence, another defender may urge, but the nature and proper end of man, to which on more than one occasion Weaver turns as basis from which to criticize the disorders of our day. And the lamentable last chapter is without doubt an effort to furnish us with a better notion of man than we can get if we base our concept of man on an evolutionary basis. But where does Weaver go for his idea of man? Weaver has no difficulty: He tells us that "religious, philosophical, and literary studies of man" concur in their teaching about him. Notice that neither the positive nor the social sciences are mentioned. But let that pass. Are we to assume that Jesus concurs with Mohammed, Loyola with Jansen, that Plato concurs with Epicurus, Kierkegaard with Dewey? That Calderon concurs with Marlowe, and Jane Austen with Kafka? Clearly the problem cannot be disposed of that easily.

But nothing can be gained by continuing the *exposé*. For the value of the book easily transcends the animadversions one might level at it. What then are its virtues? For one reader, the first is the quality of the author's thought. The quality of thought for which philosophers have so little regard, comes, in Weaver's case, from the coherent and fully examined attitudes of the author. The man's mind as expressed in his work gives off the bouquet of an *Edelwein*. There is a sturdy, yeoman's commonsense to the way in which this rhetor quietly shows us what the liberal ethos takes to be the highest virtues of our world are deplorable vices. But in back of the judgments there is something for which I have no other term than "instinct." His sub-intellectual reaction is coherent and not to be deceived by the mendacities and sentimentalities that are the liberal values. One gathers the feeling that here is a man who whether right or wrong about the formulation and argumentation of his indictment of our age was not bamboozled by the lies that assault us. His arguments were not always the best, but the attitudes from which his rejections and acceptances issued were for the most part unerring. Weaver was authentic in the original sense of the term. He possessed a character and a mind that were "written with the author's own hand."

For this reason there is another positive value to Weaver's work: Although not an original thinker, the way in which he put his ideas to use and the ends to which he was dedicated were original. When he turned his mind to a subject he did so because the deeper layers of his personality were aroused. His encounters with the world at the intellectual level were never mere SR responses. His thinking arose out of a personal need for intellectual order and moral excellence and not out of a careerist desire to acquire off-prints to put on the dean's desk.

Finally, for one of his admirers at least, the high value of his work lies in its courage. Dick Weaver had the gifts that would have enabled him, had he chosen, to have had an easy and successful career as a regular professor and a popular writer. Had he chosen the easier path, had he become one of the sycophants of the *Zeitgeist,* one of the boot-licking, liberal court-historians of his generation, flattering it while he pretends to criticize it, he would have been one of the big shots of the university and would have been invited to contribute to the organs of the Establishment. He chose the harder path. And he paid the price in slow academic recognition and in the size of audiences he reached. But in the end he won. He earned promotion in the field, into the leadership of a band of rebels—they are pitifully few, but what an elite squad!—who have been teaching us to value truth and to eschew the lie.

Note

1. *Visions of Order: The Cultural Crisis of our Time* (Baton Rouge: Louisiana State University Press, 1964).

5

The South Wisely Perceived

Allan C. Brownfeld

The South for many years has occupied a special place in the American imagination. Those in other parts of the country have romanticized about the almost medieval chivalry of the plantation days and the heroic era of the Civil War. Figures such as Washington, Jefferson, Madison, Monroe, and Robert E. Lee have been distinctively Southern, creating the American Republic in its earliest days in the image of Virginia. In this century, our literature has been largely dominated by its Southern writers—William Faulkner, Tennessee Williams, Thomas Wolfe, Flannery O'Connor, Carson McCullers, Eudora Welty—the list goes on and on.

But the South of the American imagination has other dimensions as well. The South, in the post-Civil War years, became synonymous with backwardness and provincialism and, in particular, with racial bigotry and exclusiveness. It was labeled an intellectual wasteland and rejected as hostile to the American notion of progress, business, and industrial civilization.

In the end, both of those who romanticized the South and those who make of it a scapegoat for all of the narrowness of mankind may have been mistaking their own faulty visions for the Southern reality. That reality is indeed unique and, in many ways, quite the opposite of what may be found in other areas of the United States. It also is unique in ways quite different from those many have attributed to it.

The essays in this book explore those differences with a depth and grace rarely to be found, and they are permeated with an affection which endears them to the reader.[1]

The author, Richard Weaver, was both a man of the South and a man of letters. His academic career, as professor of rhetoric at the University of Chicago, was a notable one, and his books—including *The Ethics of Rhetoric* and *Ideas Have Consequences*—have been widely recognized as important contributions to the defense of the higher culture of Western Civilization against those who would shatter it.

In an essay included in an earlier selection of Weaver's writings, *Language is Sermonic* (Louisiana State University Press, 1970) Professor Ralph T. Eubanks writes that

> Richard M. Weaver was one of those rare souls who had thought deeply about what he was doing. He had settled for himself a vast number of things about the meaning of his life and the world. And he was therefore left free to follow his "duty and destiny" in the Carlylian sense. "He believed, and passionately so, that the inherited traditions of our society were in process of rapid disintegration. And Reinhold Niebuhr regarded his seminal analysis, *Ideas Have Consequences,* as 'a profound diagnosis of the sickness of our culture." The heart of Weaver's mission was restoration of respect for what T.S. Eliot once called "the permanent things." The final sanction of his case was intuitive. "We begin our other affirmations," he wrote, "after a categorical statement that life and the world are to be cherished." Thus it was that Weaver was inevitably thrust into opposition to the Jacobin mentality.

Eubanks notes that,

> ...in a very real sense Weaver's life was a crusade to reestablish belief in the reality of transcendentals.... His defense of orthodoxy began and ended with the Southern idea of life. Weaver was a man of the South. Yet, true to his conception of the rhetor-as-cultural-critic, he exiled himself from his native South. His most mature thought was really the product of his years at the University of Chicago—years in a climate he found so hostile that he often wore two overcoats. Ironically, only a few months before his death Weaver had accepted an appointment at Vanderbilt in his beloved South.

The pieces gathered together in the current collection appeared in such journals as *The Sewanee Review, The Georgia Review, The South Atlantic Quarterly, Modern Age,* and *The Texas Quarterly.* Most of them have been out of print for years.

Richard Weaver attended Vanderbilt University, from which he received the M.A. degree, arriving during the high tide of Agrarianism, the intellectual movement sparked by the publication in 1930 of *I'll Take My Stand,* a volume of twelve essays written mainly by Vanderbilt professors and their former students. The editors of this volume, George M. Curtis III and James J. Thompson, Jr., write that "This reassertion of

Southern tradition against the fragmentation and anomie of urban industrial society captured Weaver's interest.... Agrarianism provided him with a bedrock upon which to ground his subsequent thinking."

The Agrarians, Weaver argued, were not simply a group that sought to turn back the clock:

> No one beyond the first grade in philosophy believes that time can be reversed. What the Agrarians, along with people of their philosophic conviction everywhere, were saying is that there are some things which do not have their subsistence in time, and that certain virtues should be cultivated regardless of the era in which one finds oneself born. It is the most arrant presentism to say that philosophy cannot be practiced because that philosophy is found in the past and the past is now gone. The whole value of philosophy lies in its detachment from accidental conditions of this kind and its adherence to the essential.

The conflict the Agrarians faced was one between the Old South and its traditions and values and the New South of industrialization and commerce. This conflict has, Weaver writes, been a focal point in the novels of William Faulkner:

> William Faulkner had observed the two worlds, and had made their struggle the underlying theme of his body of powerful fiction.... The entire mythology of Faulkner grows out of the contest of Sartoris and Snopes.... The Agrarians are Sartorises, not necessarily through family or inheritance, but necessarily through sympathy with a socio-ethical pattern. One has to recognize them as traditional Southerners, publicly confessing belief in the ethically responsible will. But this traditional Southerner dwells in an increasingly Snopes-ordered world; he is faced with an opponent of terrifying vitality, pushing up from below, seizing the substance of the land even as he shatters old forms and amenities. He represents the animalism which is bound to hold sway when the old gods have gone and no new gods have arrived. Snopes is immeasurably aided by the fact that he carries no baggage of sentiment (in his world business is always business and sentiment is always "false sentiment"). The modern dissolution of values has so prepared the way for him that the contest is ridiculously unequal.... We can no longer avoid seeing that this little upheaval is not a regional affair, or an American affair, but a particular instance of a movement that is taking place all over the world. It is...a phase of the general retreat of humanism before universal materialism and technification. And this is the real reason that geographic residence has ceased to be an important fact about Agrarians.

In an essay concerning Southern literature, Weaver discusses the charge that this literature abounds unduly in monsters. He writes:

> ...this literature's willingness to depict monsters is one of its strongest claims to validity. Monstrosity is one of the authentic modes of existence. The world regularly produces monsters, and to recognize them is part of the truth of art. The litera-

tures of Greece and Rome certainly had no difficulty accommodating them, and the plays of Shakespeare contain some shocking ones. It is my impression that Southern writers, instead of rationalizing away monstrous evil, as the sociologists do, or averting their gaze from it, as the romantics try to do, choose to give it epical proportions.... It may well be that this acceptance of monsters is closely related to a belief in heroes and heroism. If there is a centaur, there must be a Thesus; if the hydra exists, a Hercules must be found. It is one of the most certain signs of a collapse of values that the true hero is disappearing from modern imaginative life. After all, a hero is a man apart from the crowd, the man who refuses to participate in its cowardice and servile emotions.... The Southern writers deal with something that the modern world seems increasingly prone to deny: the presence of tragedy in life.

In the end, Weaver argues, the Southern experience is not abnormal, as some have claimed, but is "more normal than that of other sections of America. The South is the region that history has happened to. People who have never experienced tragedy are the deviants. Southern writers have told much of that tragedy, and in doing so they have told us important things about the human condition."

The typical American represents what Weaver describes as "the victorious man." He has amassed great wealth and material goods, has worshipped at the altar of progress and has not been disappointed. For this American, all things are possible and defeat is not even to be considered. The Southerner, by contrast, "has had to taste a bitter cup which no American is supposed to know anything about, the cup of defeat. Thus in a world where the American is supposed to be uniformly successful, he exists as an anomalous American."

Looking back to the legacy of the Civil War, an effort which failed despite his best efforts, the Southerner has learned lessons from history which are the opposite of those learned by other Americans: "...a supreme act of his will was frustrated, and that as a consequence of that defeat he had to accommodate himself to an unwanted circumstance. And that, of course, is the meaning of failure. Therefore in the national legend the typical American owes his position to a virtuous and effective act of his will; but the Southerner owes his to the fact that his will was denied; and this leaves a kind of inequality which no amount of political blandishment can remove entirely."

The South was invaded, its cities burned down, its citizens disenfranchised, its society "reconstructed." No other section of the country has endured such humiliation. As a result, Southerners have become much like the men and women of other regions of the world—understanding that all things may not be possible, that history's lessons are complex and sometimes tragic.

In an essay titled "Aspects of the Southern Philosophy," written in 1952, Weaver is prophetic in predicting that the time may come when the American society will be in need of the lessons the South has learned and the values it has not abandoned:

> If the world continues its present drift toward tension and violence, it is probable that the characteristic Southern qualities will command an increasing premium. While this country was amassing its great wealth, those qualities were in comparative eclipse; but the virtues needed to amass wealth are not the virtues needed to defend it. Such is our ambiguous position today that the possession of the greatest wealth in the world is going to require an amplitude of those qualities developed in the school of poverty and deprivation and in that of rural living. Important among these 'enforced' virtues are fortitude and the ability to do without. But perhaps most important of all is the Southerner's discipline in tragedy. Belief in tragedy is essentially un-American; it is in fact one of the heresies against Americanism; but in the world as a whole this heresy is more widely received than the dogma and is more regularly taught by experience.

Richard Weaver concluded that "Just as certainly as the United States grows older, it will have to find accommodation for this ineluctable notion.... If we are in for a time of darkness and trouble, the Southern philosophy, because it is not based on optimism, will have better power to console than the national dogmas."

Where in the South of today, however, can one find the values of Richard Weaver believed to be uniquely Southern? To visit modern day Atlanta, or Birmingham, or Charlotte is to see the final triumph of industry and commerce. Yet, even when the Agrarians were writing, Weaver points out, "they were becoming homeless." He compares the rejection by the New South of the older values with the welcome given by the people of London to the restored monarch Charles II just as John Milton was publishing *A Ready and Easy Way to Establish a Free Commonwealth*: "A shallow observer could well have thought that this meant the end of free commonwealths and also exposed the folly of arguing for them. The authors of *I'll Take My Stand,* who saw their compatriots turn away in large numbers from their recommendations, should not have felt any more absurd than Milton. Nor any less like prophets."

What would Richard Weaver say if he had lived through the defeat in Vietnam, the rise of crime and pornography and drugs and abortion, a growing divorce rate, shattered families, and a society more and more in disarray? Perhaps he would argue that we had finally reached the time when older values would be needed to see us through an era when optimism and materialism seem hollow indeed.

It is good to have these essays to ponder at a time when the American society seems to have lost its way. "The destruction of sentiment," Weaver wrote, "leaves us not animals, who have their own nobility, but ruined men.... Between the expression 'our people,' euphemistic though it may have been, and the modern abstraction 'manpower,' lies a measure of our decline in humanity."

Note

1. *The Southern Essays of Richard M. Weaver* (Indianapolis: Liberty Press, 1987).

II
The Rhetor

6

Richard M. Weaver on the Nature of Rhetoric: An Interpretation

Richard L. Johannesen, Rennard Strickland, and Ralph T. Eubanks

Modern philosopher Eliseo Vivas uses the ancient term "rhetor" to describe the late Richard M. Weaver. Vivas contends that Weaver saw the importance of rhetoric, in its classical sense, as "no other thinker among us...has seen it."[1] Weaver remains, no doubt, one of the most stimulating and controversial rhetorical theorists of our time. From the outset of his career he has provided, as Paul Tillich observes of his first work, "philosophical shock—the beginning of wisdom." Over the years, Weaver's views on the nature of rhetoric have had increasing influence among rhetorical scholars.[2]

Weaver as a social critic has sought to clarify the role of rhetoric in improving a declining modern culture. At one point in *Visions of Order* he described himself as a "kind of doctor of culture," a description which could also serve as a virtual self-portrait of his own function. Even though a member of that culture, this "doctor" in some degree had estranged himself from his culture though study and reflection. He had "acquired knowledge and developed habits of thought which enable him to see it in perspective and to gauge it."[3]

Although he wrote a large number of articles, essays, lectures, books and book reviews both on academic and political subjects,[4] Weaver's views on rhetoric can be gleaned primarily from the following published sources: *Ideas Have Consequences,* a post World War-II critique of American society; *The Ethics of Rhetoric*; *Composition,* a college textbook; "Language is Sermonic," a lecture delivered to a graduate speech seminar at the University of Oklahoma; *Visions of Order,* a posthumously published critique of our present society; *Life without Prejudice and Other Essays,* a collection of previously published essays; "Relativism and the Use of Language"; "Concealed Rhetoric in Scientistic Sociology"; and "To Write the Truth."[5]

Weaver held two basic orientations that are of prime importance to an understanding of his rhetorical views.[6] First, politically he was a conservative of some note. Leading conservatives such as Russell Kirk and Willmoore Kendall held him in esteem.[7] Weaver was, for example, an associate editor of the conservative *Modern Age,* a contributor to *National Review,* a trustee of the Intercollegiate Society of Individualist, and a recipient in 1962 of a national award from the Young Americans for Freedom. In his public lectures, such as "How to Argue the Conservative Cause," he actively advocated rational conservatism.

In his mid-twenties Weaver had moved from arch-socialist to ardent conservative.[8] A product of southern upbringing and education in North Carolina, Kentucky, Tennessee and Louisiana, he defended Southern Agrarian traditions.[9] At Vanderbilt University he was exposed to the Southern Agrarian ideas of John Crowe Ransom, Robert Penn Warren, Donald Davidson and Allen Tate.[10] Kendall contends that Weaver was more a commentator on southern Agrariaism than a devotee of its ideals.[11] Weaver himself admitted that at Vanderbilt he felt a "powerful pull" toward the Agrarian ideals of the individual in contact with nature, the necessity of the small-property-holding class, and a pluralistic society.[12] He left Vanderbilt poised between the opposites of socialism and Southern Agrarianism and by the early 1940s had firmly opted for conservatism generally and some particular facet of Southern Agrarianism.[13] For example, Weaver championed the Agrarian ideal of individual ownership of private property and disdain of science as inadequate to deal with values.[14] He desired in society law, order, and cohesive diversity. The just and ideal society, he believed, must reflect real hierarchy and essential distinctions. An orderly society following the vision of a Good Purpose, with men harmoniously functioning in their proper stations in the structure, constituted Weaver's goal.[15]

Secondly, Weaver was a devoted Platonic idealist.[16] Belief in the reality of transcendentals, the primacy of ideas, and the view that form is prior to substance constituted his philosophical foundation.[17] While not a Platonist in all matters, he yet looked for societal and personal salvation to ideals, essences, and principles rather than to the transitory, the changing, and the expedient. His view was antipragmatic and antiutilitarian. While general semanticist S. I. Hayakawa attacks Weaver's Platonic idealism, Russell Kirk praises Weaver as a "powerful mind given to meditation upon universals."[18]

The ultimate goods in society were of central concern to Weaver.[19] Reality for him was a hierarchy in which the ultimate Idea of Good constituted the value standard by which all other existents could be appraised for degree of goodness and truth. Truth to him was the degree to which things and ideas in the material world conform to their ideals, archetypes and essences. He contended that "the thing is not true and the act is not just unless these conform to a conceptual ideal."[20] What the ultimate Good was and how it is known through intuition, Weaver never really made clear. What comprised his ultimate Good was likewise unclear. But he viewed freedom, justice and order as ideals toward which men and cultures must strive. The reality of nature he saw as a dualistic paradox of essences and transformations. "Whatever the field we gaze upon," he observed, "we see things maintaining their identity while changing. Things both *are* and *are becoming*. They are because the idea or general configuration of them persists; and they are becoming because with the flowing of time, they inevitably slough off old substance and take on new."[21]

Weaver held a complex conception of the nature of knowledge. He partially agreed with Mortimer Adler that there are three "orders" of knowledge. First is the level of particulars and individual facts, the simple data of science. Second is the level of theories, propositions and generalizations about these facts. Third is the level of philosophic evaluations and value judgments about such theories.[22] At this third level, Ideas, universals and first principles function as judgmental standards. Knowledge based on particulars alone and on raw physical sensations is suspect since it is incomplete knowledge. True knowledge is of universals and first principles. Weaver adopted at one point the absolute position that "there is no knowledge at the level of sensation, and that therefore knowledge is of universals...the fewer particulars we require in order to arrive at our generalization, the more apt pupils we are in the school of wisdom."[23] In two other books he suggested that Knowledge of universals comes through dialectic, the ability to differentiate existents into categories, and through institution, the ability to grasp "essential correspondences."[24]

Weaver believed man's essential nature encompasses fixed elements, yet for him the good man seemed more an ideal than an actuality. He held that man's fundamental humanness is founded in four faculties, capacities or modes of apprehension.[25] Man possesses a rational or cognitive capacity which gives him knowledge; an emotional or aesthetic capacity which allows him to experience pleasure, pain and beauty; an ethical capacity which determines orders of goods and judges between right and wrong; and a religious capacity which provides yearning for something infinite and gives man a glimpse of his destiny and ultimate nature.

Weaver used a tripartite division of body, mind and soul to further explain man's essential nature. The body, man's physical being, houses the mind and soul during life but extracts its due through a constant downward pull toward indiscriminate and excessive satisfaction of sensory pleasure. The body is self-centered and disdainful of worthy goals.[26] Man's mind or intellect provides him with the potential to apprehend the structure of reality, define concepts and rationally order ideas. While giving man the capacity for knowledge and order, the mind is guided toward good or evil by the disposition of the soul.[27] Man's soul or spirit—depending upon whether it has been trained well or ill—guides the mind and body toward love of the good or toward love of physical pleasure. Weaver found the concept of soul difficult to explain; it seemed for him to encompass man's ethical and religious capacities.[28] The elements of man's essential nature he viewed as fixed. Yet he implied that the dominance of one component over others is determined by man's training, environment and culture.

Weaver underscores two additional concepts in his analysis of man's uniquely human characteristics.[29] Man's capacity for choice-making affords him his dignity—if judiciously exercised in selecting means and ends. And as the symbol-using animal—although the definition is a partial one—man rises above the sensate and can communicate knowledge, feeling, and values.

In readily accepting the label of conservative, Weaver emphasized that a conservative believes there is a structure of reality independent of his own will and desire and accepts some principles as given, lasting and good.[30] The true conservative for Weaver was one "who sees the universe as a paradigm of essences, of which the phenomenology of the world is a sort of continuing approximation. Or, to put it another way, he sees it as a set of definitions which are struggling to get themselves defined in the real world."[31]

These two fundamental orientations, political conservatism and Platonic idealism, led Weaver in *Ideas Have Consequences* and *Visions of Order* to indict contemporary Western culture for having lost faith in an order of "goods." Among the societal weaknesses and vices he condemned were the following: scientism, nominalism, semantic positivism, doctrinaire democracy, uncritical homage to the theory of evolution, radical egalitarianism, pragmatism, cultural relativism, materialism, emphasis on techniques at the expense of goals, idolization of youth, progressive education, disparagement of historical consciousness, deleterious effects of the mass media, and degenerate literature, music and art.

Weaver outlined the program he thought necessary for the restoration of health to Western culture. Among his positive suggestions were the development of a sense of history; balance between permanence and change; reestablishment of faith in ideas, ideals, and principles; maintenance of the "metaphysical right" of private property; education in literature, rhetoric, logic and dialectic; respect for nature, the individual, and the ideals of the past; reemphasis on traditional education; and control (but not elimination) of war.[32]

From this vantage point Weaver expounded his view of the nature, function and scope of rhetoric. As his writings on rhetoric show, he was familiar with the ancient theories of Plato, Aristotle, Cicero and Quintilian.[33] And Plato's views on the subject held a special attraction for him. The influence of Kenneth Burke is also clearly reflected in Weaver's writings on rhetoric.[34] At one point Weaver views rhetoric as a process of making identifications and he widens the scope of rhetoric beyond linguistic forms to include a rhetoric of "matter or scene," as in the instance of a bank's erecting an imposing office building to strengthen its image.[35]

In Weaver's view, rhetoric makes convictions compelling by showing them in the contexts of reality and human values. Rhetoric, he wrote, is "persuasive speech in the service of truth"; it should "create an informed appetite for the good."[36] It affects us "primarily by setting forth images which inform and attract." And generally, rhetoric involves questions of policy. It operates formally at the point "where literary values and political urgencies" can be combined. "The rhetorician," he observed, "makes use of the moving power of literary presentation to induce in his hearers an attitude or decision which is political in the very broadest sense."[37]

Weaver explained the "office" of rhetoric at some length:

> Rhetoric seen in the whole conspectus of its function is an art of emphasis embodying an order of desire. Rhetoric is advisory. It has the office of advising men with reference to an independent order of goods and with reference to their particular situation as it relates to these. The honest rhetorician therefore has two things in kind: a vision of how matters should go ideally and ethically and a consideration of the special circumstances of his auditors. Toward both of these he has a responsibility.[38]

The duty of rhetoric, then, is to combine "action and understanding into a whole that is greater than scientific perception." Weaver the Platonic idealist believed that "rhetoric at its truest seeks to perfect men by showing them better versions of themselves, links in that chain extending up toward the ideal which only the intellect can apprehend and only the soul have affection for."[39]

Rhetoric, held Weaver, is axiological; it kneads values into our lives.[40] Rhetoric is the cohesive force that molds persons into a community or culture. Because man is "drawn forward by some conception of what he should be," a proper order of values is the "ultimate sanction of rhetoric." Rhetoric involves the making and presenting of choices among "goods" and a striving toward some ultimate Good. By its very nature, he emphasized, "language is sermonic;" it reflects choices and urges a particular "ought." The "noble rhetorician," in Weaver's view, functions to provide a better version of what we can become. The true rhetorician attempts to actualize an "ideal good" for a particular audience in a specific situation primarily through "poetic or analogical association." He demonstrates, for instance, how an action, urged as just, partakes of ideal justice.

Weaver, therefore, condemned most social scientists for pretending to avoid value judgements in their writings while actually making such judgments.[41] He particularly attacked general semantics for its relativist "truth" and its attempt to denude language of all reflections of value tendencies.[42] He also realized that rhetoric can be perverted to employ base techniques and to serve base ends. Such perversion, he believed, occurs in much modern advertising. Against these possibilities, Weaver strove in all his writings on rhetoric. For he was certain that "all things considered, rhetoric, noble or base, is a great power in the world."[43]

Like Aristotle, Weaver perceived a close relationship between dialectic and rhetoric.[44] Dialectic, he maintained, is a "method of investigation whose object is the establishment of truth about doubtful propositions." It is "abstract reasoning" upon the basis of propositions through categorization, definition, drawing out of implications, and exposure of contradictions. Dialectic involves analysis and synthesis of fundamental terms in controversial questions. Both dialectic and rhetoric operate in the realm of probability. Rhetoric is joined with "that branch of dialectic which contributes to choice or avoidance"—that branch of dialectic which examines ethical and political questions. Good rhetoric presupposes sound dialectic. A successful dialectic secures not actuality but possibility; "what rhetoric thereafter accomplishes is to take any dialectically secured position...and show its relationship to the world of prudential conduct."[45] Weaver's criticism of the semantic positivists suggests that dialectic alone, without a succeeding rhetoric, is "social agnosticism." With dialectic unaided by rhetoric, man "knows" only in a vacuum. Thus, as earlier noted, "the duty of rhetoric is to bring together action and understanding into a whole that is greater than scientific perception." Rhetoric seeks actualization of a dialectically secured position in the existential world.

Weaver knew that logos, pathos, and ethos must combine in sound rhetoric.[46] For him "the most obvious truth about rhetoric is that its object is the whole man." It presents its arguments first to the rational aspect of man. Yet a complete rhetoric goes beyond man's cognitive capacity and appeals to other facets of his nature, especially to his nature as an emotional being, "a being of feeling and suffering." In addition, he realized that a "significant part of every speech situation is the character of the speaker." For Richard Weaver, then, the function of rhetoric was to make men both feel and believe and to perceive order, first principles and fundamental values.

He seemed committed to the proposition that as a man speaks, so he is—or that that style is the man. A person's typical modes of argument and his stylistic characteristics Weaver saw as keys to that person's philosophical orientation. An analysis of a person's rhetorical style, for example, illuminated his world view.[47] Frequent use of the conjunction "but" indicates, for example, a "balanced view" as a habit of mind. Again: A person's level of generality in word choice tells us something about his approach to a subject.

"A man's method of argument is a truer index of his beliefs than his explicit profession of principles," Weaver held as a basic axiom.[48] "A much surer index to a man's political philosophy," he felt, "is his characteristic way of thinking, inevitably expressed in the type of argument he prefers." Nowhere does a man's rhetoric catch up with him more completely than in "the topics he chooses to win other men's assent." At one point Weaver elaborated his fundamental view at some length:

> In other words, the rhetorical content of the major premise which the speaker habitually uses is the key to his primary view of existence. We are of course excluding artful choices which have in view only *ad hoc* persuasions. Putting the matter now figuratively, we may say that no man escapes being branded by the premise that he regards as most efficacious in argument. The general importance of this is that major premises, in addition to their logical function as part of a deductive argument, are expressive of values, and a characteristic major premise characterizes the user.[49]

From the Aristotelian *topoi* Weaver selected and ranked certain "topics" or regions of experience to which an advocate could turn for the substance of persuasive argument. These "topics" are the "sources of content for speeches that are designed to influence."[50] By ranking them from the most to least ethically desirable, based on his philosophic conception of reality and knowledge, he outlined a hierarchy of topics which a persuader might use and which a critic could employ to assess the rhetoric of others.[51]

A speaker would make the highest order of appeal by basing his argument on genus or definition.[52] Argument from genus involves arguing from the nature or essence of things. It assumes that there are fixed classes and that what is true of a given class may be imputed to every member of that class. In the argument from genus the classification already is established, or it is one of the fixed concepts in the mind of the audience to which the argument is addressed. In argument from definition, the work of establishing the classification must be done during the course of the argument, after which the defined term will be used as would a genus. Further: Definitions should be rationally rather than empirically sustained. Good definitions should be stipulative, emphasizing what-ought-to-be rather than operational, what-is. Under argument from genus or definition, Weaver also included argument from fundamental principles and argument from example. An example, he felt, always implies a general class. He believed that arguments from genus or definition ascribe "to the highest reality qualities of statis, immutabilty, eternal perdurance."

He admitted that his preference for this mode of argument derived from his Platonic idealism. This mode of argument, he felt, was also a mark of the true conservative. To argue from genus or definition was to get people "to see what is most permanent in existence, or what transcends the world of change and accident. The realm of essence is the realm above the flux of phenomena; and definitions are of essences and genera."[53]

Weaver applied this viewpoint in his evaluation of the rhetoric of Abraham Lincoln.[54] He explicitly cited over a dozen examples of Lincoln's rhetoric. Yet unfortunately he did not indicate whether he based his generalizations on a careful examination of the entire corpus of the martyred president's oratory. Weaver's analysis led him to conclude that, although sometimes arguing from similitude, as in the Gettysburg address, and gain from consequence and circumstance Lincoln characteristically argued from genus, definition and principle. His greatest utterances, for example, were "chiefly arguments from definition." And in Weaver's view, therefore, Lincoln was a true conservative.[55] In contrast, many of Lincoln's contemporary Whigs were conservative, Weaver argued, only in the negative sense that they opposed Democratic proposals. Naturally Weaver praised Lincoln's rhetoric and his philosophical position.

As second in rank among the topics Weaver placed argument from similitude.[56] In this mode of argument are embraced analogy, metaphor, figuration, comparison, and contrast. Metaphor received focused attention from Weaver: to him it was often central to the rhetorical process.[57] Some of our profoundest intuitions concerning the world around us, he noted, are expressed in the form of comparisons. His Platonic idealism again helped him rank this topic. The user of an analogy hints at an essence he cannot at the moment produce. Weaver asserted that "behind every analogy lurks the possibility of a general term."

Argument from cause and effect stands third in Weaver's hierarchy of topics, and includes argument from consequences.[58] Although casual reasoning is a "less exalted" source of argument, we "all have to use it because we are historical men." This method of argument and its subvarieties, he felt, characterized the radical and the pragmatist. Casual argument operates in the realm of "becoming" and thus in the realm of flux. Argument from consequences attempts to forecast results of some course of action, either very desirable or very undesirable. These results are a determining factor for one in deciding whether or not to adopt a proposed action. Arguments from consequences, Weaver observed, usually are completely "devoid of reference to principle or defined ideas."

At the very bottom of Weaver's hierarchy stands argument from circumstances, another subvariety of causal reasoning.[59] This mode of argument, in his view, is the least "philosophical" of the topics because it admits of the least perspicaciousness and theoretically stops at the level of perception of fact. Argument from circumstances characterizes those who are easily impressed by existing tangibles, and such argument marks, he believed, the true liberal.[60] The arguers from circumstance, concerned not with "conceptions of verities but qualities of perceptions," lack moral vision and possess only the illusion of reality. We are driven back upon this method of argument when a course of action cannot be vindicated by principle or when effects cannot be demonstrated. The argument simply cites brute circumstance; it suggests expedience. "Actually," he explains, "this argument amounts to a surrender of reason. Maybe it expresses an instinctive feeling that in this situation reason is powerless. Either you change fast or you get crushed. But surely it would be a counsel of desperation to try only this argument in a world suffering from aimlessness and threatened with destruction."[61]

Weaver employed this topic to analyze the rhetoric of Edmund Burke, commonly classified as a conservative.[62] He conceded that many of Burke's observations on society have a conservative basis. On the other hand, he contended that when Burke came to grips with concrete policies, his rhetoric reflected "a strong addition to the argument from circumstance." Weaver concluded, "When judged by what we are calling aspect of argument," Burke was "very far from being a conservative."[63] Burke was at his best, Weaver argued, when defending immediate circumstances and "reigning" circumstances. And until the time of the French Revolution when he felt the need for "deeper anchorage," Burke's habitual argument from circumstances marked him philosophically as a liberal.[64] Weaver held Burke in low esteem as a conservative.

Again, while Weaver cited some dozen examples of Burke's rhetoric, he failed to indicate whether his generalizations rested on a scrutiny of all Burke's speeches, letters, and essays. It is in this connection also worthy of note that Russell Kirk has levied several objections to Weaver's evaluation of Burke.[65] First, the true conservative described by Weaver, contends Kirk, represents Weaver's ideal and ignores the historical fact that a true conservative is a follower of Edmund Burke, no matter what his typical mode of argument. Second, Kirk alludes to one of Burke's speeches to indicate that while Burke disdained "abstraction," he did praise genuine "principle." Here Kirk ignores Weaver's axiom that the important index is not what one says, but how one characteristically argues. Third, Kirk claims that although Abraham Lincoln often may have argued from principles and definition, he also often acted from circumstances and consequences. Finally, Kirk sees Burke's prosecution of Warren Hastings and his attack on French errors during the Revolution as "instances of argument and action from definition."

Weaver's central premise of a typical pattern of argument for a speaker implies simply frequency of usage, as reflected in his use of the terms "characteristic" and "habitual." But some speakers may not have a clearly predominant mode of argument; they may blend a number of types of argument mentioned by Weaver. Judgment of the speaker is then more difficult. More important, some speakers may use arguments from consequences and circumstances more frequently than other types and yet use a few arguments from genus or principle as the fundamental arguments underlying all others.[66] Finally, Weaver fails to explain how a critic may determine whether a given line of argument is a metaphysical choice reflecting a speaker's philosophical stance or an "artful" choice necessitated by the practicalities of audience adaptation.

The use of characteristic mode of argument as the prime standard for rhetorical criticism represents an overly simplistic approach to evaluation of rhetorical practice. Such analysis promotes the slighting of other relevant factors in the rhetorical process. In the dramatistic terms proposed by Kenneth Burke, Weaver overemphasizes "agency" at the expense of "agent," "act," "scene," and "purpose." His typology of the "aspect" of argument can afford valuable insights, but it must not be taken as a well-rounded critical system. Yet in fairness to him it must be admitted that he did not intend his system to serve as the universal criterion of rhetorical criticism.

In addition to the hierarchy of "internal" sources of argument is the "external topic" of argument from authority and testimony.[67] Statements made by observers and experts take the place of direct or logical interpretation of evidence. Such testimony often embodies arguments from genus or definition, cause-effect, consequences, and circumstances, and thus can be judged by the standards appropriate to such arguments. But also involved is the more general question of the status of the authority. Thus a sound criterion, wrote Weaver, is that an argument from authority is only as good as the authority itself.

In his writing and teaching Weaver constantly strove to train his students in ethical rhetoric. Hence knowledge of rhetoric and skill in its use provided a defense against base rhetoric and propaganda.[68] In rhetorical education he placed prime emphasis on invention and style. Argumentation, including induction, deduction and a modernized set of *topoi* adapted from Aristotle, formed a crucial part of rhetorical education.[69] The enthymeme received focused attention in Weaver's philosophy of rhetoric.[70] The rhetorician, he observed, enters into a oneness with his audience by tacitly agreeing with one of its perceptions of reality. Weaver noted further that the enthymeme functions only when the "audience is willing to supply the missing proposition."[71]

In *Composition,* a college textbook, Weaver treated the following "topics": genus, or definition, cause and effect, similitude, comparison, contraries, circumstance, testimony and authority. As could be expected, a major part of Weaver's text was devoted to style, including grammar and composition. His persistent efforts stimulated introduction of units of logic and the revitalized "topics" into the freshman English course in the College of the University of Chicago.[72]

Edward P. J. Corbett credits the article by Bilsky, Weaver and others in *College English* (in 1953)—"Looking for an Argument"—with providing "perhaps the first suggestion of the value of classical rhetoric for the Freshman Composition Course." Corbett claims that the treatment of the *topoi* in Weaver's *Composition* "represented the first instance of the use of the topics in a freshman rhetoric since the appearance of Francis P. Donnelly's books in the 1930's."[73]

Weaver's writings on rhetoric emphasize the processes and techniques of invention and the elements of effective style, giving minor place to organization and none to the classical canons of delivery and memory. He aims indeed at revitalizing invention and argumentation. To Weaver true rhetoric involves choices among values and courses of action; it aims at showing men "better versions of themselves" and better visions of an ultimate Good. As Platonic idealist and political conservative, he praised the ideal, the essence, the unchangeable, and condemned the particular, the transitory, and the expedient. A speaker's characteristic use of argument from genus, definition, principle, similitude, cause and effect, consequences and circumstances, Weaver regarded as an index to the speaker's philosophical viewpoint and ethical stature.

By reaffirming and refining the essential connection between dialectic and rhetoric, Weaver illuminated the true province of rhetoric. Indeed, Weaver's theory pointed the way to the current rapprochement between philosophy and rhetoric.[74] Some of Weaver's political, philosophical, and rhetorical assumptions may be questioned in whole or in part. Still, there is little doubt that Weaver's theory, rooted as it was in a dialectic of the "true nature of things," has helped to reestablish rhetoric as a substantive discipline—a discipline concerned with matters of "the real world" and with the preservation of "the permanent things."

Notes

1. Eliseo Vivas, "The Mind of Richard Weaver," *Modern Age* 8 (Summer 1964): 309; Vivas, "Introduction," in Weaver, *Life without Prejudice and Other Essays* (Chicago: Regnery, 1965), xiii-xiv. When Weaver died at age fifty-three, April 3, 1963, he was professor of English in the College of the University of Chicago.
2. For the influence of Weaver's ideas on other rhetorical theorists see Maurice Natanson, "The Limits of Rhetoric," *Quarterly Journal of Speech* 41 (April 1955): 133-39; Virgil Baker and Ralph Eubanks, *Speech in Personal and Public Affairs* (New York: David McKay, 1965), viii, 74, 80, 113; Ralph Eubanks and Virgil Baker, "Toward an Axiology of Rhetoric," *Quarterly Journal of Speech* 48 (April 1962): 157-68; Walter R. Fisher, "Advisory Rhetoric; Implications for Forensic Debate," *Western Speech* 29 (Spring 1965): 114-19; Donald Davidson, "Grammar and Rhetoric: The Teacher's Problem," *Quarterly Journal of Speech* 39 (December 1953): 424-36; Ralph T. Eubanks, "Nihilism and the Problem of a Worthy Rhetoric," *Southern Speech Journal* 33 (Spring 1968): 187-99; W. Ross Winterowd, *Rhetoric: A Synthesis* (New York: Holt, Rinehart and Winston, 1968), 9-10, 13. Some of Weaver's essays now are being reprinted in anthologies on rhetoric. See, for example, Joseph Schwartz and John Rycenga, eds., *The Province of Rhetoric* (New York: Ronald Press, 1965), 275-92, 311-29; Dudley Bailey, ed., *Essays on Rhetoric* (New York: Oxford University Press, 1965), 234-49; Maurice Natanson and Henry W. Johnstone, eds., *Philosophy, Rhetoric, and Argumentation* (University Park: Pennsylvania State University Press, 1965), 63-79.
3. Although most of his writings on rhetoric have this thrust, one of his most clearly focused essays was "The Cultural Role of Rhetoric," in *Visions of Order* (Baton Rouge: Louisiana State University Press, 1964), chap. 4. See also page 7.
4. The editors wish to acknowledge the cooperation of Louis Dehmlow, compiler of Weaver's papers, and the late Kendall Beaton, literary executor, in securing a bibliography of Weaver's writings and copies of some of Weaver's unpublished manuscripts. A complete bibliography of Weaver's published writings appears in

his *The Southern Tradition at Bay,* edited by George Core and M. E. Bradford (New York: Arlington House, 1968), 401-18.
5. Weaver, *Ideas Have Consequences* (Chicago: University of Chicago Press, 1948); *The Ethics of Rhetoric* (Chicago: Regnery, 1953); *Composition: A Course in Writing and Rhetoric* (New York: Holt, Rinehart and Winston, 1957); "Language is Sermonic," in Roger E. Nebergall, ed., *Dimensions of Rhetorical Scholarship* (Norman: University of Oklahoma Department of Speech, 1963); *Visions of Order; Life without Prejudice and Other Essays*; "Relativism and the Use of Language," in H. Schoeck and J. W. Wiggins, eds., *Relativism and the Study of Man* (New York: Van Nostrand, 1961), 236-54; "Concealed Rhetoric in Scientific Sociology," *Georgia Review* 13 (Spring 1959): 19-32; "To Write the Truth," *College English* 10 (October 1948): 25-30.
6. James Powell, "The Foundations of Weaver's Traditionalism," *New Individualist Review* 3 (1964): 3-7; E. Victor Milione, "The Uniqueness of Richard M. Weaver," *Intercollegiate Review* 2 (September 1965): 67.
7. Russell Kirk, "Richard Weaver, R I P," *National Review* 14 (23 April 1963): 308; Willmoore Kendall, "How to Read Richard Weaver," *Intercollegiate Review* 2 (September 1965): 77-86. In fact Kendall argues that Weaver was so unique that he was virtually the only true American conservative on the contemporary scene.
8. Weaver discusses this transition in his autobiographical article "Up from Liberalism," *Modern Age* 3 (Winter 1958-59): 21-32. Starting in 1932 he was a formal member of the American Socialist Party for at least two years.
9. Weaver, "The Southern Tradition," *New Individualist Review* 3 (1964): 7-17. Born in Asheville, North Carolina, in 1910, he received his B.A. from the University of Kentucky in 1932, M.A. from Vanderbilt University in 1934, and Ph.D. from Louisiana State University in 1943.
10. For statements of Southern Agrarian precepts, including those of Ransom, Warren, Davidson, and Tate, see *I'll Take My Stand: The South and the Agrarian Tradition,* by Twelve Southerners (New York: Harper, 1930); see also Herbert Agar and Allen Tate, *Who Owns America? A New Declaration of Independence* (Boston: Houghton Mifflin, 1936). Ransom, Warren, Davidson, and Tate, who led the influential literary group known as the "Nashville Fugitives," reflect on their participation in the Southern Agrarian movement in Rob Roy Purdy, ed., *Fugitives' Reunion: Conversations at Vanderbilt* (Nashville: Vanderbilt University Press, 1959), 177-218. Ransom directed Weaver's M.A. thesis on "The Revolt Against Humanism." A recent analysis of the Southern Agrarian philosophy is Alexander Karanikas, *Tillers of a Myth: Southern Agrarians as Social and Literary Critics* (Madison: University of Wisconsin Press, 1966).
11. Kendall, "How to Read Richard Weaver," 78.
12. Weaver, "Up from Liberalism," 23; Weaver, "The Confederate South, 1865-1910: A Study in the Survival of a Mind and Culture" (Ph.D. dissertation, Louisiana State University, 1943), 517. In a slightly revised form this dissertation has been published as *The Southern Tradition at Bay.*
13 Weaver, "Up from Liberalism," 23-24; Weaver, "The Tennessee Agrarians," *Shenandoah* 3 (Summer 1953): 3-10.
14. Agar and Tate, *Who Owns America?,* 182-83, 325-26; Weaver, *Ideas Have Consequences,* chap. 7.
15. Weaver, *Ideas Have Consequences,* 20, 35-51, 74-75; Weaver, *Visions of Order,* 13, 22-39.

16. Weaver, *Ideas Have Consequences*, 3-5, 12-17, 22-23, 34, 52, 60, 73 119, 130-32, 146-47, 154; Weaver, *Visions of Order*, 20-21, 38, 134-35; Weaver, "Language is Sermonic," 55; Weaver, *Ethics of Rhetoric*, 3-26.
17. Weaver, Foreword to *Ideas Have Consequences* (paperback, 1959), v; Weaver, *New York Times Book Review* (March 21, 1948), 29.
18. S. I. Hayakawa, *Symbol, Status, and Personality* (New York: Harcourt, Brace, and World, 1963), 154-70, 182-85; Russell Kirk, "Ethical Labors," *Sewanee Review* 62 (July-September 1954): 489.
19. Weaver, *Ideas Have Consequences*, 17, 51-52; Weaver, *Ethics of Rhetoric*, 212-32.
20. Weaver, *Ideas Have Consequences*, 130, 4. For many of the insights in the following paragraphs concerning Weaver's philosophy of reality and knowledge, the authors wish to acknowledge the research of Thomas D. Clark. See Thomas D. Clark, "The Philosophical Bases of Richard M. Weaver's View of Rhetoric" (M.A. thesis, Indiana University, 1969).
21. Weaver, *Visions of Order*, 23.
22. Weaver, *Ethics of Rhetoric*, 30-31; *Ideas Have Consequences*, 18.
23. Weaver, *Ideas Have Consequences*, 12-13, 3, 27.
24. Weaver, *Visions of Order*, 12; Weaver, *Ethics of Rhetoric*, 49-54, 45-57, 203-204.
25. Weaver, *Visions of Order*, 85; Weaver, "Language is Sermonic," 50-51; Weaver, *Life without Prejudice*, 146.
26. Weaver, *Visions of Order*, 9, 144; *Life without Prejudice*, 146; Weaver, *Ideas Have Consequences*, 18.
27. Weaver, *Visions of Order*, 24, 50, 85; Weaver, *Ideas Have Consequences*, 19-20; Weaver, *Life without Prejudice*, 45-46.
28. Weaver, *Visions of Order*, 43-44, 47, 85, 144; Weaver, *Ideas Have Consequences*, 19-20; Weaver, *Ethics of Rhetoric*, 17, 23.
29. Weaver, *Visions of Order*, 135; Weaver, *Ideas Have Consequences*, 167; *Life without Prejudice*, 45-47. For Kenneth Burke's analysis of man as the symbol-using animal, see Burke, *Language as Symbolic Action* (Berkeley: University of California Press, 1966), 3-24.
30. Weaver, *Life without Prejudice*, 157-59.
31. Weaver, *Ethics of Rhetoric*, 112.
32. Some of Weaver's positive suggestions were propounded in *Ideas Have Consequences* and *Visions of Order*; others were presented in some of his articles such as "The Humanities in a Century of Common Man," *New Individualist Review* 3 (1964): 17-24. See also *Life without Prejudice*, 15-64, 99-120; *The Southern Tradition at Bay*, 29-44, 388-96.
33. Wilma R. Ebbitt, "Richard M. Weaver, Teacher of Rhetoric," *Georgia Review* 18 (Winter 1963): 417. These ancient sources are reflected, for example, in Weaver's *Ethics of Rhetoric*, 128, 174, 203; *Composition*, 212; and "Language is Sermonic," 62. Chapter one of *Ethics of Rhetoric* is a perceptive analysis of Plato's *Phaedrus*.
34. Weaver, "Concealed Rhetoric in Scientistic Sociology," 20-24, 28-30; *Ethics of Rhetoric*, 12, 22, 128, 225; "Language is Sermonic," 60-61; *Composition*, 43; *Visions of Order*, 105; *Life without Prejudice*, 46-47.
35. Weaver, "Concealed Rhetoric in Scientistic Sociology," 20, 22.
36. Weaver, *Life without Prejudice*, 116-18.
37. Weaver, *Ethics of Rhetoric*, 16, 17, 115; Weaver, "Language is Sermonic," 63.
38. Weaver, "Language is Sermonic," 54. Rhetoric must integrate the realism of Ideas and Particulars, of Being and Becoming.

39. Weaver, *Ethics of Rhetoric*, 24-25. The infusion of Weaver's philosophy into his view of rhetoric bears out his premise that our "conception of metaphysical reality finally governs our conception of everything else." Weaver, *Ideas Have Consequences*, 51.
40. Weaver, *Ethics of Rhetoric*, 18, 23, 24, 211; "Language is Sermonic," 58, 60-63; *Ideas Have Consequences*, 3, 19-20, 153, 167; *Visions of Order*, 67-69, 135; *Life without Prejudice*, 118. Weaver made a detailed analysis of ultimate "god terms" and "devil terms" which have potency in contemporary American discourse. See *Ethics of Rhetoric*, 211-32.
41. Weaver, "Concealed Rhetoric in Scientistic Sociology," 19-32. Weaver also analyzed the "sources of pervasive vices" in the rhetoric of social scientists, sources which make their prose difficult to understand and seemingly divorced from reality. See *Ethics of Rhetoric*, chap. 8.
42. Weaver, *Ideas Have Consequences*, 4-5, 150-60; Weaver, *Visions of Order*, 67-70; Weaver, "Relativism and the Use of Language," 236-54; Weaver, "To Write the Truth," 25-30.
43. Weaver, *Ethics of Rhetoric*, 11-12, 18-24, 217, 232; Weaver, *Ideas Have Consequences*, 153; *Life without Prejudice*, 121-28.
44. Weaver, *Ethics of Rhetoric*, 15-22, 25, 27-29; *Composition*, 120-23; *Visions of Order*, 55-72. For an example of Weaver's use of dialectic see *Visions of Order*, 92-112. As a rhetorical critic, he analyzed the use of rhetoric and dialectic by John Randolph of Roanoke, Henry David Thoreau, and by Bryan and Darrow in the Scopes Trial. See Weaver, *Life without Prejudice*, 65-97; *Ethics of Rhetoric*, chap. 2.
45. Weaver, *Ethics of Rhetoric*, 27-28.
46. Weaver, "Language is Sermonic," 51, 59-60; *Ethics of Rhetoric*, 134; *Ideas Have Consequences*, 19, 21, 165-67; *Visions of Order*, 70-72.
47. Weaver, *Ethics of Rhetoric*, 115-42, 167. As a rhetorical critic, Weaver used a stylistic analysis to probe the "heroic" prose of John Milton and to illuminate the "spaciousness" of American oratory in the 1840s and 1850s. See *Ethics of Rhetoric*, chaps. 5 and 6.
48. This and the following quotations are from *Ethics of Rhetoric*, 58, 112, 114, 55.
49. Ibid., 55-56. Although Weaver excludes "artful choices," the point can be raised that rhetoric by definition is artful in its adaptation to audience and situation and in its conscious effort at success. For an interesting attempt to test Weaver's axiom, without prior knowledge of Weaver's view, see Edwin S. Shneidmann, "The Logic of Politics," in Leon Arons and Mark May, eds., *Television and Human Behavior* (New York: Appleton-Century-Crofts, 1963), 177-99.
50. Weaver, "Language is Sermonic," 53; *Composition*, 124.
51. Weaver, "Language is Sermonic," 55.
52. Ibid., 53, 55-56; Weaver, *Composition*, 124-27; *Ethics of Rhetoric*, 27, 56, 112-14; *Visions of Order*, 6. For Weaver's own extensive use of argument from genus or definition see, for example, *Ideas Have Consequences*, 43-44, 101, 129, 172; *Visions of Order*, chaps. 1, 2, and 8.
53. Weaver, "Language is Sermonic," 55; *Life without Prejudice*, 158-59.
54. Weaver, *Ethics of Rhetoric*, 85-114. The user of arguments from genus, principle, and definition often realizes that on some issues there is no middle ground, only right and wrong. Lincoln, for instance, knew that honest and long-run political success on the slavery issue depended upon avoiding major middle-road po-

sitions. But the failure of Stephen Douglas on the slavery question, believed Weaver, was that he chose an untenable position in the "excluded middle." See *Ethics of Rhetoric*, 94-95, 105-10.
55. Weaver saw George Washington as the "archetypal American conservative." Weaver, *Life Without Prejudice*, 165.
56. Weaver, "Language is Sermonic," 53, 56; *Ethics of Rhetoric*, 56-57; *Composition*, 129-32. For examples of Weaver's own use of argument from similitude see *Visions of Order*, chaps. 2 and 7.
57. Weaver, *Ethics of Rhetoric*, 18, 23, 127-35, 150-52, 202-206; *Composition*, 248-58; *Visions of Order*, 142.
58. Weaver, "Language is Sermonic," 53, 56; *Composition*, 127-28; *Ethics of Rhetoric*, 57; *Life without Prejudice*, 142, 145; Weaver, "A Responsible Rhetoric," (address delivered March 29, 1995, to a Great Issues Forum of students at Purdue University), 4. See *Visions of Order*, chaps. 1 and 2, for examples of his use of causal reasoning. And to a degree his *Ideas Have Consequences* is an argument from consequences; violation of certain ideals, values, and principles has led to destructive consequences.
59. Weaver, "Language is Sermonic," 57; *Ethics of Rhetoric*, 57-58; *Composition*, 128-29; *Ideas Have Consequences*, 151. An example of Weaver's infrequent personal usage is in *Ideas Have Consequences*, 134.
60. Weaver's major redefinition of the terms "liberal" and "conservative" seems to violate the type of linguistic covenant which he espouses as necessary in "Relativism and the Use of Language," 247-53.
61. Weaver, "Language is Sermonic," 57.
62. Weaver, *Ethics of Rhetoric*, 55-84; Weaver, "The People of the Excluded Middle" (unpublished and undated manuscript), 12. Weaver felt that although circumstance was no more than a retarding factor in Lincoln's considerations, circumstance was for Burke the deciding factor. See *Ethics of Rhetoric*, 95.
63. Weaver, *Ethics of Rhetoric*, 58.
64. Weaver, "The People of the Excluded Middle," 12.
65. Russell Kirk, "Ethical Labor," 485-503.
66. See, for example, Richard L. Johannesen, "John Quincy Adams' Speaking on Territorial Expansion, 1836-1848" (Ph.D. dissertation, University of Kansas, 1964), 304-50.
67. Weaver, "Language is Sermonic," 54, 57; *Composition*, 132-34.
68. Weaver, *Composition*, iii-iv; *Ethics of Rhetoric*, 232; "To Write the Truth," 25-30.
69. Weaver, *Composition*, 90-120, 123-34.
70. Weaver, *Ethics of Rhetoric*, 173-74; *Visions of Order*, 63-64; *Composition*, 118-20; "Concealed Rhetoric in Scientistic Sociology," 29-31.
71. For a similar view see Lloyd Bitzer, "Aristotle's Enthymeme Revisited," *Quarterly Journal of Speech* 45 (December 1959): 399-408. American oratory in the 1840s and 1850s was characterized by the use of "uncontested terms" and ideas "fixed by universal consensus" as unstated premises already accepted by audiences. This characteristic marked the "spaciousness" of the rhetoric of that era. See *Ethics of Rhetoric*, 164-74.
72. Ebbitt, "Richard M. Weaver, Teacher of Rhetoric," 417. Insight into argumentation and the *topoi* as taught to the freshman is gained from Manuel Bilsky, McCrea Hazlett, Robert Streeter, and Richard Weaver, "Looking for an Argument," *College English* 14 (January 1953): 210-16. Many of Weaver's personal classroom

concerns are reflected in an unpublished paper, "The Place of Logic in the English Curriculum."
73. Edward P. J. Corbett, "Rhetoric and Teachers of English," *Quarterly Journal of Speech* 51 (December 1965): 380.
74. Natanson, "The Limits of Rhetoric," 136-37. Witness the increased recent interest in scholarly scrutiny of philosophical-rhetorical issues. See, for example, Otis Walter, "On Views of Rhetoric, Whether Conservative or Progressive," *Quarterly Journal of Speech* 49 (December 1963): 367-82, and the journal, *Philosophy and Rhetoric,* published by the Pennsylvania State University Press.

7

Dialectic Rhetorician

Bruce A. White

"From speaking truthfully to speaking correctly to speaking usefully—is this not the rhetorician's easy descent to Avernus?" Richard M. Weaver's sober rhetorical query, with its analytical progression and classical allusion, capsulates his great obsessions: the dissolution of Western language and civilization; the appealing order of an idealized past; and the political relationship between dialectic and rhetoric. A Socialist Party member who became a conservative crusader, a Southern Agrarian who exiled himself to a northern megalopolis, and an academic rhetor who dialectically dissected contemporary culture, Weaver was a complex individual who believed that "to establish the fact of decadence is the most pressing duty of our time." This he sought to do in his many essays and his increasingly influential trilogy: *Ideas Have Consequences; The Ethics of Rhetoric;* and *Visions of Order: The Cultural Crisis of Our Time.*

Frank S. Meyer extolled the publication of *Ideas Have Consequences* (1948) as "the *fons et origo* of the contemporary American conservative movement." The book was a heartfelt response to the nihilism of World War II as Weaver notes in his autobiographical essay, "Up from Liberalism": "I recall sitting in my office...in 1945 and wondering whether it would not be possible to deduce, from fundamental causes, the fallacies of modern life and thinking that had produced this holocaust and would insure others. In about twenty minutes I jotted down a series of chapter headings, and this was the inception of...*Ideas Have Consequences.*"

Establishment critical reaction to this affront to "modern life and thinking" was pronounced and usually disparaging. Although John Fermatt praised it "unanswerable logic and lucidity," H. M. Jones dismissed the book as a "sincere, fanatical, and, for my money, irresponsible piece of writing," and J. O. Hertzler complained that "the nostalgia for and flight to the ideas and 'conditions' of the Middle Ages, leaves one cold." Fermatt wrote for the *Catholic World*, and Jones's review appeared in the *New York Times*: Hertzler's criticism, which appeared in the *Annals of the American Academy of Political and Social Science*, possibly carries more weight as it was not so ideologically biased. Weaver's own assessment of the book underwent revision. Originally he considered it a work of philosophy to the extent that it tried to refer "many features of modern disintegration... to a first cause"; years later, however, he felt it to be "rather an intuition of a situation."

The book's premises regarding the modern "situation" are that "the world is intelligible and... man is free," but that, at the same time, "modern man has become a moral idiot." The "fundamental cause" for this moral imbecility was the "defeat of logical realism in the great medieval debate" by the nominalism of William of Occam. After the fourteenth century "logic became grammaticized, passing from a science which taught men *vere loqui* to one which taught *recte loqui*." Symptomatic of modernity, which, according to M. E. Bradford, "meant to him at bottom institutionalizing most of the Seven Deadly Sins," is the idolatry of "the gods of mass and speed," the prevalence of social meliorism and "hysterical optimism," and the popular servitude to "the great stereopticon" machinery of the press, the motion picture, and the radio, a machinery which Weaver interprets as "a translation into actuality of Plato's celebrated figure of the cave." This attack on the banality of mass media is, of course, not original. Thoreau, with whom Weaver has something in common, had remarked, "I am sure that I never read any memorable news in a newspaper.... If you are acquainted with the principle, what do you care for a myriad instances and applications?" Weaver's social criticism, while not startlingly original, is nonetheless original in its fresh, vivid and timely approach; he often sounds like a latter-day Thomas Carlyle, whom he quotes in a chapter epigraph, and the book could be seen as something of an American version of *Past and Present*.

The final three of the book's nine chapters profess to "present means of restoration." Chapter 7 argues for the preservation and greater exercise of "the last metaphysical right," the right of private property. The next chapter, "The Power of the Word," claims that "ultimate definition is, as Aristotle affirmed, a matter of intuition," and pleads for the dual training of man in both "literature and rhetoric...(and) logic and dialectic." In the last chapter Weaver bemoans the passing of gentlemen and ladies, condemns the modern "contempt for the past," and issues an impassioned plea for the reinstatement of the disciplines of "piety and justice."

In *The Ethics of Rhetoric* (1953), Weaver alludes to Plato's *Phaedrus* and defines noble rhetoric (as opposed to base rhetoric) as consisting of "truth plus its artful presentation." Such truth is not "a truth of facts" but of ideas, and those who argue from facts or circumstance he considers the least philosophical of rhetoricians. Ironically, such an argument from circumstance was utilized by Weaver himself in his radical switch from the advocacy of socialism to the espousal of private property as "the last metaphysical right." He relates this transformation (evocative of that undergone by the Italian novelist Ignazio Silone) in "Up from Liberalism," the title of which, alluding to Booker T. Washington's autobiography, implies that liberalism is intellectual slavery: "I discovered that although the socialist program had a certain intellectual appeal for me, I could not like the members of the moment as persons.... It began to dawn on me uneasily that perhaps the right way to judge a movement was by the persons who made it up rather than by its rationalistic perfection and by the promises it held out." It is well that Weaver admits that such a procedure for assessing political movements came to him "uneasily," for it is a dangerous one. (If he himself had not gone to Vanderbilt University, but fallen in with amiable liberals instead, would he have written *Ideas Have Consequences*?) Perhaps his long graduation from philosophy to intuition, as alluded to earlier in his evolving assessment of his first book, helps to account for his vulnerability to his own charge, "least philosophical of rhetoricians." In any event, it was after this reasoning *ad hominem* that Weaver, borrowing the subtitle of John Crowe Ransom's *God without Thunder*, began his unorthodox defense of orthodoxy.

As an example of such unorthodox defense, Weaver employed both his analytical and his intuitive gifts to analyze the speeches of Edmund Burke and Abraham Lincoln, an apparent coupling of a conservative with a liberal. Observing that "the rhetorical content of the major premise which the speaker habitually uses is the key to his primary view of existence,"

Weaver notes that Burke tended to employ the argument from circumstance, which, in Weaver's dialectic, is the mode "philosophically appropriate to the liberal." Lincoln, on the other hand, tended to argue from genus or definition. Thus Lincoln was essentially more conservative than Burke, according to his criterion: "The true conservative is one who sees the universe as a paradigm of essences, of which the phenomenology of the world is a sort of continuing approximation.... He sees it as a set of definitions which are struggling to get themselves defined in the real word."

In the final chapter of *The Ethics of Rhetoric*, "Ultimate Terms in Contemporary Rhetoric," Weaver discusses the "god terms," "devil terms," and "charismatic terms" of the present age. He cites "progressive," "science," "modern," and "efficient" as popularly accepted "god terms," and "un-American" and "Communist" as "devil terms." "Freedom" and "democracy" are given as examples of "charismatic terms," those words which "have a power which is not derived, but which is in some mysterious way given." After nearly twenty years, it would appear that these terms still retain much of their same connotations. Alluding to George Orwell's study of abbreviated and telescoped words and phrases, Weaver warns that when "the ultimate terms become a series of bare abstractions, the understanding of power is supplanted by a worship of power," which results inexorably in state worship. And echoing Thoreau's famous essay, he concludes by asking "whether the real civil disobedience must not begin with our language." Every conservator of meaningful language is of necessity, he implies, a linguistic insurgent.

The final chapter of *Visions of Order: The Cultural Crisis of Our Time* (1964), the last opus of his trilogy, addresses "the image of culture," and how the style of culture assets itself "against the world of meaningless 'democratic' existence." Here he states that the task of the conservative "in our time" is "to expose as erroneous attempts to break down the discriminations of a culture," cautioning that "if no reasonable cultural unification is offered, an unreasonable one may be invented and carried to frightful lengths," as occurred before and during World War II. Weaver, who preferred to do his farming in Weaverville, North Carolina, with a horse-drawn plow, and refused on principle to take advantage of air travel and to use typewriters for works in progress, repeats his attack on "speed and mass," charging that these slogans "are the antithesis of culture." He defines cultured style as "elaboration, rhythm, and distance, which demand activity of the imagination and play of the spirit." If a culture would remain civilized, it cannot stress "function" (the feature of change) at the expense of "status" (the feature of permanence); moreover, a functional society fails utterly "in its unwillingness to ask, 'What is man?'" Turning to the role of language in society, he insists that an "axiological view of language is...necessary to recover the source of status," since this view accepts the poetic and mythopoeic nature of language. Metaphor and myth are, in his meta-political theory, the supreme analogizing modes of intellect and intuition, uniting symbolically what is partially known with what is unknown.

In one chapter, "The Cultural Role of Rhetoric," Weaver postulates that the reason Socrates was condemned is because he "had excited the rhetoricians against him." One can, after all, become "too committed to dialectic for his own good and the good of those whom he influences," for "dialectic alone in the social realm is subversive." The reason why early Christianity made such rapid headway, in his estimation, is because "a society cannot live without rhetoric," as it cannot live without a culture that satisfies its psychic needs, and "Christianity provided all that Greek dialectic left out." He declared rhetoric *ipso facto* "the most humanistic of all the disciplines," and prophesied that in "the restored man dialectic and rhetoric will go along hand in hand." As Eugene Davidson noted tellingly of Weaver, his "syllogisms were always humane."

The preceding chapter and that on "A Dialectic on Total War" are considered the best two of the book in a review by Eliseo Vivas. Assailing the democratization of war, Weaver notes poignantly that the "obliteration bombings carried on by both sides in the Second World War put an end to all discrimination." In lieu of the "abstract, windy, and demagogic apostrophes of the present day to brotherhood," he proposes the concept and practice of chivalry, which did not end wars, but controlled them through ritualized canalization. He cites the "liberal" Roosevelt's stipulation of "unconditional surrender" as an instance of unchivalrous and irrational conduct. And given the "absoluteness" of atomic weapons, he continues, he fears that if dialectic and rhetoric do not join hands, we may yet "witness the truth of Poe's line, 'The play is the tragedy,' Man."

Another target of Weaver's social criticism is progressive, practical education, which he condemns as "a wholesale apostasy, involving abandonment of fundamental and long-held beliefs about man and the world." He calls modern educationists "gnostic educators," and blames Emerson and Thoreau, and New England Transcendentalism in general, for the decline of modern education. In an article in *Modern Age,* "Two Types of American Individualism," Weaver attacks Thoreau for his failure to "see the consequences" of his "individual isolation" and insists upon the need for a "social bond" individualism exemplified by John Randolph. Something in Thoreau seemed to draw frequent fire from Weaver, though their similarities may outweigh their differences. Thoreau, an earlier proponent of agrarianism, had no more enthusiasm for his age than Weaver had for his; to Thoreau the nineteenth century was "restless, nervous, bustling, trivial." Perhaps certain facets of Thoreau's personality reflected uncomfortably in Weaver's own. Both shared a tendency to intensity of purpose, and both were reclusive aristocrats given to idealization of the past and disdain for the present. In any event, Weaver must have realized that Thoreau would have been just as distressed as he at the decline in education; Thoreau was another reverent student of the classics who had complained of not having anyone at hand to discuss Greek passages, and lambasted the anemic educational and cultural milieu of Concord. Thoreau, then, wanted "uncommon" schools, as Weaver wanted "uncommon" teaching.

Weaver is clearly not attacking transcendentalism *per se;* we have noted his description of the conservative's task as the vision of "the universe as a paradigm of essences." Furthermore, in "Language is Sermonic," his last major essay, Weaver reiterates his belief in the realm of essence and states that "the cosmos is one vast system of analogy." What he does object to is the democratization of the classroom, and he reminds his readers that "democracy is not a way of life but a form of government." The teacher must never abdicate his superior office as the Adam to his students; for "teaching people to speak the truth...can be done only by giving them the right names of things." When teachers stop believing in objective truth, their pupils can learn only sophistry and etiquette; it is through the "status" of cultural transmission that teachers "teach names which are indexes to essences," thereby becoming philosophers and not mere instructors of philosophy. Such teachers assign not only names, but values, for "language is a system of imputation, by which values and precepts are first framed in the mind and are then imputed to things." Thus true teachers preach, "bearing the sword of division" between utility and teleology. Had Socrates in his salutation to Phaedrus not asked what he did, but "Where do you hail from...and where are you bound?"

In assessing Weaver's work, so much of it consisting of "Truth plus its artful presentation," it can be asserted that he convincingly and eloquently established the fact of decadence in his time. Such decadence, sadly, is no less factual in ours; to cite one example, only a "moral idiot" and a lexical pervert could employ the oxymoron of "smart bomb" with nonchalance. As to Vivas's criticism that Weaver's definition of the conservative's task is not new, Weaver might have been among the first to admit its pertinence. Such criticism misses the point when applied to a rhetorician from the school of Platonic idealism, for the same, old ideas, in appropriate garb, must ever be exhorted anew to each age. Where Weaver is more original is in his meta-political theories and his dialectics of rhetoric. To quote again from "Language is Sermonic," rhetoric operates "at that point where literature and politics meet, or where literary values and political urgencies can be brought together. The rhetorician... induces in his hearers an attitude or decision which is political in the very broadest sense." That is to say, ideas *do* have consequences.

Vivas's charge that Weaver disregarded "his limitations" is more substantive: "A rhetor doing the work of a philosopher, he tackled problems for which he was not equipped." That is the risk hazarded by Weaver, who could have made a niche for himself in any of a half dozen academic disciplines, when he chose to be "a man writing as a man." And it is a risk that more professional men of his stature and insight need to take. Donald Davidson argued in his review of Weaver's *Life without Prejudice and Other Essays* that we need more men "who will step outside their 'fields' onto the public terrain,... willing to become 'amateurs' as Richard Weaver was." Concerned with "the whole man," Weaver had displayed his humanness in his reasoning *ad hominem,* which resulted in his ideological about-face from socialism to conservatism. He had declared his humanity in leaving "dry, insistent people of shallow objectives" for those who were "more humane, more generous, and considerably less dogmatic." In him, dialectic and rhetoric, intellect and intuition, head and heart, struggled to go along hand in hand.

8

Rhetoric and the Tyrannizing Image

John Bliese

Richard Weaver was, among other things, a Southerner, a conservative and a rhetorician. The relationship between his Southern background and his analysis of contemporary social and political issues has been much discussed and has been perhaps best summarized by M. E. Bradford.[1] But the relationship between his political and rhetorical theories has been largely overlooked. Conservatives writing about Weaver tend to ignore his rhetoric almost entirely. For example, John P. East presents an excellent analysis of Weaver's politics. But rhetoric is conspicuous by its absence from his list of those things essential to understanding Weaver's "conservative mind."[2] Wilmoore Kendall, reviewing *Visions of Order*, claims it should have the "political equivalent of biblical status" for conservatives, but he merely mentions Weaver's discussion of rhetoric in that work.[3] And Frank S. Meyer observes that for Weaver "rhetoric itself [was] an essential component of civilizational being, an element the Ancient World and Europe through the Renaissance understood, but of which we are today woefully ignorant." He notes that for Weaver there was a close connection between rhetoric and his analysis of our society, but Meyer does not develop that connection.[4]

Likewise, rhetoricians consider Weaver's rhetorical theories while largely ignoring his politics. Richard L. Johannesen mentions that Weaver was a conservative, claims that this is significant in understanding his rhetoric, and then drops the point.[5] In my summary of Weaver's rhetoric, although some of his practical advice for conservative persuasion is presented, the relation of rhetoric to his political theory is mentioned at only a few places.[6] Bruce A. White's summary of Weaver's rhetoric and dialectic similarly touches on this relationship but briefly.[7] None of these does full justice to Weaver's thought on this crucial point, for he perceives an intimate relationship between rhetoric—the art of persuasion—and culture, especially our Western culture. Since it is conservatism's highest mission to preserve that culture, his rhetoric is of central significance in understanding his political theory.

One of Richard Weaver's major recurrent themes was his belief that Western culture is in deep trouble. He believed that the West has been in steady decline since the time of William of Occam in the fourteenth century.[8] He agreed with T. S. Eliot that the decline continues today; "that the standards of culture are lower than they were fifty years ago; and that the evidences of this decline are visible in every department of human activity."[9]

Yet when Weaver describes specifically how our culture is declining, he gives two contradictory answers. Often he tells us that our culture is disintegrating, fragmenting and descending into chaos. "For four centuries every man has been not only his own priest but his own professor of ethics and the consequence is an anarchy which threatens even that minimum consensus of value necessary to the political state."[10] He makes the same judgment in relation to the recent past: "It is now a truism that the homogeneity of belief which obtained three generations ago has largely disappeared."[11] He refers to "the fact that our world is disintegrating rapidly."[12]

On the other hand, almost as frequently Weaver claims that, far from coming apart, we are being increasingly forced into the sterile mold of the mass man. He warns: "It cannot be too often said that society and mass are contradictory terms and that those who seek to do things in the name of mass are the destroyers in our midst."[13] The advertisers' goal of happiness through comfort has been so widely accepted that it is virtually impossible to teach anything else; our culture has deteriorated into a conformist mass with consumption as its only goal in life.[14] Moreover, "not only is the single human individual being pushed toward conformity, but the individual group or culture is met with the same demand to go along, to become more like the generality, and so to give up character."[15]

Whether our culture is descending into chaos or mass conformity is never resolved by Weaver. However, we should not be too hasty to reject his analysis simply because of this contradiction. Rather we should take our cue from Weaver himself:

> To show that a political system or a political thinker exhibits contradictions is not nearly so serious a charge...I will hazard that such can be proved more or less about any comprehensive system which has ever been put forward. What the contradictions may, and certainly in many cases do indicate is that the author of the system is at grips with reality. The contradictions are not of course good things in themselves, but they are evidences of a referential relationship to the world, and they may be resolved on a higher level. Thus they are often signs of vitality.[16]

Weaver's belief that the West is declining, no matter how, led him, at a higher level to make a profound analysis of the general nature of culture and its constituent parts. In this analysis, rhetoric is very closely tied to culture: Whenever he writes of culture, rhetoric is not far in the background and vice versa.

All men, at all times, have fashioned for themselves ideational environments to humanize their worlds. We call these creations cultures. They are ultimately based on our innate capacity to create values, for we "are born into history, with an endowment of passion and a sense of the *ought*."[17] We collectively idealize this "sense of the ought" in what Weaver early in his career called "metaphysical dreams." "Without the metaphysical dream it is impossible to think of men living together harmoniously over an extent of time. The dream caries with it an evaluation, which is the bond of spiritual community."[18] Later he referred to this cultural center as:

> A "tyrannizing image" which draws everything toward itself. This image is the ideal of its excellence. The forms that it can take and the particular manifestations that it can find are various. In some instances it has been a religious ritual; in others a sacred scripture; in others a literature which everyone is expected to know; codes of conduct (and even of warfare) may be the highest embodied form. But examine them as we will, we find this inward facing toward some high representation. This is the sacred well of culture from which inspiring waters like magnetic lines of force flow out and hold the various activities in a subservience of acknowledgment. Not to feel this magnetic pull toward identification and assimilation is to be outside the culture.[19]

Many of Weaver's rhetorical concepts are based on the notion of a tyrannizing image that provides a culture with its ideals and goals. The analysis of ultimate terms in chapter 9 of *The Ethics of Rhetoric* is a clear case. Certain terms bear extremely favorable or unfavorable connotations and the mere use of them as labels is a forceful and persuasive attempt to get an audience to accept, or reject, the thing labelled. These "ultimate terms" are names for the central values, or their opposites, of the culture's tyrannizing image. Moreover, there is "some system of relationship among the attractive and among the repulsive terms, so that we can work out an order of weight and precedence in the prevailing rhetoric once we have discovered the 'rhetorical absolutes'—the terms to which the very highest respect is paid." The highest positive terms is the "god term," "that expression about which all other expressions are ranked as subordinate and serving dominations and powers. Its force imparts to the others their lesser degree of force and fixes the scale by which degrees of comparison are understood." Its negative counterpart is the "devil term." Weaver, in 1953, believed the god term of contemporary America was "progress"; therefore to label some proposal as "progressive" was to invoke the highest value in its favor.[20]

Weaver's hierarchy of arguments also is closely related to his concept of the tyrannizing image. The type of argument one habitually employs, he contends, is the surest index to one's philosophy, and some kinds of arguments are more ethical than others.[21] At the top of the hierarchy, the most ethical appeal is the argument from principle or genus or definition. (All three are essentially similar.) Often the rhetor takes a genus or definition contained within the tyrannizing image and uses it as a predicate in a categorical proposition. Thus, Abraham Lincoln's argument defining Negroes as men derives its force from the prevailing beliefs of what it means to be a man.[22] If the tyrannizing image of his time had not included beliefs such as that man should be free, Lincoln's argument from definition would not have had the desired force. This type of appeal is the proper one for conservatives.

The argument from similitude is also good and is ranked second, for its searches for a genus or principle. Causal arguments rank third. They are lower since their impact derives less from the cultural ideal than from purely pragmatic consideration. At the bottom are appeals based on circumstances. They ignore ideals entirely and appeal merely to brute fact. This last line of argument is the proper one for liberals and one fatal for conservatives. Weaver uses the history of the Republican Party to illustrate the fate of conservatives when they abandon their proper appeals from definition and principle in favor of arguments from circumstances. The Party began with Lincoln as its leader, appealing to principles: "the moral idea of freedom and the political idea of union." Later the Party degenerated to appealing to circumstances, arguing: "Look how prosperous the country has become." The prosperity vanished with the Depression, leaving the Party without even this source, so it shifted to charges that the incumbent Democrats had "bungled." The result is well known: The Party was reduced to minority status, without any principle from which to oppose the majority. Its platforms deteriorated to promising just what the Democrats did, only a little bit less.[23]

We may also note Weaver's analysis of the rhetorical syllogism or enthymeme.[24] This is a syllogism with one of the premises missing, for "it is presumed to exist already in the mind of the one to whom the argument is addressed."[25] These propositions which a rhetor simply assumes will often be value judgments contained the culture's tyrannizing image. Rhetoric, we have seen, relies on the cultural focal point for its effectiveness. If an orator cannot operate on the basis of common, accepted, uncontested terms and premises, he has no fulcrum for leverage in moving his audience. Without mutual assent to a tyrannizing image, he may never be able to get his premises accepted, "at least not as orator."[26]

While rhetoric depends on the tyrannizing image for its effectiveness, the relation is not simply linear but reciprocal. The image in turn depends on rhetoric for its force. While rhetoric utilizes appeals to the values of the image, without the resources of rhetoric the cultural ideal would be merely a sterile, abstract idea, unrelated to the world. The image supplies the focal point for a culture; rhetoric provides adhesion to that point. Weaver explains: "A society cannot live without rhetoric. There are some things in which the group needs to believe which cannot be demonstrated to everyone rationally. Their acceptance is pressed upon us by a kind of moral imperative arising from the groups as a whole.... Such beliefs always come to us couched in rhetorical terms, which tell us what attitude to take."[27] Rhetoric, that is, has a crucial function as cultural glue; it "supplies the bond of community, for community rests upon informed sentiment."[28]

Not only is rhetoric intimately related to culture at its central core, the relationship permeates many aspects of culture. Weaver uses a number of key terms which cluster around the word "culture." He writes that culture is an expression of values, often religious values; culture is exclusive, integrating; it is a form, and form equals style; it is hierarchic and aristocratic. Each of these aspects of culture is, in turn, related to rhetoric.

Weaver recognizes an intimate relationship between religion and culture: "A culture nearly always appears contemporaneously with the expression of religious feeling."[29] He refers to a mediating function of culture, similar to rhetoric's mediation between the tyrannizing image and individuals: "Cultural fulfillment never seems complete without some kind of religious orientation. Culture has been described as a bridge between strictly religious ideas and the mundane concerns of life."[30]

The Christian religion is by nature rhetorical, which accounts for its historical success. Weaver contrasts the strongly dialectical Hellenic philosophy with Christianity, which "provided all that Greek dialectic left out. It spoke to the feelings, and what seems of paramount significance, it has its inception in a historical fact.... Dialectic has been present because it is never absent from rational discourse, but rhetoric and poetry were there to make up the winning combination." The current "decay" of Christianity as a "great support of Western culture is closely connected with the decline of rhetoric."[31]

Weaver repeatedly emphasizes that a tyrannizing image unites a community while excluding other communities. "A culture...operates on a principle of exclusiveness and can operate on no other.... The principle of exclusiveness of a culture is simply its integrity. It is an awareness of the culture that it is a unity of feeling and outlook which makes its members different from outsiders."[32] A culture flourishes only as a unity. It "is like an organic creation in that its constitution cannot tolerate more than a certain amount of what is foreign or extraneous."[33] Consequently, rhetoric must function both as a unifying force within a culture and as a divisive force against outside influences.

Although a culture must be restrictive, it is not necessarily a uniformly compressed mass. On the contrary, a healthy culture is hierarchic, including considerable differentiation oriented toward one center.[34] It consists of classes, each person knowing his own status within the structure. The structure of a flourishing culture is not rigid; it allows upward—and downward—mobility, based on rational criteria. But its class structure is clear.[35] It is the function of rhetoric to bond these different strata together by relating them to one another and, ultimately, to the tyrannizing image that unites the entire culture.

Since each culture is a unique form, it will exhibit its own particular style. "In a highly developed culture this sense of style permeates everything; it is in dress and manners, in art and institutions, in architecture and cookery. It imparts tone to the whole of society by keeping before its members a standard of the right and not right."[36]

As a culture has its own style, conversely a particular style asks its audience to respond according to the style's dominating image. Weaver is bothered by the deterioration of style in our time: it is both a symptom of cultural decline and a further impetus to decline.³⁷ He criticizes style in many areas. His dislike for jazz, modern art, and the obscene is well known. Perhaps less well known is his criticism of our broadcasters.

> Not to be overlooked in any gauging of influence is the voice of announcer and commentator. The metaphysical dream of progress dictates the tone, which is one of cheery confidence, assuring us in the face of all contrary evidence that the best is yet to be. Recalling the war years...who has not heard the news of some terrible tragedy, which might stagger the imagination and cause the conscientious artist to hesitate at the thought of its description, given to the world in the same tone that commends a brand of soap or predicts fair weather for the morrow? There were commentators, it is true, who got the spirit of gravity into their speech, but behind them stood always the announcer, denying by his formula of regular inflection the poignancy of their message.³⁸

This indictment was written in 1948. Our broadcasters today are no better: one need only to consider the television coverage of any major disaster. Surely we must agree with Weaver that use of a particular tone asks the audience to adopt a corresponding attitude which the speaker deems appropriate. We may also agree that we hear in these broadcasters "the voice of the Hollow Men who can see the toppling walls of Jerusalem, Athens and Rome without enough soul to sense tragedy."³⁹

Weaver's concern for style focuses on language, because language is "one of the supremely important elements in a culture."⁴⁰ Man is basically linguistic and it is the linguistic "faculty which has enabled men to create cultures and civilization."⁴¹ Weaver believes that language is inherently rhetorical, that "language is sermonic."⁴² He refers to "a fundamental proposition of Aquinas: 'Every form is accompanied by an inclination.' Now language is a system of forms, which both singly and collectively have this inclination or intention."⁴³

As cultures can be healthy or diseased, developing or declining, so can languages. Weaver fought a constant battle against the general semanticists, because they were attempting to eliminate feelings, values, tendencies from language. They would deprive language of its rhetorical dimension, which is necessary to relate the tyrannizing image to the individual.⁴⁴ But his concern extends far beyond the semanticists: "The English language today is losing character, strength and resonance. What I am chiefly conscious of is the loss of resonance, and I think that this loss is owing mainly to the fact that the modern style shuns anything suggestive of value. Or, if this generalization must be qualified, it admits only values of the narrow, strident kind, such as might be expected to survive after positivism has done its work."⁴⁵

He compares our more limited linguistic resources with those of an earlier age:

> If we seat a typical modern before a chapter of the King James Bible, or a passage from an eighteenth century oration, it is problematical how much of what is there he can get. The wonderful wealth of pleonasm, metonymy, synecdoche, antithesis, isocolons, anaphoras, inversions, and climactic orders—a veritable orchestration for the soul—is, I believe, puzzling to him. His reaction, I suspect, is that the writer of the passage is saying it the best way he could, and must be pardoned, being of a primitive time. The way to say it would be in the style of *Look*, or of an editorial in the New York *Daily News*, with words of flat signification, with syncopated syntax, and with none of the broadly ruminative phrases which have the power to inspired speculation. The essential sterility of such a style is one of the surest signs we have that modern man is being desiccated.⁴⁶

If a society breaks down completely, its language can suffer a similar destruction. In an unpublished lecture, Weaver quotes Thucydides' account of a civil war which became increasingly bloody. Then Weaver continues: "And one of the results which he is concerned to stress is that following the breakdown of community, words ceased to have their old meanings and in many cases were applied to things whose previous meaning were opposite.... When a people are beside themselves, as it were, with anger and fear, the dialectic of language, which in a normal situation our conscience tells us to regard, is abandoned in favor of passion and action."⁴⁷

Since language is so critical an aspect of culture, one may think that simply by tinkering with language one could rescue a declining culture. A tempting thought, but it would not work. "Something will have to be done first about man's representation of himself, because that representation broadens or narrows the vocabulary and the rhetoric which he thinks he can use." However, if we do not want to contribute to cultural decline, we need to be aware of our own linguistic usage. "It is very easy to pick up unconsciously a tone, or to fall into a vocabulary, or to make use of figures and analogies, whose implications are opposite to the views we really hold. Any style moves along on a set of hidden or half-hidden premises, and there is a great if unconscious pressure to accept the premises of a style in popular use." We can, at least, avoid using "the kind of discourse that carries just below its surface a contempt for all values."⁴⁸

Several of Weaver's ideas on the relationship between rhetoric and culture have now been presented. In evaluating them we should consider two problems in his analysis. First, Eliseo Vivas notes a basic equivocation in Weaver's use of the word "culture." In reviewing *Visions of Order,* Vivas writes: "Infecting it with incoherence is a defect that runs like a geological fault throughout the whole of the book's length. Early in chapter one, the reader becomes aware that Weaver oscillates between the sociological and the honorific meaning of the term 'culture.'" This ambiguity raises a considerable difficulty. "Weaver wanted to criticize the crisis of our world. But which of the two cultures was open to criticism?"[49] The same ambiguity may be found in Weaver's other works as well. However, it does not significantly affect his analysis of the role of rhetoric. We have here been concerned almost exclusively with the sociological meaning of "culture," but insofar as the term may be used "honorifically," rhetoric still plays an important role. In the latter case, creating "cultured" people or raising the standards of culture is a rhetorical process. It is rhetoric that shows us "better versions"[50] of ourselves and that leads us upwards toward the tyrannizing ideal.

Second, Weaver treats cultures as far more exclusive than they probably are. He often seems to believe cultures are isolated monads that can only be contaminated by contact with other monads. Surely Christopher Dawson is far closer to the truth when he traces the diverse ways in which cultures can interact, even combine with phenomenally creative results.[51] Again, this defect does not seem to affect Weaver's ideas on the role of rhetoric as the bond of culture. At most, it means rhetoric has less of a divisive role in relation to other cultures.

Overall, however, we must admire Weaver's efforts to revitalize rhetoric as a crucial step in stemming our cultural decline. He reminds us that rhetoric is a fundamental dimension of humanity that we are all "born rhetoricians."[52] As we are cultural by nature, so also are we rhetorical—and these dimensions of humanity are closely interrelated.

In his own "unorthodox defense of orthodoxy"[53] Weaver saw himself as one of "the embattled friends of traditional rhetoric," one of those men who were "the prime conservators of the values essential to culture cohesion."[54] For rhetoric is not a mere bag of tricks for getting one's way in the world. On the contrary, our linguistic style essentially embodies our tyrannizing image, the outlook on the world which we accept and would have others accept as well.[55] The kinds of arguments we habitually employ are not merely random or strategic choices, but the embodiment of our philosophies on their logical forms. And so with the other aspects of rhetoric as well. Rhetoric is "the most humanistic of the disciplines,"[56] and it must be restored if our culture is to be preserved.

Notes

1. M. E. Bradford, "The Agrarianism of Richard Weaver: Beginnings and Completions," *Modern Age* 14 (1970): 249-56.
2. John P. East, "Richard M. Weaver: The Conservatism of Affirmation," *Modern Age* 19 (1975): 339.
3. Willmoore Kendall, "How to Read Richard Weaver: Philosopher of 'We the [Virtuous] People,'" *The Intercollegiate Review* 2 (1965-66): 81 f.
4. Frank S. Meyer, "Richard M. Weaver: An Appreciation," *Modern Age* 14 (1970): 246 f.
5. Richard L. Johannesen, "Richard Weaver's View of Rhetoric and Criticism," *Southern Speech Journal* 32 (1966-67): 133-45.
6. John R. Bliese, "Richard M. Weaver: Conservative Rhetorician," *Modern Age* 21 (1977): 377-86.
7. Bruce A. White, "Richard M. Weaver: Dialectic Rhetorician," *Modern Age* 26 (1982): 256-59.
8. Richard M. Weaver, *Ideas Have Consequences* (Chicago, Ill., 1948), 3.
9. Richard Weaver, "The Image of Culture," *Modern Age* 8 (1964): 187.
10. Weaver, *Ideas Have Consequences*, 2.
11. Richard Weaver, *The Ethics of Rhetoric* (Chicago, 1953), 167.
12. Richard Weaver, "Up from Liberalism," in *Life without Prejudice and Other Essays* (Chicago, 1965), 154.
13. Weaver, *Ideas Have Consequences*, 35.
14. Ibid., 105.
15. Richard Weaver, "Reflections of Modernity," in *Life without Prejudice*, 111.
16. Richard Weaver, "Illusion of Illusion," *Modern Age* 4 (1960): 318.
17. Richard Weaver, *Language is Sermonic*, ed. Richard L. Johannesen, Rennard Stickland, and Ralph T. Eubanks (Baton Rouge, La., 1970), 221. Italics in the original.
18. Weaver, *Ideas Have Consequences*, 18.
19. Richard Weaver, *Visions of Order* (Baton Rouge, La., 1964), 11 f.
20. Weaver, *Ethics of Rhetoric*, 212.
21. See Weaver, *Ethics of Rhetoric*, chaps. 3 and 4; and Weaver, *Language is Sermonic*, 208 f.
22. Weaver, *Ethics of Rhetoric*, 91.
23. Ibid., 80 f.
24. Ibid., 173 f.
25. Weaver, *Visions of Order*, 63.
26. Weaver, *Ethics of Rhetoric*, 174.
27. Weaver, *Visions of Order*, 65.
28. Weaver, "Reflections of Modernity," 118.
29. Richard Weaver, "The Importance of Cultural Freedom," in *Life without Prejudice*, 15.

30. Richard Weaver, "Contemporary Southern Literature," *Texas Quarterly* 2 (1959): 133. See also Weaver, "Importance of Cultural Freedom," 15 f.
31. Weaver, *Visions of Order*, 66 f.
32. Weaver, "Reflections of Modernity," 110.
33. Weaver, "Importance of Culture Freedom," 18.
34. Weaver, *Visions of Order*, 16 f.
35. See especially Weaver, *Visions of Order*, chap. 2
36. Weaver, "Importance of Cultural Freedom," 197 f.
37. Weaver, "Image of Culture," 197 f.
38. Weaver, *Ideas Have Consequences*, 103.
39. Ibid.
40. Weaver, "Reflections of Modernity," 111.
41. Richard Weaver, "Education and the Individual," *The Intercollegiate Review* 2 (1965): 70.
42. Weaver, "Language is Sermonic," in *Language is Sermonic*, 201-205.
43. Weaver, *Ideas Have Consequences*, 153.
44. See for example, *Ideas Have Consequences*, chap. 8.
45. Richard Weaver, "Individuality and Modernity," in *Essays on Individuality*, ed. Felix Morley (Philadelphia, Pa., 1958), 76 f.
46. Ibid., 77.
47. Richard Weaver, "The Strategy of Words," unpublished address given 13 February 1962, at the Lake Bluff Women's Club.
48. Weaver, "Individuality and Modernity," 77 f.
49. Eliseo Vivas, "The Mind of Richard Weaver," *Modern Age* 8 (1964): 309.
50. Weaver, *Ethics of Rhetoric*, 25.
51. For summaries of Dawson's systematic analysis of the subject, see the introduction to *The Age of the Gods* (London, 1933); John J. Mulloy's closing essay in Dawson's *The Dynamics of World History*, ed. John J. Mulloy (New York, 1962); and John Bliese, "Christopher Dawson: His Interpretation of History," *Modern Age* 23 (1979): 259-65.
52. Weaver, *Language is Sermonic*, 221.
53. Weaver adopted this phrase from John Crowe Ransom.
54. Ralph T. Eubanks in *Language is Sermonic*, 4.
55. See, for example, his analysis of memory, one of the ancient canons of rhetoric in *Visions of Order*, chap. 3.
56. Weaver, *Visions of Order*, 71.

III

The Southern Conservative

9

The Agrarianism of Richard Weaver: Beginnings and Completions

M. E. Bradford

Though his worth and stature were early established among them, while yet living Richard M. Weaver was something of a puzzle for his friends within the American "conservative establishment." And despite some valuable consideration of his work occasioned by his death and the posthumous publication of composition left upon his desk with that untimely event, the original confusion persists, perhaps even deepens.[1] Southern origins, humanistic training, and a deep, special learning (plus long exposure to Chicago and its university) offer only a modicum of clarification. And earned reputation for dour sobriety adds but a little more. Only in the strictest sort of intellectual history are there appropriate instruments for the necessary explanation/remedy. Such is here undertaken.

Weaver himself in the autobiographical "Up from Liberalism" pointed the way for the work at hand.[2] There he specified how his life had turned upon his first acquaintance with the Agrarians of *I'll Take My Stand*, with his reading of their books and papers and his experience of their tutelage.[3] These facts are well-known to Weaver's admirers: the facts, but not their significance. I suspect the process of their reception goes something like this:

> In Nashville, Weaver accepted being Southern; Baton Rouge finished the job. That was predictable. There was nothing particularly intellectual about the change. Even after persuasion to the contrary, they all come to it—or else go mad. And we know "good" Southerners ordinarily "lean to the right"—though they don't think about it much. Besides, some of those fellows were poets. I've read a little of them, once or twice.

Such obfuscation is not vicious or even ill-intentioned. It is only the usual, historically explicable Yankee (and most identified American conservative intellectuals are Yankees) short cut, a short cut that transcends ideology. The Agrarians are only names to most of the spokesmen for the company Weaver joined soon after World War II. Vigorous and informed regionalism intimidates them, sets back at arm's length their "should-be" allies. And Southerners are of course, by definition, intellectually unimportant. They may distinguish themselves in literature, politics or the church; but that's not what we mean by intellectual. In accepting the Weaver of Chicago, his new friends therefore found it impossible to make a serious attempt at explaining the North Carolinian who had surfaced curiously in their midst. Hence for two reasons an orderly exposition of Agrarian doctrine and application of that overlay to Weaver's total production is at this time in order: first, because it might help stifle the sort of reflex before Southern men and materials illustrated above; second, because Weaver deserves the intelligibility it should provide for his career.

Since it is not possible to survey here the variety of Agrarian teaching in detail, the reader must permit me the liberty of a private synthesis from their writing. For my comment, the obvious focus lies in the 1930 manifesto itself and more specifically in the "Statement of Principles" with which *I'll Take My Stand* was prefaced and to which all twelve of its contributors subscribed.[4] What I choose to emphasize in the way of implicit moral and political philosophy is not, however, merely a concession to convenience, a preparation for study of Weaver in his own right. For my argument is not simply that Weaver had so and such intellectual antecedents. Instead I contend that what was essential to the Agrarian enterprise—fundamental though often concealed in an emphasis on this or that topical difficulty—found its final competition in Weaver's more general and sustained excursions into social theory, rhetoric, educational philosophy, intellectual history, and related fields. That Weaver knew he was doing this is evident in his correspondence with Southern friends during the years he labored on *Ideas Have Consequences, The Ethics of Rhetoric,* and *Vision of Order.*[5] Evident there, and in his decision to return upon historic (and other Southern) subjects, once that work of theory was done. But more of this hereafter.

To being, *because they were Southern* (and hence rather more European by inheritance than American intellectuals from north or west) the political vision of the Agrarians conformed not at all to the familiar native political categories: in a word, they were neither "liberty men" nor "equality men." Yet neither were they rank Tories. Their measure of any polity was its human (and not its legal or economic) product. As a body they were doubtful about "Progress"—and even doubtful that the appearance of the "progressive," postbellum United States on the stage of history was in the long run to be of certain benefit to Western man. And though respectful of human dignity, they were submissive before "the frame of Creation" in a way that would seem to most Americans not of their regional patrimony both radical and surprising. Reason therefore was not their "strange god." However, they were eminently "reasonable" and made few prescriptive appeals to custom or usage alone.

Industrialism and applied science were the immediate villains in the Agrarian analysis of Southern difficulties after the crash of 1929. In this season of ecology and runaway conservation, it is more or less difficult to write off Agrarian alarm concerning such aggression against nature: at least more difficult than at any other time in the last four decades. But unlike contemporary enthusiasms for "clear water in the sun," Agrarian suspicion of the Faustian temptation as it made an appearance among their kinsmen was utterly unsentimental. Indeed it was just the opposite— based on the assumption that external nature was *for* man's use and keeping, to be cooperated with, not controlled (and certainly not remade into a refugee from peculiarly human responsibilities). Moreover that suspicion was consistent with the group's position on other matters. All agreed that industrialism and its instruments were in themselves morally neutral, dangerous only insofar as they encourage men to misconceive of their condition. Yet because of what brought them into being, the results of the new juggernaut had been for the United States worse than apostasy or abolition. And, law or history aside, they were, for these specifically philosophical reasons, certainly to be resisted by a pious people. The Book does not anticipate good fortune for the children of Pride. And the modern economy, come southward by the way of Manchester and then Lowell, appeared to go with the hegemony of that breed. To submit to them was damnation by adoption, an immigration to the Cities of the Plain. Pride was, obviously, for the Agrarians the identifying vice of the modern dispensation. And this was reason enough for their "thundering negations."[6]

Though he conceded nothing concerning Agrarian tactics for specific reformations (and defended their proposals in a variety of practical connections), Richard Weaver chose to continue the work of his masters by tracing their "contextually colored" positions back to the first principles out of which those positions emerged. And, more importantly, he attempted to give order and connection to these principles, to supply the lack of system and depth of thought which he always identified as the great weakness of his people in their dealing with mortal enemies.[7]

After early graduate study at Vanderbilt, an interval of teaching, and completion in 1943 of work on his terminal degree at Louisiana State University (work that led to *The Southern Tradition at Bay: A History of Postbellum Thought*), Weaver turned back in time to consider the sources and the unfolding of those ideas, hostile and friendly, which "had consequences" in the life of the South.[8] For he sensed from the first that the record of his own subculture was a late chapter in a very long story. Moreover he had learned from his survey of Southern thought in the decades just before hard nationalizing set in that all major cultural changes are "moral creations" and issue for the "obscure depths of men's wanting" and from the ontological or religious posture they assume in answering those needs of flesh and spirit.[9] The reception given some of his early Agrarian essays and the imperception with which the major university press of his native state greeted his dissertation forced Weaver to create his own intellectual history of the West—or at least a history of those ideas on which turned his arguments concerning the Southern past. John Crowe Ransom's *God without Thunder* (the most important of Agrarian documents for Weaver) had anticipated *Ideas Have Consequences,* as had a few other pieces by members of the group.[10] But it is true that his first book publication "got Weaver going." In addition it did what Ransom's astonishingly prophetic (and previous) exposure of utopian ideology failed to accomplish: divested the Agrarian calculus of its diverting topically and "merely regional" connotations.

There were also other important factors influencing the direction taken by Weaver's career after original immersion in things Southern: the breakup of Agrarianism as a movement; a deepening interest in the theology and in the true nature of the liberal education; the full flowering of the Southern Literary Renascence and of a body of criticism which accounted for it; the fresh spate of political attacks on the Southern "regime" after World War II; and the appearance of (along with his personal involvement in) a nationwide network of intellectuals on the Right. However, more significant than all of these influences toward complexity and sophistication was the discovery behind the next stage in his development. Stated briefly, that discovery was of a casual link between corruption of the language, rhetorical illiteracy, and the characteristic modern errors of doctrine: the general contemporary acceptance of debilitating materialism or gnostic conceptions of man's condition, nature, and destiny. Out of this revelation came Weaver's least understood work, *The Ethics of Rhetoric*.[11] In this connection he authored a fine textbook; and he also began to practice the part of rhetor, both in political journalism and on the platform.[12]

In all these undertakings Weaver followed well established Agrarian precedent.[13] Yet none of the original dozen (nor, indeed, any later recruits) became professional rhetoricians. Weaver did, even earning the respect of authorities in the discipline who shared nothing but that interest with him. Once again, the necessity for depth and organization (plus a willingness to go the long and certain way around) determined Weaver's course. Implicitly, in this vocational detour, he acknowledged that more than philosophical penetration was required for the counterattack in which he had enlisted.[14] For the vehicle which carries it affects the purchase and authority of any wisdom that deserves circulation. And, as Weaver insisted, most of the accepted vehicles, the systems or "universes" of discourse available for his use in the mid-twentieth century, were perverted by a built-in hostility to his purposes. Nominalism, primitivism, egalitarian fancies and their pseudo-scientific derivatives had poisoned the wells of truth, forbidden the teaching of logic and the rules of discourse, undermined man's ancient faith in the imagination, derided custom, and in general spread sentimentality and barbarism. Which is to say nothing of the strictly social implications to the "democratic" public school. A concern for valid rhetoric and honest dialectics remains as an ingredient in everything Richard Weaver wrote after 1948. With these instruments perfected and a backdrop in the history of ideas sketched out, he was ready to work toward certain positive, normative statements: essays focusing upon pressure points inside what remains of the permanent in the going order, essays toward the restoration of a civil polity. *Visions of Order* is what resulted.[15]

At the time of his death Weaver was finally ready to make his case for the South. He had established an audience to hear it and a content to insure its plausibility. Moreover he was once again ready to submit for publication the work with which his scholarly career began. As is indicated by the manuscripts Weaver left (plus certain late publications), he had organized his life out of that original effort, his understanding of the Southern experience. And he intended much more in the same vein: a series on Southern letters; an American Plutarch, comparing exemplary Southern and Northern types; a collection of papers on American rhetorical landmarks; a study of conflict in the American churches over slavery; and a few other items reaching out toward a transregional definition of the national character. A sample of this material is the "Two Orators," printed in this same issue; and there is more, in print and forthcoming.[16]

Weaverville's loyal son, therefore, may be said to have moved, twice over, "out and then back." The total pattern of his life almost fits the old Hegelian diagram: from unself-conscious immersion, to conscious alienation, and from thence again to the point of beginning, to subsist there finally, *but this time on purpose*.[17] Yet the Weaver we confront in his writings belongs only to the last of these stages. The variety of his interests described above was, as I have already inferred, only apparent. Always Weaver remained inside the tradition he appropriated through the Agrarians, a tradition always "at bay" and always defensible. And there was another difference in his second "returning." For in making public the reasoning which "paved his way home" he made it possible for *a whole people* to come along behind, to discover and to accept themselves in an act of mind. In truth, he became much of the Southern philosopher for whose appearance he had called since 1943. He supplied the central lack on which he placed the blame for the South's prolonged and unamenable "embattlement." The men who had pointed him this way were, by and large, delighted. I believe that they alone recognized from the beginning what Weaver was up to.[18]

A few unmistakable points of tangency identifying my subject with his immediate forbears in spirit are worth special attention. A brief glance in their direction should leave few doubts among close readers of both that such a connection exists. Apart from the dissertation and compositions overtly in tribute to (or analysis of) the Agrarians, Weaver is closest to them in such works as "Aspects of the Southern Philosophy," "The South and the American Union," "Lee the Philosopher," "Life without Prejudice," The Regime of the South," "Ultimate Terms in Contemporary Rhetoric," "The Spaciousness of the Old Rhetoric," "The Southern Tradition," "Status and Function," "Forms and Social Cruelty," "Piety and Justice," and one or two other papers appearing finally in *Life with-*

out Prejudice.[19] Weaver had his nationalist side. Often he spoke as one generically American[20] (*why* I shall explain in concluding). But it is unlikely that any citizen of the Republic not a Southerner—and a Southerner "educated" by the Nashville brotherhood—would have written this group of essays. For one thing, Weaver's emphasis on roots, on memory, on cultural pluralism (or regionalism), on ineradicable human differences, and on the right of a regime to protect itself—a right balanced by its duty to avoid "over-formalization"—reduces easily to the social paradigms rendered in works such as Donald Davidson's *Attack on Leviathan,* "The New South and the Conservative Tradition," or his cultural analyses in *Still Rebels, Still Yankees;* John Donald Wade's "The Life and Death of Cousin Lucius," "The Dugonne Bust" and "What the South Figured: 1865-1914"; Frank Owsley's "The Pillars of Agrarianism," "The Soldier Who Walked with God," and "Democracy Unlimited"; John Crowe Ransom's "Happy Farmers," "Reconstructed but Unregenerate," and "What Does the South Want?"; Andrew Lytle's comments on Calhoun of Carolina, John Taylor of Virginia, Lee, and Nathan Bedford Forrest; Robert Penn Warren's portrait of John Brown; and Allen Tate's biographies of Jeff Davis and Stonewall Jackson (to say nothing of another hundred kindred affirmations or of the oblique evidence from poetry and fiction issuing from Agrarian inspiration).[21]

Even after selection, this is an unmanageable mass of documentation. There is however one common denominator uniting everything contained in both lists. For every item in them articulates a horror of atomistic man and therefore of the arrangements (economic, political, pedagogical, and aesthetic) that tend to produce him. Weaver spoke of the phenomenon as "depersonalization."[22] Its domestic face is statism, a passion for "Union." In the international framework it appears as ideological imperialism, an armed doctrine on the march. In art, Mr. Tate has appropriately named it "angelism."[23] In commerce it is any system which defines the species in terms of goods and services. And in the schools its aim is "life adjustment." The thrust behind all these phantasms seeking form is a fusion of those old enemies of the Godsweal, perfectionalism and its twin, the envious and cowardly dream of uniformity: the impulse to "fix everything" and thus pretend to create it, to cover with uniforms and affix numbers. Of course, I return again to the yardstick with which I began this essay—Pride. Southerners like Weaver and his predecessors attempt to keep clear of this first error by "seconding God's motion," by approving the variety inside of being, what the theologians call "plentitude." They doubt that the given world requires repairing. The Turkish qualities of Turkey, the flatness of plains and the vaulting upreach of mountains call forth from them no restless ingenuity. Their uneasiness about "homogenizing" schools is notorious. The poetics' operative in their just concluding half-century of literary flowering has been well called "submissive."[24] And they can wait for heaven.

Why Weaver claimed his homeland was the "last nonmaterialistic civilization in the western world" should by now be clear.[25] Modernity to him meant at bottom *institutionalizing* most of the Seven Deadly Sins; and each of those follies, in its turn, presupposes a denial of the finiteness of finitude, of "contingency" (to use a favorite Agrarian word). It has never been difficult to prove that the South was slow in "getting modern." In his life, it remained, though declining, as a facet of the nation's conscience—or, if you like, of its sanity. Hence Weaver addressed much of his Southern (yet more than Southern because well examined) argument to the nation at large. As he sometimes remarked, the South was never more loyally American than when it was being most Southern—even in secession.[26] These were Agrarian assumptions.[27] And where the present South did not suit well their admonitory ends, Weaver and the Agrarians were quick to use even its decline for instruction. Which brings me to my last point.

Richard Weaver never lost interest in defending what survived of this historic Southern order. His political journalism plus certain of his papers in opinion document this devotion. Indeed it was so strong as to move Weaver into a dangerous public support of the South's position in racial matters. For he perceived from its start that this Second Reconstruction had objectives far more ambitious (and perhaps other than) "justice for the Negro": in a word, abolition of the subculture itself could not survive such coercive dislodgement of its "wisest prejudice."[28] However, the fortune of the Agrarians (and their individual experiences after dispersal) had convinced him that such defendings were in vain—that is, unless the set of mind that made them necessary be discredited at its source: unless liberalism (as we speak of it loosely) be exposed for the pathology it is. The mind informed by memory (history humanized), by literature (rendering the real, including memory), and by rhetoric (bringing memory and its rendering to bear) *cannot* find in the South only a scandal. The universities were a place for that labor, or most of it. They were a base of power. Since the English Revolution of the 1640s, the French Revolution, the American Civil War, and the Communist triumph in Russia, our wars have been wars of doctrine. They are won or lost on that ground. And what is needed for them is *aristoi,* a new version of the old idea called "gentleman"; a body of informed men and women *within* the Academy— personally loyal to one another, courageous, and indefatigable. Pelham needed only a few to man his guns, hold the high ground, and turn back hosts. Only a few, because they knew their business and could trust each other. The intellectual counterpart of that astonishing battery exists today, in part thanks to this quiet little man.

Yes, Weaver was perhaps an optimist. The gentleman is always that way, at least functionally. The alternative is bad stewardship. Moreover the Agrarians had taught him the necessity of working optimistically. For "a community...groaning under...an evil dispensation...must find the way to throw it off. To think that this cannot be done is pusillanimous. And if the whole community...thinks it cannot be done, then it has simply lost its political genius and doomed itself to impotence."[29]

Notes

1. I refer especially to Eugene Davidson's "Richard Malcolm Weaver—Conservative," *Modern Age* 7 (Summer 1963): 226-30; Eliseo Vivas' Introduction to Weaver's *Life without Prejudice and Other Essays* (Chicago: Henry Regnery, 1965), vii-xvii; James Powell's "The Foundations of Weaver's Traditionalism," *New Individualist Review* 3, no. 3 (1964); Willmoore Kendall's "How to Read Richard Weaver: Philosopher of 'We the (Virtuous) People,'" *Intercollegiate Review* 2 (September 1965): 77-86; Russell Kirk's Foreword to Weaver's *Visions of Order* (Baton Rouge: Louisiana State University Press, 1964), vii-ix, and his "Richard Weaver, RIP," *National Review* 14 (23 April 1963): 308.

    More penetrating comments have recently appeared in H. L. Weatherby's "A Southern Rebuttal," *Triumph* 4 (April 1969): 31-33; in Donald Davidson's Foreword to George Core's and this writer's edition of Weaver's *The Southern Tradition at Bay: A History of Postbellum Thought* (New Rochelle, N.Y.: Arlington House, 1968), 13-25; and in Marion Montgomery's "Richard Weaver against the Establishment," *Georgia Review* 23 (Winter 1969): 433-559.
2. Weaver, "Up from Liberalism," *Modern Age* 3 (Winter 1958-59): 21-32.
3. Weaver received his first education at the University of Kentucky, came from a poor area of North Carolina, had received a religious upbringing, and therefore fell briefly under the spell of some witches' brew called "Christian socialism" in Lexington. In some ways this interlude had prepared him for the "religious" side of the Agrarian argument.
4. Twelve Southerners, *I'll Take My Stand: The South and the Agrarian Tradition* (New York: Harper and Brothers, 1980), ix-xx.
5. I have examined a number of his letters to Randall Stewart and Donald Davidson.

6. I have purposefully drawn this reaction from Weaver's own writings about Agrarianism: "Agrarianism in Exile," *Sewanee Review* 58 (Autumn 1950): 586-606; "The Tennessee Agrarians," *Shenandoah* 3 (Summer 1952): 3-10; "The Southern Phoenix," *Georgia Review* 17 (Spring 1963): 6-17; and the aforementioned "Up from Liberalism."
7. Weaver, *The Southern Tradition at Bay*, 390.
8. I use the title of *Ideas Have Consequences* (Chicago: University of Chicago Press, 1948).
9. Weaver, "The Southern Phoenix," 16.
10. John Crowe Ransom,, *God without Thunder: An Unorthodox Defense of Orthodoxy* (New York: Harcourt, Brace and Co., 1930). The book anticipates much "neo-orthodox" theology and in part concludes (pp. 327-328) with the admonition:

    With whatever religious institution a modern man may be connected, let him try to turn it back towards orthodoxy.

    Let him insist on a virile and concrete God, and accept no principle as a substitute.

    Let him restore to God the thunder...
11. Weaver, *The Ethics of Rhetoric* (Chicago: Henry Regnery, 1953). The book, as a piece of strategy, has misled many of Weaver's admirers. Its contents emphasize what is confused in contemporary rhetoric, and maneuver to that end by disarming means (i.e., praising part of Lincoln, faulting part of Burke, etc.). It is unwise to infer over-much from his choice of illustrative materials.
12. I have no idea if unsigned Weaver appeared in *National Review*. I count thirty-seven signed items there, plus a dozen elsewhere. And he made two score public lectures in his last decade. The textbook is modestly entitled *Composition: A Course in Reading and Writing* (New York: Holt, Rinehart, and Winston, 1957).
13. Cleanth Brooks and Robert Penn Warren have a rhetoric text, *Modern Rhetoric* (New York: Harcourt, Brace, 1949). Davidson's *American Composition and Rhetoric* (New York: Scribner, 1939) is one of the best established in the field. Ransom also authored the similar *A College Primer of Writing* (New York: Holt, 1943).

    Ten of the twelve Agrarians are (or were) accomplished public speakers. Several of them defended their position in the forum, sometimes before considerable audiences.
14. Weaver, "The Tennessee Agrarians," 5.
15. Willmoore Kendall, however, has done well to insist that we take Weaver primarily as a "political theorist" ("How to Read Richard Weaver," 78).
16. An essay on William Byrd and Cotton Mather appears to be salvageable. Likewise another on Parson Weems. I will not predict what may be done with the rest of his unpublished works.
17. I say he traveled biographically (and therefore spiritually) out and back because Weaver, as an upcountry man, was the born heir of the *Tertium Quids,* the Old Republicans of the stripe of Virginia's John Randolph of Roanoke or John Taylor of Caroline and Nathaniel Macon of North Carolina. The upcountry was localistic, pious, and not at all sanguine. Historically, it came early to the Revolution proper, stood opposed to the ratification of the Constitution, remained persistently jealous of states' rights, and (when the time came) was hot for secession. Moreover it filled up the gray files of Mr. Davis' armies. As one side of the South's historic Whig/Tory (here meant in the English sense) syncretism, the yeoman counties were never Federalist and yet never unwilling (unless affronted) to be led by the gentry. Weaver's "Aspects of Southern Philosophy," with its paean of praise for

an envy-free class society, a patriarchy sans class consciousness, is clearly in the *Quid* line (pp. 14-30 of Louis D. Rubin, Jr., and Robert D. Jacobs, eds., *Southern Renascence* [Baltimore: Johns Hopkins Press, 1953]).
18. Such is the testimony of two living Agrarians. Another, now deceased, concurred with them. And there is additional evidence in the Davidson correspondence collection at Vanderbilt.
19. Weaver's "The South and the American Union" appears in Louis D. Rubin, Jr., and James Jackson Kilpatrick, eds., *The Lasting South* (Chicago: Henry Regnery, 1957), 46-68; "Lee the Philosopher" in *Georgia Review* 2 (Fall 1948): 297-303; "Life without Prejudice" on pp. 1-13 in the book by that title; "The Regime of the South" in *National Review* 6 (14 March 1959): 587-89; "Ultimate Terms in Contemporary Rhetoric" and "The Spaciousness of the Old Rhetoric" on pp. 211-32 and 164-85 of *The Ethics of Rhetoric*; "The Southern Tradition" in *New Individualist Review* 3 (1964): 17-24; "Piety and Justice" on pp. 170-87 of *Ideas Have Consequences*; "Status and Function" and "Forms and Social Cruelty" in *Visions of Order*, pp. 22-39 and 73-91.
20. For instance, see George Core's and this writer's edition of Weaver's "The American as a Regenerate Being," *Southern Review* 4 n. s. (Summer 1968): 633-46.
21. Donald Davidson, *The Attack on Leviathan* (Chapel Hill: University of North Carolina Press, 1938); "The New South and the Conservative Tradition," *National Review* 9 (10 September 1960), 141-46; and *Still Rebels, Still Yankees* (Baton Rouge: Louisiana State University Press, 1957). The Wade essays all appear in Donald Davidson's edition of *Selected Essays and Other Writings of John Donald Wade* (Athens: University of Georgia Press, 1966), 23-45, 195-207, and 82-89. Owsley's papers are all reproduced in Harriet Chappell Owsley's edition of *The South: Old and New Frontiers, Selected Essays of Frank Lawrence Owsley* (Athens: University of Georgia Press, 1969), 177-89, 235-57, and 190-204. Ransom's "Happy Farmers" first appeared in *American Review* 1 (October 1933): 513-35; his "Reconstructed but Unregenerate" on pp. 1-27 of *I'll Take My Stand*; and his "What Does the South Want?" in *Virginia Quarterly Review* 12 (April 1936): 180-94. Lytle's "John C. Calhoun" and "Robert E. Lee" are together on pp. 205-39 of his *The Hero with the Private Parts* (Baton Rouge: Louisiana State University Press, 1966); "John Taylor and the Political Economy of Agriculture" in *American Review* 3 and 4 (September, October, and November 1934): 432-47, 630-43, and 84-99. The biography here is *Bedford Forrest and His Critter Company* (New York: McDowell, Obolensky, 1960). Warren wrote *John Brown: The Making of a Martyr* (New York: Payson and Clarke, 1929). Tate authored *Jefferson Davis* (New York: Minton, Balch, 1929) and *Stonewall Jackson* (New York: Minton, Balch, 1928).
22. The word is central in Weaver's vocabulary. The act it describes entails a rejection of Creation's variety.
23. Allen Tate, "The Angelic Imagination: Poe and the Power of Words," *Kenyon Review* 14 (Summer 1952): 455-75.
24. Donald Davidson, "Why the Modern South has a Great Literature," in *Still Rebels, Still Yankees*, 159-79.
25. Weaver, *The Southern Tradition at Bay*, 391.
26. Weaver, "The South and the American Union," in *The Lasting South*, 67.
27. And remain (or remained) so with most of the original twelve, as well as with later recruits to the cause. Evidence of the continuity appears in *Conversations at Dallas: An Agrarian Reunion, April 1968*.

28. See Weaver, "The South and the American Union," in *Visions of Order,* 20 and 21; "The Regime of the South"; and "Integration is Communization," *National Review* 4 (13 July 1957): 67-68 for a sample.
29. "Statement of Principles," in *I'll Take My Stand,* xx.

10

A Southern Agrarian at the University of Chicago

Henry Regnery

He saves himself, if at all, by bringing the community around to right reason.
—Richard M. Weaver

To identify Richard Weaver with the University of Chicago and Southern Agrarianism provides a reasonably accurate approximation of the influences that determined his view of the world and the character of his work. He was born in 1910 in Weaverville, North Carolina, of a closely knit, substantial family, the first Weaver ancestor having come into the region in the 1790s when it was still a wilderness. A family history published in 1962 includes two talks given in 1950 and 1954 at the annual family gatherings by the member of the family who had become a professor at the University of Chicago. In his 1950 talk he "looks at Weaverville and the Weaver community," as he put it, "through a perspective of Chicago." He goes on to say:

> I have been condemned for the past six years to earn my living in that most brutal of cities, a place where all the vices of urban and industrial society break forth in a kind of evil flower. I sometimes think of the university to which I am attached as a missionary outpost in darkest Chicago. There we labor as we can to convert the heathen, without much reward of success.

His 1954 talk, by way of contrast, is a tribute to his uncle, Ethan Douglas Weaver, who had died a few months before at the age of ninety-seven, the father of ten children and the acknowledged patriarch of the Weaver family.

> In the whole course and tenor of his life, Uncle Doug suggests strongly the ideal citizen as he was contemplated, near the founding of this republic, by Thomas Jefferson. He was an agrarian, living on the soil; a primary producer creating things, not trafficking in the things that other men made.... In a world where so much is superficial, aimless and even hysterical, he kept a grasp upon those values which are neither old-fashioned or new-fashioned, but are central, permanent and certain in their reward. That is why we think of him as an outstanding example of the sturdy yeomanry which, though modest and self-effacing, has contributed so much to the fibre of this state.

Richard Weaver came to the University of Chicago in 1944 to teach English and rhetoric in the college; he became professor in 1957 and stayed at the university until his death in 1964 at the age of fifty-three. Before he died he had accepted a visiting professorship at Vanderbilt University which he hoped might become a permanent appointment, but for all his dislike of the city, I do not think that he was unhappy at the University of Chicago. He was a demanding but successful teacher, much respected by his students, and he enjoyed the stimulating, challenging, if not always compatible atmosphere of the University. In 1949 he was awarded the Quantrell Prize for excellence in teaching.

Weaver was of medium height, solidly built, had strongly held opinions which his rather heavy, clearly marked features reflected. He was pleasant to be with, always courteous, never forcing his opinions on others, but he was a man, I think, who found it difficult to establish close relations with others, which doubtless contributed to his loneliness at the University of Chicago. Eliseo Vivas, who was a colleague of Weaver's before becoming a professor at Northwestern University writes of him, "One impression that grew stronger the longer I knew him was that I would never get to know him intimately.... He did not put you off... but somehow you did not breach the reserve that kept his inwardness inviolate and inviolable."

As soon as the teaching term ended in the spring he abandoned his rather dingy, unkempt bachelor apartment in Hyde Park and set off for Weaverville, always traveling by train, difficult as it became as rail travel deteriorated—he would never fly unless there was no other choice. "You have to draw the line somewhere," he once remarked to me. Distrustful of "progress" and industrialism in general, he regarded the airplane with particular repugnance. He always insisted that his garden be plowed by horse or mule, which became increasingly difficult for his mother to arrange prior to his arrival. As far as it was possible for him to be in our modern world, Weaver was consistent.

Weaver entered the University of Kentucky at the age of seventeen. The professors, he tells us in his characteristically modest, honest autobiographical essay, "Up from Liberalism," were mostly "earnest souls from Middle Western universities, and many of them—especially those in economics, political science, and philosophy—were, with or without knowing it, social democrats." The university was given to the elective system, which meant that seventeen-year-old students, in effect, told the faculty what they ought to be taught. Having been given no defense against the doctrinaire position of his teachers, by the time he graduated in 1932, Weaver himself had been persuaded, as he said, "that the future was with science, liberalism, and equalitarianism, and that all opposed to these trends were people of ignorance or malevolence." In his third year he joined the Socialist Party and became secretary of the local unit, and while the socialist program had a certain appeal to him—it was then the bottom of the great depression—he soon found that he could not like the party members he met as persons—"they seemed dry, insistent people of shallow objectives."

Subsequent graduate study at Vanderbilt, where he came under the influence of the Southern Agrarians, who in 1930 had published their manifesto, *I'll Take My Stand*, and particularly of John Crowe Ransom, with whom he studied, marked a decisive turning point in his life and ended his flirtation with socialism. While he did not, at first, fully agree with these men, he liked them as persons: "They seemed to me more humane, more generous, and considerably less dogmatic than those with whom I had been associated under the opposing banner...the intellectual maturity and personal charm of the Agrarians were very unsettling to my then-professed allegiance."

The graduate degree in English he earned at Vanderbilt led to a teaching post at a large technical college in Texas where, as he described it, he "encountered a rampant philistinism, abetted by technology, large-scale organization, and a complacent acceptance of success as the goal of life." While driving back at the beginning of his third year "across the monotonous prairies of Texas," it suddenly dawned on him that he was under no compulsion to go back to a job that had become distasteful to him nor to go on professing the clichés of liberalism. At the end of the year he gave up his job and "went off," as he put it, "to start my education over, being now arrived at the age of thirty."

He had used his time in Texas to read extensively in the history of the Civil War, which he continued to do during the three years he spent at Louisiana State, giving special attention to the losing side: "It is good for everyone," he wrote in justification of his decision, "to ally himself at one time with the defeated and to look at the 'progress' of history through the eyes of those who were left behind.... The people who emerged were human, all-too-human, but there was still the mystery of the encompassing passion which held them together, and this I have not yet penetrated. But in a dozen various ways I have come to recognize myself in the past, which is at least an important piece of self-knowledge."

In the biographical essay I have referred to, Weaver speaks of two convictions which took possession of him as a result of his studies of the Civil War: that "we live in a universe which was given to us, in the sense that we did not create it"; and that "we don't understand very much of it." Following the further experience of a world war and its consequences, he came to the conclusion, after having rejected it as a ridiculous superstition when he was a young man, that there is no concept that expresses a deeper insight into the enigma of man than that of original sin, which he defines as "a parabolical expression of the immemorial tendency of man to do the wrong thing when he knows the right thing," and finally that we must recognize evil "as a subtle, pervasive, protean force." Armed with such convictions and a firmly held view of the world arrived at after careful study and long reflection, he came to the University of Chicago in 1944 well prepared to teach English and rhetoric in the college and to hold his own in what must, at times, have seemed a rather hostile environment.

It is ironical that this Southern Agrarian, with his distrust of progress and materialism and of science as the source of truth, his rejection of liberalism and socialism, and his preference for the old, backward South to the progressive, industrial North, should have spent the productive years of his life at a university founded by John D. Rockefeller, where, not long before arrived, the first chain reaction had taken place, the event that launched the age of the atomic bomb, and in the city where fifteen years before there had been a great exposition, "A Century of Progress," celebrating the achievements of science and technology. Out of place as Weaver may have been in Chicago, the challenge and intellectual stimulation of the university undoubtedly contributed to his creative achievement.

One day in the fall of 1945, after the shooting and the bombing had finally stopped and the appalling consequences of the war were becoming apparent, Weaver tells us in "Up from Liberalism," he was contemplating, from the vantage point of his office in Ingleside Hall, the actual course of events as compared with the glib promises of our wartime leaders, and wondering what it was that had gone wrong. How could it have happened, for example, that the medieval idea of chivalry, which recognized even the enemy as a man with an immortal soul and thus kept war within the bounds of civilization, could have been supplanted by total war which knows no limits and is subject to no restraint, to be followed by the demand for unconditional surrender that places the defeated at the mercy of the victor, and that, as Weaver says, "impiously puts man in the place of God by usurping unlimited right to dispose of the lives of others."

Believing as he did that the world is intelligible and that history is not accidental, nor determined by biological or economic forces, but is the result of conscious choice, he wondered if "it would not be possible to deduce from fundamental causes, the fallacies of modern life and thinking that had produced this holocaust and would insure others." To discover what went wrong and to describe its consequences is the purpose and the achievement of Weaver's first book, the beginning of which goes back to those ruminations in Ingleside Hall in the fall of 1945.

By a fortunate coincidence, the director of the University of Chicago Press when Weaver submitted his manuscript, William T. Couch, was a man who by temperament and background would have been sympathetic to Weaver's unabashed attack on the accepted positions of the post-war period. Mr. Couch's enthusiasm for the book, from the standpoint of his own career, may have been ill-advised, but however that may be, the manuscript was accepted. The publisher insisted on a different title, *Ideas Have Consequences,* on the assumption that it better represented the thesis of the book than the author's *Fearful Descent.* In the fall of 1948 the book was published by the University of Chicago Press with the strong backing of its Director, who used all the resources available to him to bring the book into the center of discussion.

The thesis of the book is far-reaching and can be said to question the basic assumptions of modern life. This thesis can be easily stated: It is the triumph of the doctrine of nominalism as propounded by William of Occam in the latter part of the fourteenth century that put Western man on the wrong path. Such a doctrine had the practical result, Weaver argues,

> To banish the reality that is perceived by the intellect and to posit as reality that which is perceived by the sense. With this change in the affirmation of what is real, the whole orientation of culture takes a turn, and we are on the road to modern empiricism.... The denial of everything transcending experience means inevitably—though ways are found to hedge on this—the denials of truth. With the denial of objective truth there is no escape from the relativism of "man the measure of all things." ... Thus began the "abomination of desolation" appearing today as a feeling of alienation from all fixed truth.... Man created in the divine image, the protagonist of a great drama in which his soul was at stake, was replaced by man the wealth-seeking and consuming animal.

Having described the changes in the percept of reality and truth which he believed began the process of dissolution Weaver goes on to describe its specific consequences: The doctrine of original sin makes way for belief in the innate goodness of man, hierarchy succumbs to equalitarianism, religion and faith to rationalism and science, discipline to comfort, the acceptance of the human condition as a given to belief that man is master of his own fate. Because society depends on distinction, "the most insidious idea," Weaver asserts, "to break down society is an undefined equalitarianism," which, among other things, puts into question the relationship between effort and reward. In a chapter called "The Great Stereopticon" Weaver expresses his strong feelings about the destructive influence of the press, radio, and movies (TV was then still in its infancy):

> What person taking the affirmative view of life can deny that the world served up daily by press, movie, and radio is a world of evil and negation? There is irony in our nature sufficient to withstand any fact that is present in a context of affirmation, but we cannot remain unaffected by the continued assertion of cynicism and brutality. Yet these are what the materialists in control of publicity gave us.

Dismal as all this sounds—and let us not forget that it was written shortly after the end of World War II when the prospects for the Western world seemed to be dismal in the extreme—Weaver "propounds," as he says, if not a whole solution, at least the beginnings of one. The last three chapters, therefore, are devoted to an account of the measures which he thinks would contribute to a recovery of sound values: the restoration of respect for private property, the restoration of the integrity of language, and the restoration of piety and justice as cardinal elements of social life, piety understood in the classical sense as respect for the order of being.

Property, Weaver unequivocally states, is "the last metaphysical right," metaphysical "because it does not depend on any test of social usefulness." Is it not, he goes on to ask, "quite comforting to feel that we can enjoy one right which does not have to answer to sophistries of the world or rise and fall with the tide of opinion?" Weaver's concept of property is specific and concrete; it involves not merely claiming the right to something, but bearing the responsibility for it. For him, however, Southern Agrarian that he was, the "last metaphysical right" does not include "the kind of property brought into being by finance capitalism," which, as an abstraction, lends itself to control by the state. I will conclude Weaver's observations on property with one last challenge to the utilitarians, levelers, liberals, or whatever their name may be: "In private property there survives the last domain of privacy of any kind. Every other wall has been overthrown. Here a unique privacy remains because property has not been compelled to give a justification of the kind demanded by rationalists and calculators."

Having determined a sanctuary in private property, Weaver goes on to speak about the nature of language and its relation to order. To demonstrate the ancient belief that there is a divine element in language, Weaver speaks of "the potency ascribed to incantations, interdictions and curses. We see it in the legal force given to an oath or a word...which can only mean that words in common human practice express something transcending the moment." What Weaver sought to restore, with all the eloquence at his command was an appreciation of language as something uniquely human, as something given to man to express his highest aspirations, not as a means to deceive others, but as the binding element of society, as "a great storehouse of universal memory" and as a way "to get at a meaning beyond present meaning."

Weaver begins the chapter "Piety and Justice," the last in the book, by extending the meaning of Plato's Euthyphro from the impiety of a son toward his father to the impiety of modern man, through technology, toward nature. This impiety takes the form of believing that the demands of man take precedence over the order of nature, as we see, for example, in the destruction of the environment. But the contempt for natural order can also take other forms, one of which, Weaver believes, is "the foolish and destructive notion of the 'equality' of the sexes." He concludes his observation on this subject with the remark, "After the gentlemen went, the lady had to go too. No longer protected, the woman now has her career, in which she makes a drab pilgrimage from two-room apartment to job to divorce court." Besides learning to regard the order of nature with piety, we must also learn to regard our neighbors with piety, and, finally, the past, by which he meant history and tradition.

It is instructive, from the distance of forty years, to consider the reception given Weaver's first book when it appeared. While there were cries of outrage from the expected sources, on the whole it must be said that the book was given the serious attention it deserved. Howard Mumford Jones in the *New York Times,* as one would have anticipated, labeled it "a sincere, fanatical, and, for my money, irresponsible piece of writing"; George R. Geiger, in the *Antioch Review,* used such terms as "pompous fraud," "essentially evil," and "notorious"; Charles Frankel, in *The Nation,* criticized Weaver's "absolutist defense of the humanistic tradition"; and both the *Annals of the American Academy* and *The Christian Century* were critical of what they considered Weaver's nostalgia for the Middle Ages. The book was warmly welcomed by William A. Orton in *Commonweal* and by Charner Perry in *Ethics*—the latter remarking: "That the author's prejudices run counter to much of modern taste is helpful." Reinhold Niebuhr judged it "a profound analysis of the sickness of our culture," and Paul Tillich pronounced it "brilliantly written, daring and radical.... It will shock, and philosophical shock is the beginning of wisdom."

Only one other book of Weaver's was published during his lifetime, *The Ethics of Rhetoric* in 1953, which he once remarked to me was his best and which Eliseo Vivas, whose judgment Weaver greatly respected, considered, "from a scholar's point of view...[his] most important contribution." The austere quality of the book may be surmised from the following observation at the beginning of the opening chapter, "The *Phaedrus* and the Nature of Rhetoric":

> Our difficulty with the *Phaedrus* may be that our interpretation has been too literal and too topical. If we will bring to the reading of it even a portion of that imagination which Plato habitually exercised, we should perceive surely enough that it is consistently, and from beginning to end, about one thing, which is the nature of rhetoric.

Weaver derives his definition of rhetoric from his discussion of the *Phaedrus*: "Rhetoric...consists of truth plus its artful presentation." He later remarks that "neuter discourse is a false idol" because the purpose of all, or most, discourse is to convince us of something, good or bad: The essential thing is to be aware of the rhetorical device being used.

In order to demonstrate the difference between dialectical and rhetorical argumentation, Weaver devotes the second chapter of the book to a discussion of the Scopes trial in Dayton, Tennessee, where, in 1925, John T. Scopes, a high school teacher, was tried for having violated a law recently passed by the State of Tennessee making it unlawful in any state-supported educational institution "to teach any theory that denies the story of the Divine creation of man as taught in the Bible." With Clarence Darrow for the defense and William Jennings Bryan for the prosecution, the case attracted national attention, the issue being represented as science and enlightenment arrayed against fundamentalism and superstition. Weaver, however, is not concerned here with the merits of evolution or the wisdom of the law forbidding its teaching in the public schools, but rather with the manner in which the case was argued. The defense, Weaver shows, "pleading the cause of science, was forced into the role of rhetorician; whereas the prosecution, pleading the cause of the state, clung stubbornly to a dialectical position." The defense brought in expert witnesses to prove the scientific truth of evolution, but a scientific theory cannot be proved or disproved in a court of law, and this, in any case, was not the issue. It was clear that the law had been enacted by the State of Tennessee and that John T. Scopes was guilty of having violated it, and so the court decided.

The law, as Weaver said, won a victory, but the defense accomplished what it set out to do: It made the law and the point of view it represented look foolish. No matter how much this victory may have been welcomed by the forces of modernism, it was a disservice to the understanding of what the true issue really was. In his discussion of the Southern heritage in his doctoral dissertation, *The Southern Tradition at Bay,* Weaver points out that the anti-evolution laws reflected the belief that "science has not usurped the seats of the prophets," and however foolish Clarence Darrow made such a belief appear to be, it is, as Weaver said a "continuum of history" and thus deserving of respect.

In his discussion of the various forms of argumentation—the argument from genus or definition, the argument from circumstance, the argument from consequence—Weaver uses Edmund Burke, to the distress of some of his conservative admirers, to illustrate the argument from circumstance, and, in spite of his Southern heritage and Confederate sympathies, Abraham Lincoln to illustrate the argument from definition. The argument from circumstance, in Weaver's opinion, is the least philosophical form of argument because it only attempts to measure current conditions and pressures. It is, therefore, an argument philosophically appropriate to the liberal. Weaver gives numerous examples of what he calls Burke's "strong addiction to the argument from circumstance": his great speech on "Conciliation with the American Colonies," Weaver says, "is from beginning to end...an argument about policy as dictated by circumstances."

In contrast to Burke, Lincoln in his state papers and speeches habitually used the argument for definition, which Weaver believed is the higher form of argument. He gives many striking examples of Lincoln's reasoning in arriving at a position and of his method of argumentation, beginning with his stand against slavery in his debates with Douglas, which he based on the nature of man and the irrefutable fact that the Negro is a man. Weaver concludes his discussion of Lincoln with the following observation:

> The heart of Lincoln's statesmanship, indeed, lay in his perception that on some matters one has to say "Yes" or "No," that one has to accept an alternative to the total exclusion of the other, and that any weakness in being thus bold is a betrayal.

This may be true, but like every other rigid position it is true only within limits. If Lincoln had been less unbending in his conduct of the war, had been willing to consider the circumstances of Southern society, some of the worst excesses could have been avoided and eventual reconciliation made less difficult. A rigidly logical position is all very well, but we live in the world as it is. Edmund Burke states the issue with wonderful clarity: "A statesman, never losing sight of principles, is to be guided by circumstances; and judging contrary to the exigencies of the moment he may ruin his country forever."

Having defined his subject, Weaver devotes the rest of *The Ethics of Rhetoric* to a masterful study of the nature of rhetoric and its relation to civilized discourse. In the chapter "Grammatical Categories" he describes the characteristics of the various parts of speech and demonstrates how the proper use of words and of sentence structure adds to the effectiveness of writing: He compares the use of the adverb by Thomas Carlyle with that of Henry James. And to show how effective the proper use of the word "and" can be Weaver refers to its use in the King James Bible to join long sequences of verses, giving one "the feeling that the story is confirmed and inevitable.... When this pattern is dropped, as it is in a recent 'American' version of the Bible, the text collapses into a kind of news story." There is a demanding but rewarding chapter, "Milton's Heroic Prose," which makes a sharp contrast to the chapter that follows, "The Rhetoric of the Social Sciences," a rhetoric, it becomes clear, which is neither heroic nor effective.

The last chapter, "Ultimate Terms in Contemporary Rhetoric," includes Weaver's description of "God terms" and "Devil terms," words or phrases which through use or association have acquired, or have been given, a force which goes beyond their original meaning. As examples of God terms he cites "progress," "fact," "science," "modern." An example of a "Devil term" is "prejudice," which, Weaver says, is an "uncontested term"—and who in public life would admit to being prejudiced?—that "disarms the opposition by making all positional judgments reprehensible." The present use of "racist" serves the same purpose. God terms, Weaver asserts, still have some relationship to their original meaning, to what he calls their "referent," but there is another term, to which he gives the name "charismatic," whose referents are virtually impossible to discover because "it is the nature of the charismatic term to have a power which is not derived but which is in some mysterious way given." Weaver's rhetorical sensibility led him to believe that one of the principal charismatic terms of our time is "freedom." Our political leaders, he goes on to say, make the greatest demands in the name of freedom, in the form of military service, higher taxes, abridgement of rights—one need only think only of Franklin D. Roosevelt's "Four Freedoms"—while carefully avoiding any attempt to clarify what it refers to. Another major charismatic term, in his opinion, is "democracy," which people seem to resist any effort to define for fear that to define it would deprive it of its charisma.

Except for a textbook, *A Rhetoric and Handbook, Ideas Have Consequences,* and *The Ethics of Rhetoric* were the only books of Weaver published during his lifetime. A third book, *Visions of Order,* was in manuscript when he died and appeared the following year; although he had made arrangements for its publication, he had no opportunity to make final corrections. As in his previous books, his concern is with the disintegration of society, and in making his case he further develops many of the themes he had alluded to in his previous books. In considering the prospect of the total destructiveness of war made possible by the development of modern science, Weaver refers again to the example of chivalry, by means of which, in a period of comparable moral chaos, it was possible to put a limit on destructive impulses. All this, it is clear, is another aspect of what he considers to be the destructive nature of the idea of equality, about which he has more to say in the chapters "The Image of Culture" and "Status and Function." By its very nature, he believed, culture is exclusive. There can be no such thing as a "democratic" culture. "Without the power to reject that which does not understand or acknowledge its center of force, it would disintegrate."

One of the strongest chapters in the book is "The Cultural Role of Rhetoric." Just as he used the Scopes trial in his earlier book to demonstrate the differences between rhetorical and dialectical argumentation, in *Visions of Order* he goes back to the trial of Socrates to illustrate his contention that dialectic, when used in disregard of accepted beliefs and traditions, can be destructive:

> By turning his great dialectical skill upon persons and institutions, Socrates could well have produced the feeling that he was an enemy of the culture which the Greeks had produced.... The trial itself can be viewed as a supremely dramatic incident in the far longer and broader struggle between rationalism on the one hand and poetry and rhetoric (and belief) on the other.

And to demonstrate further the place of rhetoric he adds:

> The triumph and continuance of Christian culture attests the power of rhetoric in holding men together and maintaining institutions. It is generally admitted that there is a strong element of Platonism in Christianity. But if Plato provided the reasoning, Paul and Augustine provided the persuasion. What emerged from this could not be withstood even by the power of Rome.

The subject of the final chapter of *Visions of Order* is the imminence of "such a dark night of the mind" as man has experienced in those periods in the past when he seemed to lose sight of the knowledge of his own nature he had previously won. One of the things man has learned about himself, Weaver says, is that he is a creature of choice, which realization gives him a sense of his own worth and dignity. These two qualities, he concludes, give man the capability to create a rational civilization. Now Weaver was strongly of the opinion, and this is the theme of his concluding chapter, that the most serious threat to the concept of man as a creature enjoying the privilege of making choices, and therefore of freedom, comes from science, and in various guises. From the realization that the earth is not the center of the universe, but a minuscule part of it, it has been concluded that the fate of man is of little moment. The consequence of evolution, as Weaver puts it, is "to place man squarely in the animal kingdom." Finally, having gone this far, the next step is to make man entirely subject to the material causality. "If his being and shape were due to natural laws, which could be studied as phenomena, why not account for the whole of him, including his famous free will, in the same way?" The effect of this diminishing of man in his own estimation can be clearly seen, Weaver believed, in his representation in literature and religion: "If the story of man was but the story of an animal, was it really deserving of the sublime treatment it had been given in religion and literature?"

Weaver's answer to all this is to question the validity of the Darwinian hypothesis, which he does in a number of ways, the most convincing of which in his mind, apparently, is the mystery of language, which cannot be explained, Weaver believed, in any other way than as a gift. His criticism of the theory of evolution must have been convincing to him, but it did not convince his old friend and colleague Eliseo Vivas who, in an otherwise very positive review in *Modern Age* (vol. 8, no. 3, 307-10) called his attack on evolution "An embarrassing performance...it would have taken far more science and philosophy than he had at his command to undermine successfully the work of Darwin and his heirs."

From the standpoint of the strict philosopher, Vivas may well be correct. But it should also be said that the basis of Weaver's attack on evolution is not philosophy but instinct, and as Vivas remarks in the same review: "...back of his judgments there is something for which I have no other term than 'instinct.'...His arguments were not always the best, but the attitudes from which his rejections and acceptances issued were for the most part unerring." For the attitude from which his rejection of evolution issued we have not far to seek: It is clearly stated in Weaver's first published essay, "The Older Religiousness in the South," which is included in the *Southern Essays of Richard M. Weaver*:

> Nature is a vast unknown; in the science of nature there are constantly appearing emergents which, if allowed to affect spiritual and moral verities, would destroy them by rendering them dubious, tentative, and conflicting. It is therefore impera-

tive in the eyes of the older religionists that man have for guidance in this life a body of knowledge to which the "facts" of natural discovery are either subordinate or irrelevant. This body is the "rock of ages," firm in the vast sea of human passion and error.

While Weaver was not a church-goer, I have no doubt that the "body of knowledge" he referred to was one of the givens of his view of the world.

For all his foreboding about the imminence of "a dark night of the mind," Weaver believed that our best hope lies not in science or politics, but in culture, and that "literature is the keystone of culture." This is so, he said, not only because literature is the most various, searching, and complete of the forms of culture, but because "it is the form in which an intellectual culture stores the ideas from which society derives its rhetoric of cohesion and compulsion."

Besides his doctoral dissertation, *The Southern Tradition at Bay,* three other books were published after Weaver's death, all collections of essays: *Life without Prejudice* in 1965, *Language is Sermonic* in 1970, and *Southern Essays of Richard M. Weaver* in 1987. The eight essays included in *Life without Prejudice* include many of Weaver's most strongly held convictions, which, presented in the concise form of the essay, are sharply and succinctly expressed. "Life without prejudice," he says in the title essay, "were it ever to be tried, would soon reveal itself to be a life without principle.... For prejudices...are often built-in principles. They are the extract which the mind has made of experience." In the essay "Education and the Individual" he makes the following observation, which on reflection will be seen to be completely in opposition to the position of "progressive" education:

> Education thus has a major responsibility to what we think of as objectively true. But it also has a major responsibility to the person. We may press this even further and say that education must regard two things as sacred: the truth and the personality that is to be brought into contact with it. No education can be civilizing and humane unless it is a respecter of person.

In another essay, "Two Types of American Individualism," he compares what he considers to be the socially irresponsible individualism of the New Englander Henry David Thoreau with the more realistic, principled individualism of the irascible Southern eccentric John Randolph. It is not surprising that Russell Kirk considers this to be the "liveliest essay" in this collection, nor that Eliseo Vivas, in his introduction, remarks that it contains "some essays that fully and completely express the man and his thought,... [and] may rank as his best book."

The four books of which I have tried to give some idea reflect the rhetorician and the University of Chicago professor who had thought deeply about the social crisis of our time, its causes and what might be done about it. The *Southern Essays of Richard M. Weaver* reflect the Southerner whose attitude and loyalty to the South are most clearly represented, perhaps, by the position of Southern Agrarianism, which, he said in the chapter "The Tennessee Agrarians," was "one of the few effective challenges to a monolithic culture of unredeemed materialism." The South, it must be said, with the mechanization of cotton farming and its industrial development, is far more industrialized now and, doubtless, more materialistic than it was when the Southern Agrarians issued their manifesto in 1930. Even if he had lived to see what has happened since then, Weaver could not have given up the belief that the sort of change the Agrarians strove for was possible. At the end of the same chapter he writes:

> There have been revolutions in human affairs which appear miraculous in the light of the conditions which preceded them. Ultimately it is the human psyche which determines the kind of world we live in, and history is marked by radical changes of phase which could undermine even so seemingly impregnable a thing as our modern scientific-technological order.

The truth of the matter was that in making a case for the kind of life the Agrarians espoused, as Weaver himself realized, they had become intellectuals, and in so doing, had isolated themselves. 'The South no longer had a place for them, and the flight to the North completed an alienation long in process." In writing this he may well have been thinking of the boy from Weaverville, North Carolina, who, after the University of Kentucky, Vanderbilt, and Louisiana State, ended up condemned to earn his living, as he said, "in the most brutal of cities," even though Chicago gave him the intellectual stimulus and the platform he may not have found in the South.

The doctoral dissertation that resulted from Weaver's thorough study of the "losing side" was discovered several years after his death and published in 1968 as *The Southern Tradition at Bay*. George Core of the University of Georgia and M. E. Bradford of the University of Dallas carefully, and I am sure, lovingly edited the manuscript; and to make its Southern origin unmistakable, Donald Davidson wrote an appreciative foreword for what he called his former student's "wise, good-tempered book." It was Weaver's purpose to discover what it was about the South that sets it apart and makes it a distinct region, what it fought for in the war which Weaver thought of as its War of Independence, and then in his study of the postwar period, the time euphemistically called "Reconstruction," how it was that the South, despite defeat and the humiliation of military occupation, was able to resist spiritual disintegration. It is not a book about events, but rather an attempt to discover what people believed, what the "encompassing passion" was, as Weaver called it, that held the South together through four long years of war. For one brought up in a Northern community, where the righteousness of the Civil War as a war to free the slaves and save the Union was accepted as an article of faith, where, in school, to commemorate Lincoln's birthday, one sang "The Battle Hymn of the Republic" and "Marching Through Georgia," it is an illuminating and rewarding experience to read Weaver's account of how it appeared from the other side.

Richard Weaver was not the sort of professor whose picture appears on the cover of *Time* or whose books receive rave reviews in the *New York Times*, but his work has had a profound influence which will continue. *Ideas Have Consequences* is one of the three books, with F. A. Hayek's *Road to Serfdom* (1944) and Russell Kirk's *The Conservative Mind* (1953), which provided the intellectual basis for the modern conservative movement. A program of scholarships, the Weaver Fellowships, demonstrates the influence of Weaver by the quality and achievement of the students the program has sponsored, and the Rockford Institute has named one of the two Ingersoll Prizes it gives annually for contributions to literature and scholarly letters for Richard Weaver, the other for T. S. Eliot.

How much he was recognized or how highly regarded he may have been at the University of Chicago I have no way of knowing, but he was much respected as a teacher. In a letter written in 1959 to Russell Kirk he mentions that he was Chairman of the English course in the college and had been invited to teach the course the next year in the history of Western civilization. On the other hand, an old friend and former colleague of Weaver's told me that when the Dean gave him the Quantrell Prize for excellence in teaching he remarked, 'Weaver, I hope you will take the money and go some place else."

Although *Ideas Have Consequences* was a commercial success and, however much it may have disturbed some people, was recognized as a book of intellectual distinction, the University of Chicago Press never published another book by Weaver. The head of the press who published Weaver's first book, William T. Couch, was rudely dismissed several years later, but the press has kept his book in print. When Weaver died, Robert E. Streeter, Professor in the Department of English and Dean of the Division of the Humanities said of him: "Richard M. Weaver for two decades gave University of Chicago undergraduates an understanding of what it means to think, speak, and to write with full responsibility."

The Richard Weaver I knew as a friend, not as a professor, was a modest, unassuming man of great integrity. He was rather reticent, but always good company and pleasant to be with. During the last winter or two of his life several of us who were involved with the quarterly *Modern Age*, which was then published in Chicago, would meet on Friday afternoons in the modest office of the magazine to look over the manuscripts that had come in and to talk about the problems associated with such a venture—what might be done to make it more appealing to the readers we wanted to reach, whether we should try to obtain advertising, which books we should review, in short, what we should do to give it substance. Weaver always seemed to enjoy such occasions, took a lively part in the conversation, and added to the pleasure we all took in each other's company. It was on a Monday following such an occasion that I received the sad news of his death.

As his life and work make clear, Weaver had strongly held convictions and made no concessions to the intellectual fashions of the day, however much his position in the academic community might have been helped by doing so. He gave freely of himself in his teaching and in his willingness to write for publications he respected and to lecture to groups he felt were serious, irrespective of the honorarium or prestige involved. In his essay "Agrarianism in Exile," he remarks that no man save himself alone: "He saves himself, if at all, by bringing the community around to right reason." This Richard Weaver tried manfully to do, and with more success, it seems fair to say, than he himself realized.

11

The Conservativism of Affirmation

John P. East

Born in Asheville, North Carolina, in 1910, Richard Malcolm Weaver was raised in Lexington, Kentucky. Elected to Phi Beta Kappa, Weaver graduated from the University of Kentucky in 1932. In that year he joined the American Socialist Party; however, from the outset Weaver was disenchanted with that association, and his flirtation with socialism was brief: "I could not like the members of the movement as persons. They seemed dry, insistent people, of shallow objectives."[1] He attended graduate school at Vanderbilt University where he obtained his M.A. degree in 1934. At Vanderbilt, Weaver was influenced by the Fugitive-Agrarians who were assembled there. In particular, he was deeply moved by one of the most eminent of that group, John Crowe Ransom. Weaver contended that Ransom's *God without Thunder,* published in 1930, was "the profoundest of books to come out of the Agrarian movement."[2] The subtitle of Ransom's work was "An Unorthodox Defense of Orthodoxy," and in his analysis Ransom warned against "the watered theology of the advanced moderns": he proposed that we "do what we can to recover the excellences of the ancient faith." Weaver wrote his M.A. thesis, "The Revolt against Humanism," under the direction of Ransom.

Weaver obtained his doctorate in English from Louisiana State University in 1943. His dissertation, "The Confederate South, 1965–1910: A Study in the Survival of a Mind and Culture," was directed by Cleanth Brooks, who was assisted by, among others, Robert Penn Warren. Having joined the faculty at the University of Chicago in 1944, Weaver was a professor of English at that institution at the time of his death in 1963. At his death, one admiring colleague wrote, "His success was extraordinary: he was, I think, the most distinguished teacher of writing this institution has had in the last twenty years."[3]

Weaver became a powerful intellectual force in the American conservative movement of the post-World War II period. His best-known work, *Ideas Have Consequences*, was published in 1948. Frank S. Meyer described the book as "the informing principle of the contemporary American conservative movement."[4] Subsequently, Weaver wrote *The Ethics of Rhetoric*, probably his most scholarly work, and *Visions of Order*, which Willmoore Kendall characterized as deserving "the political equivalent of biblical status" out of all American conservative books.[5] Weaver's dissertation was published in 1968 under the title *The Southern Tradition at Bay*, and he dedicated the book to "John Crowe Ransom, subtle doctor."

Aside from these key works, Weaver published numerous reviews and articles. An anthology of among the best of the latter is found in *Life without Prejudice and Other Essays*. Included among the selections is Weaver's "Life without Prejudice," originally published as the lead article for the first issue of *Modern Age* in 1957. *Language is Sermonic*, appearing in 1970, is an anthology dealing exclusively with Weaver's works on rhetoric. Unquestionably, Weaver's works has had a profound impact upon the intellectual development of the American conservative movement; indeed, in keeping with Meyer's and Kendall's observations, it can be argued that intellectually he is the founding father. In the words of Russell Kirk, "Richard Weaver sowed deep his intellectual seed; and though there are no heirs of his body, the heirs of his mind may be many and stalwart."[6]

Weaver accepted the label "conservative" as descriptive of his philosophical position:

> The modifier which has been most frequently applied to my own writings is "conservative." I have not exactly courted this but I certainly have not resented it, and if I had to make a choice among the various appellations that are available, this is very likely the one that I would wind up with. I must say that I do not see any harm in it, and in this I am unlike some of my friends, unlike some people with whom I agree on principles, but who appear to think that the term is loaded with unfavorable meanings or at least connotations.[7]

The principal connotations of Weaver's conservatism are the Platonic and religious strains of Western thought. Weaver succinctly explained: "The way for any writer to show responsibility is to make perfectly clear the premises from which he starts...I maintain...that form is prior to substance, and that ideas are determinants. I am quite willing to be identified with the not inconsiderable number of thinkers in the Platonic-Christian tradition who have taken the same stand."[8] As Weaver viewed it, the "fearful descent" of the modern age had been precipitated by "nominalism," which was a rejection of the Platonic-Christian heritage, and the formidable task of restoration rested upon the capacity of the West to rediscover the verities inherent in that heritage. In the American setting, Weaver looked upon the Southern legacy as uniquely valuable in providing the philosophical based needed for the imposing work of revitalization. To understand the conservative mind of Richard Weaver, it is essential then to analyze his positions on Platonism, religion, nominalism, and the significance of the Southern experience.

I.

Throughout Richard M. Weaver's work is found a profound appreciation of Plato and his contribution to the Western heritage. Indeed, Weaver's best-known and probably most influential work, *Ideas Have Consequences,* is a book-long lament that Western modernism has departed from the Platonic tradition. Plato, Weaver wrote, "possessed the deepest divining rod among the ancients."[9] In Plato, Weaver found the personification of that philosophical bent which pursued an understanding of "the structure of reality":

> From the time of the Greeks there have existed in most periods "wise men," philosophers, or scholars who make it their work to seek out the structure of reality, and to proclaim it by one means and another to the less initiated. The first Greeks began looking for the structure of reality in the constitution of matter: What was the prime element out of which all other things were made?[10]

Weaver reasoned that a mature conservatism would follow in that tradition:

> It is my contention that a conservative is a realist, who believes that there is a structure of reality independent of his own will and desire. He believes that there is a creation which was here before him, which exists now not by just his sufferance, and which will be here after he's gone.... Though this reality is independent of the individual, it is not hostile to him. It is in fact amenable by him in many ways, but it cannot be changed radically and arbitrarily. This is the cardinal point. The conservative holds that man in this world cannot make his will his law without any regard to limits and fixed nature of things.[11]

In keeping with the Platonic view, Weaver argued this "structure of reality" was composed of things which have "essential natures" and that these natures were "knowable." Moreover, we have an "intuitive feeling that existence is not meaningless."[12] It is, then, the function of the philosopher to discern the realities—the essential nature of things— and hopefully to perceive, even though dimly and imperfectly, the meaning and purpose of existence. As it was with Plato, so it was with Weaver, that philosophy was the highest calling whereby through "right reasoning" knowledge, understanding, wisdom and ultimately truth were to be pursued.

Consistent with the Platonic view, Weaver contended that basic and inherent in the "nature of things" was a dualism:

> The first positive step must be a driving afresh of the wedge between the material and the transcendental. This is fundamental: without a dualism we should never find purchase for the pull upward, and all idealistic designs might as well be scuttled.... To bring dualism back into the world and to rebuke the moral impotence fathered by empiricism is then the broad character of our objective.[13]

The material side of this dualism related to specifics and concretes, to the impermanent and transitory. The transcendental facet pertained to first principles, essences, universals, forms, and finally to unchanging Ideals: Truth, Beauty, Justice, and Goodness. In Weaver's words: "Plato reminded us that at any state of an inquiry it is important to realize whether we are moving toward, or away from, first principles."[14] Similarly, Weaver wrote, "Belief in universals and principles is inseparable from the life of reason," and he noted, "[We] invariably find in the man of true culture a deep respect for forms."[15] In this regard, probably Weaver's best-known observation was:

> The true conservative is one who sees the universe as a paradigm of essences, of which the phenomenology of the world is a sort of continuing approximation. Or, to put this in another way, he sees it as a set of definitions which are struggling to get themselves defined in the real world.[16]

Weaver's embrace of the Platonic concept of the transcendent led to his observation that "the conservative image of history arises out of primal affection and a desire to follow transcendental ideals of justice. And it is this that gives content to the philosophy of conservatism."[17] In the final analysis, the pursuit of ideals is the Platonic quest for standards and values:

> Standard means, first of all, something of general application and validity. A standard is something that is set up as measure for all. It is not contingent upon this man's preference, or whim, or that man's location in space and time.... A standard, is, therefore, something of uniform and universal determination. This is one of the aspects of the meaning. But in addition to this, the term standard in its more general usage has the imperative sense of an ideal.[18]

We must, Weaver argued, have ideals, standards, and values in order that we can distinguish and evaluate: "Before we can have the idea of relative evaluation at all, we must have a *tertium quid,* a third essence, an ideal ideal, as it were. This is why a humanism which is merely historical-minded can be learned, but cannot in the true sense be critical."[19]

"Evaluation"—this is the ultimate objective of our pursuit, and through this quest we are seeking to reassert "the ancient affirmation that there is a center of things": "The reason for this is that every culture polarizes around some animating idea, figment, or value, toward which everything that it produces bears some discoverable relation."[20]

The most significant thing about a society is its conception of value; this conception "imparts tone to the whole of society by keeping before its members a standard of right and not right."[21] In brief, according to Weaver, this conception of value is "the centripetal image of an ideal of perfection and goodness," and "[t]he task in our time of the conservative is to defend this concentration and to expose as erroneous attempts to break down the discriminations of a culture."[22] Clearly, a key "conservative principle" is a "belief in the primacy of ideas and values," and to the extend that anyone "tries to pull back toward a position of value, he becomes a conservative."[23]

In his concern for values and evaluation, Weaver, in the tradition of Plato, admonished, "There must be a source of clarification, or arrangement and hierarchy."[24] Or to state the matter otherwise: "in the final reach of analysis our problem is how to recover that intellectual integrity which enables men to perceive the order of goods."[25] And what is the position of conservatism on these matters of "hierarchy" and "the order of goods?" "The word is *order.* Order, or harmony as an expression of order,... is the goal which most if not all conservative thinking has in view."[26] Undeniably, as Weaver perceived it, conservatism had "its passion for an order reflecting a meaningful hierarchy of the goods." This is keeping with that ultimate of the Platonic ideal which conceives of Justice as the proper ordering of things which in turn is productive of balance, proportion, and harmony—all contributing immeasurably to the health and stability of the well-ordered society. In fact, Weaver concluded, "Civilization is measured by its power to create and enforce distinctions.... The man of a civilized tradition, therefore, will find nothing strange in the idea of hierarchy."[28]

With this Platonic emphasis upon the importance of a hierarchy of values, Weaver warned, "[C]onservatives should treat as enemies all those who wish to abolish the sacred and secular grounds for distinctions among men."[29] Egalitarianism and leveling were insidious ideas; in a statement that is the quintessence of Platonism, Weaver elaborated:

> A just man finds satisfaction in the knowledge that society has various roles for various kinds of people and that they in the performance of these roles create a kind of symphony of labor, play, and social life. There arises in fact a distinct pleasure from knowing that society is structured, diversified, balanced, and complex. Blind levelers do not realize that people can enjoy seeing things above them as well as on a plane with them.[30]

In sum, "It is an historic truth...that culture has developed from the liberty of the superior individual to love superior things."[31] Certainly the founder of the Academy would not have dissented from these observations.

II.

In addition to its roots in Platonism, Weaver's conservatism is firmly based upon the religious heritage of Western thought. Reflecting this religious perspective, Weaver wrote, "Man has an irresistible desire to relate himself somehow to the totality, to ask what is the meaning of his presence here made the great empirical fact of the universe," and "[t]hrough religion [man] reveals his profoundest intuition regarding his origin, his mission on earth, and his future state."[32] Nor could there be any doubt that a religious bent of mind is found in Weaver's rhetorical question: "How could simple environmental influence have called forth the giraffe, the centipede, the butterfly, the orchid, the sunflower?" Likewise, Weaver said, "I found myself [over the years] in decreasing sympathy with those social and political doctrines erected upon the concept of a man-dominated universe and more and more inclined to believe with Walt Whitman that a "mouse is miracle enough to stagger sextillions of infidels."[33] And could there be any question as to the religious character of this observation: "The final solution must accommodate the ideas lying behind our feeling that the appearance of man on earth was a destined miracle."[34] Moreover, with affection, Weaver wrote, "No one can study Greek philosophy or medieval Christianity or the other great religions of the world without realizing that these saw man as a creature fearfully and wonderfully made, and that each tried to lead him with appropriate imagination and subtlety."[35] If any doubt lingers as to the religious based of Weaver's thinking, it should be removed by Weaver's unequivocal and moving instruction: "But the road away from idolatry remains the same as before; it lies in respect for the struggling dignity of man for his orientation toward something higher than himself which he has not created."[36]

This religious character of Weaver's mind perhaps could be explained as merely another manifestation of Platonism, for after all Plato too yearned for glimpsing and understanding the mysteries of the transcendent and eternal; he above all the ancients sought to escape beyond the material confines of his earthly existence. The more fundamental question is: was Weaver a Christian? Weaver never concretely stated, "I am a Christian," but then Weaver was too subtle in his thinking to resolve the ultimate question in such a simple declaratory form. In Weaver's own words: "Literalism is the materialism of religion."[37] To Weaver, the truth of Christianity was not something resolved by dialectic; human reason and language were inadequate to that formidable task. Christianity is a matter of "rhetoric"; that is, it is a matter of the perceived, the felt, and the intuited. More particularly, the matter of faith is not resolved through the abstract dialectic of debate; rather, it is established by the mind's grasp and reverence for the ineffable miracle of creation.

A careful reading of Weaver's works yields up a position that is markedly, if not openly, Christian. For example, Weaver's esteem for Christianity is reflected in his observation that there are "reasons for believing that Christianity made a cultural and ethical contribution surpassing even the high-water mark of the Greeks."[38] Similarly, with eloquence he maintained:

> The Greeks could out-argue the Christians and the Romans could subject them to their government, but there was in Christianity an ethical respect for the person which triumphed over these formalizations. Neither the beauty of Greek culture nor the grandeur of the Roman state system was the complete answer to what the people wanted in their lives as a whole.[39]

Elsewhere, Weaver asserted, "[B]ut being a great writer does entail having the Christian-like view of man, which sees him as a dual creature, possessing the capacity for glory and damnation."[40] Even more revealing was this sweeping observation.

> It was inevitable that, lacking one vital element, the ancient governments should have collapsed into despotism. That vital element was introduced by Christianity. This was belief in the sacredness of the person and thus in a center of power distinct from the state. What the pagan philosophers in all their brilliance had not been able to do, that is, set effective barriers to the power of the state, was done in response to that injunction: "Render unto Caesar the things that are Caesar's and unto God the things that are God's." This instituted a basis of freedom upon which the world since that time has been able to build.[41]

Concerning a personal commitment to Christianity, perhaps most revealing was Weaver's review of Bertrand Russell's *The Impact of Science on Society*. In this work Russell reluctantly acknowledged the indispensability of Christianity in dealing with the "wide diffusion of malevolence" in the world. Regarding Russell's grudging admission, Weaver remarked:

> It seems a long way around to find something which might have been discovered on the threshold. But sometimes we are firmer in our convictions for having surveyed the possible alternatives. Let us hope that this is true of all who like Lord Russell in this book make the long circuit to learn that society is not saved by bread alone.[42]

There is evidence Weaver considered Christianity the logical fulfillment of Platonism, Weaver had agreed that "Plato built the cathedrals of England," and, even more pointedly, he stated: "It is generally admitted that there is a strong element of Platonism in Christianity. But if Plato provided the reasoning, Paul and Augustine supplied the persuasion. What emerged from this could not be withstood even by the power of Rome."[43]

This reference to St. Augustine as the fulfillment of Plato is dramatically suggestive of Saint Augustine's own reasoning in *The City of God:* "For none of the other philosophers has come so close to us as the Platonists have, and, therefore we may neglect the others.... Some of our fellow Christians are astonished to learn that Plato had such ideas about God and to realize how close they are to the truths of our faith." This striking similarity between St. Augustine's and Weaver's views does not end here. More specifically, the orthodox Christian concepts of original sin, evil and "the tragic sense" go to the core of Weaver's conservatism.

In his classic autobiographical essay, "Up from Liberalism," Weaver wrote:

> It has been said that disillusionment with human nature most often turns the mind toward Christianity. I know that in my period of jejune optimism the concept of original sin seemed archaically funny. Now, twenty years later [1958], and after the experience of a world war, there is no concept that I regard as expressing a deeper insight into the enigma that is man.[44]

What is original sin?

> Original sin is the parabolical statement that man is somehow originally flawed. He has the temptation, known allegorically as the curse visited upon the descendants of Adam, to do what he knows he ought not do. This flaw is no respecter of person or place or station.[45]

Sin leads to evil in the world, and it is great error to believe "that man is by nature good, and therefore not responsible for evil"; in addition, it is an error to assume "that man is merely the creature of circumstances, and again not responsible for evil.... The denial of evil is a very great heresy."[46]

Weaver contended that evil and "the tragic sense" were inseparable: "Hysterical optimism will prevail until the world again admits the existence of tragedy, and it cannot admit the existence of tragedy until it again distinguishes between good and evil."[47] Weaver was deeply religious and conservative in dealing with the problem of tragedy. Unequalled in this regard is the following assessment:

> The herd man never grows reconciled to the fact that life is a defeat, and that this defeat is its real story.... It does finally require some discipline of mind to accept the fact that life is not a triumphal progress, but a sadly mixed affair with many a disenchantment.[48]

Similarly, he wrote, "[M]an is born to suffer, to endure his passion, and to find redemption, if he finds it, through effort and struggle."[49] He summarized:

> Perhaps there is nothing in the world as truly educative as tragedy. When you have known it, you've known the worst, and probably also you have had a glimpse of the mystery of things. And if this is so, we may infer that there is nothing which educates or matures a man or a people in the way that the experience of tragedy does. Its lessons, though usually indescribable, are poignant and long remembered.[50]

In fact, "education in tragedy" is a lesson "with which other educations are not to be compared, if you are talking about realities."[51] To Weaver tragedy was the fundamental datum of the human experience. However, out of tragedy did not emerge anguish or despair; rather, Weaver's position was remarkably similar to that articulated by Saint Paul in his letter to the Romans: "[W]e rejoice in our suffering, knowing that suffering produces endurance, and endurance produces character, and character produces hope, and hope does not disappoint us." In Weaver's words: "The noble view of life...tends always to be pessimistic.... It could not be otherwise, for...the...very plot of tragedy depends upon the 'good' man struggling in a net of evil."[52] The Pauline "hope" lies in the "good man" overcoming "the net of evil" by directing his vision to the transcendent and thereby comes Good. As Weaver explained in the final paragraph of *Ideas Have Consequences*: "It may be that we are awaiting a great change, that the sins of the fathers are going to be visited upon the generations until the reality of evil is again brought home and there comes some passionate reaction, like that which flowered in the chivalry and spirituality of the Middle Ages."[53]

Together the Christian ideal and Platonism produced in Weaver's conservatism the final key concept of piety, which Weaver described as "one of the oldest and deepest human attitudes."[54] "I would define piety," he wrote, "as an attitude of reverence or acceptance toward some overruling order of some deeply founded institution which the mere individual is not to tamper with."[55] Or to put the proposition somewhat differently: "Piety comes to us as a warning voice that we must think as mortals, that it is not for us either to know all or to control all. It is a recognition of our own limitations and a cheerful acceptance of the contingency of nature, which gives us the protective virtue of humility."[56] A thinker imbued with a sense of piety will realize "[i]n the figure once used by a philosopher, we are inhabitants of a fruitful and well-ordered island surrounded by an ocean of ontological mystery. It does not behoove us to presume very far in this situation.... Therefore, make haste slowly. It is very easy to rush into conceit in thinking about man's relationship to the created universe."[57] Weaver warned, "[Man] must not, like the child, expect all delights freely; he must not...expect all paradoxes to be resolved for him. He must be ready to say at times with Thomas Hooker: 'The point is difficult and the mystery great.'"[58]

Concerning Plato's contribution to the "ancient virtue of *pietas*," as a quotation introductory to "Piety and Justice," the final chapter of *Ideas Have Consequences,* Weaver quoted from Plato's Laws: "Let parents, then, bequeath to their children not riches, but the spirit of reverence."[59] In this chapter Weaver discussed Plato's dialogue *Euthyphro,* which was devoted to the theme of "piety and impiety":

> It is highly significant to learn that when Plato undertakes a discussion of the nature of piety and impiety, he chooses as interlocutor a young man who is actually bent upon parricide. Euthyphro, a youth filled with arrogant knowledge and certain that he understands "what is dear to the gods," has come to Athens to prosecute his father for murder. Struck by the originality of this proceeding, Socrates questions him in the usual fashion. His conclusion is that *piety, which consists of co-operation with the gods in the kind of order they have instituted, is part of the larger concept of justice.* It can be added that the outcome of the dialectic does not encourage the prosecution. The implication is that Euthyphro has no right, out of his partial and immature knowledge, to proceed contemptuously against an ancient relationship.[60]

Elsewhere Weaver wrote that in understanding the meaning of piety it had "proved impossible to dispense with appeal to religion," he emphasized:

> Every legend of man's fall is a caution against presuming to know everything, and an indirect exhortation to piety; and the disappearance of belief in original sin has done more than anything else to prepare the way for sophistical theories of human nature and society. Man has lost piety toward nature in proportion as he left her and shut himself up in cities with rationalism for his philosophy.[61]

The concept of piety permeates Weaver's works, and it is the key to his philosophy. As Weaver explained, "The recovery [of a sense of piety] has brought a satisfaction which cannot be matched, as far as my experience goes, by anything that liberalism and scientism have to offer."[62] Weaver contended there was a "structure of reality" called creation. Man was not the Creator; he was not self-produced. Man is a creature limited in his potential. Confronted with choices between evil and good, man frequently chooses evil with its accompanying anguish, and this condition is compounded by that ever-present matter of tragedy. In view of these imposing realities, would not wisdom and prudence dictate that man ought to be modest, restrained, and humble—in a word, pious? Should he not stand in reverence and awe before this miracle called life? Without equivocation, according to Weaver, the philosopher and theologian will answer that question in the affirmative, and the result is that "ancient virtue of *pietas*."

III.

Weaver reasoned it was the emergence of nominalism, the departure from Platonism and Christianity, which produced the intellectual heresies leading to the trauma and anguish of the modern era. "It was," he elaborated, "William of Occam who propounded the fateful doctrine of nominalism, which denies that universals have a real existence," and as a result, "For four centuries every man has been not only his own priest but his own professor of ethics, and the consequence is an anarchy which threatens even that minimum consensus of value necessary to the political state."[63] Weaver concluded, "Whether we describe this as decay of religion or loss of interest in metaphysics, the result is the same; for both are centers with power to integrate, and, if they give way, there begins a dispersion which never ends until the culture lies in fragments."[64]

Platonism and Christianity acknowledged there was "a center of things." The center suggested transcendent Ideals: Truth, Beauty, Justice and the Good. Life had meaning and purpose, and the Platonic-Christian view allowed man to relate, to discern his position in the scheme of things; and it facilitated humaneness in the human condition, for man knew his nature and could be himself. But the spirit of modernity, rooted in nominalism, undercut that view. It rejected the notion that there was "a center of things," and it turned in "flight toward periphery."[65] There was no longer an integrating Ideal; the pull of intellectual forces was "centrifugal" rather than "centripetal." Conceptually the life of the mind became "fragmented," and the press to the "periphery" became a powerful "obsession." There emerged a preoccupation with the factual and concrete—positivism manifested that trait. There was no desire to synthesize, to relate, to conceptualize, or to project notions of meaning and purpose. In fact, there emerged a profound hostility to the contention that essences—Truth, Beauty, Justice, Good—even existed, let alone could be defined. As Weaver explained, "The modernistic searcher after meaning may be likened to a man furiously beating the earth and imaging that the finer he pulverizes it, the nearer he will get to the riddle of existence." And to what end?[66]

It is a politics of infinite dispersion. Everything goes flying off in its own direction; liberalism becomes ever more liberal; hierarchies are toppled so that there is no longer any means of judging one thing as better or worse than another. Moral order is collapsed into something like the universe of modern astrophysics, with everything moving away centrifugally, nobody knows where or why. And this goes on forever.[67]

"It is," Weaver summarized, "just as if Plato's philosopher had left the city to look at the trees and then had abandoned speculative wisdom for dendrology."[68] This intellectual flight of the modern mind from the Platonic-Christian perspective is lamentable, for "[w]isdom does not lie on the periphery."[69]

Nominalism infected the American political character through its agent of relativism. Denying the notion that there were ultimate essences and absolutes by which judgments and evaluations were to be made, nominalism led inexorably to the premise that all values were relative:

> Relativism denies outright that there are any absolute truths, any fixed principles, or any standards beyond what one may consider his convenience. A theory is true only relative to the point of view of the individual, or to the circumstances which prevail at the moment. Truth is forever contingent and evolving, which means, of course, that you can never lay hands on it. Relativism is actually the abdication of truth.[70]

And as to the political implications of relativism, Weaver observed:

> The greatest injury that the idea of relativism had done to political thinking... lies in the encouragement it gives to middle-of-the roadism.... Middle-of-the-roadism is the departure of intellect from political thinking.... A political philosophy takes a stand in favor of certain values and the arrangements that follow from them.... Now the truth about the middle-of-the-road position is that it has no such character.... It doesn't see with its own eyes. It tries to get along by borrowing a little from those who have done the hard work of seeing the principles through.[71]

Weaver had no quarrel with the need to compromise "at the level where concrete facts [were] encountered." However, he added, "But I do deny strenuously that compromise itself is a political philosophy. After all, one has to have something to compromise *from*."[72] Relativism had produced the "Whig theory of history" which taught "that the most advanced point in time is the most advanced in development," and the demanding mistress Progress emerged as the new Goddess.[73] More pointedly, relativism had produced contemporary American liberalism. Concerning the latter, Weaver wrote, "[T]he essence of the liberal's position is that he has no position."[74] Moreover "[w]here no conception of a moral absolute exists, authority has no real basis" and this has ominous implications for the ideal of "human freedom and dignity"; Weaver asserted, "I am entirely convinced that relativism as a doctrine must eventually lead to a regime of force. The relativist has no outside authority, no constraining transcendent idea to appeal to or to be deterred by. For him 'all things flow.'"[75]

In addition to spawning the "Whig theory of history," nominalism had other devastating effects upon cultural life in the West and in America in particular. First, contrary to the Platonic-Christian patrimony, by "denying that universals [had] a real existence," nominalism destroyed the traditional conception of education. "Traditional education," Weaver wrote, "has always been based on the assumption that there is a world of data, a fixed reality, which is worth knowing and even worth reverencing."[76] Furthermore, in keeping with the Platonic-Christian view, traditional education felt "the upward pull of definite religious and cultural ideals," and, as a consequence, "Its content and method have been designed to develop the mind and the character in making choices between truth and error, between right and wrong."[77] Nominalism substituted "progressive education" for the traditional form. In promoting the "flight toward the periphery," Nominalism reduced education to a formless, unstructured ritual void of substance. "The new education," Weaver explained, "is rather something dreamed up by romantic enthusiasts, political fanatics, and unreflective acolytes of positive science."[78] As there were no principles, no essences, no universals, no objective structure of reality, education, under the guidance of John Dewey and his disciples, became a fragmented and purely subjective personal experience: "In brief, learning is to be foregone in favor of the child's spontaneous desires and unreflective thoughts."[79] Weaver further noted:

> The boasts of the innovating "progressive" schools is that they prepare the youth for a changing world. *Would it not be incomparably more sensible to prepare the youth to understand why the world is changing?* This is what the humanities do. There is little appeal here to the exponents of progressive education because they have no desire to rise above the confusion.[80]

Progressive education, Weaver lamented, "[N]either encourages reflection nor inspires a reverence for the good," and he concluded, "The conflict between [it] and the principal teachings of the Judeo-Christian-classical heritage of the West will be immediately apparent."[81] As the educational system was a key bearer of culture, the ravages of nominalism had been carried into the vital center of the American experience.

Beyond education, nominalism had taken a heavy cultural tool in journalism, painting, music and rhetoric. The world of journalism, including that of the newspaper, radio, and television, projects a "sickly metaphysical dream. The ultimate source of evaluation ceases to be the dream of beauty and truth and becomes that of psychopathia, of fragmentation, of disharmony and nonbeing."[82]

In turning from any notion of an integrating ideal or center, modern journalism had sought refuge in a preoccupation with the specific and fleeting. Weaver compared the world of journalism with that of the Platonic cave.[83] In the cave the multitude sits with eyes fixed upon the wall where shadows rise and fall. The wall of shadows is the world of the ephemeral and trivial. As Plato instructed, it was the philosopher who sought to turn from the wall and to go out of the cave into the sun, into the world of the true and enduring. In contrast, the function of the modern journalist is to keep the focus of the multitude upon the wall. To accomplish this end, the journalist employs that giant machine, The Great Stereopticon.[84] As Weaver observed, "It is the function of this machine to project selected pictures of life in the hope that what is seen will be imitated.... We are told the time to laugh and the time to cry."[85] To keep all eyes fixed upon the wall, the journalists—the operators of The Great Stereopticon—must war upon memory, form, and the reflective. The need was to gain and keep attention through "titillation"; all reserve was sacrificed, and "[p]roud of its shamelessness, the new journalism served up in swaggering style matter which heretofore had been veiled in decent taciturnity."[86] In making a "virtue of desecration," license is taken whereby "a certain recklessness of diction, with vivid verbs and fortissimo adjectives, creeps into the very language," and "substance itself is changed to appeal to appetites for the lurid, the prurient, and the sadistic."[87] Weaver concluded:

> What humane spirit, after [exposure to some form of contemporary journalism] has not found relief in fixing his gaze upon some characteristic bit of nature? It is escape from the sickly metaphysical dream. Out of surfeit of falsity born of technology and commercialism we rejoice in returning to primary data and to assurance that the world is a world of enduring forms which in themselves are neither brutal nor sentimental.[88]

Likewise, modern painting had suffered extensively under the imprint of nominalism: "For when we plumb the deepest springs of the artistic impulse, we find a source much akin to that of philosophy. All philosophy, Aristotle declared, begins with wonder, and it appears equally true that the artist is a wonder-struck being."[89] However, modern art, in following contemporary philosophy, retreated from the notion of a transcendent ideal at the center and opted for an obsession with fragments. Painting no longer had an integrating ideal, and there commenced a shift of emphasis to technique and to the subjective world of sensation. The ultimate in the decline of art is "[t]he movement of Impressionism, which is the revolutionary event of modern painting.... This meant the acceptance of life as good and satisfying in itself, with a consequent resolution to revel in the here and now. The world of pure sensation thus became the world of art."[90] Weaver asserted, "My interpretation is that Impressionism brings nominalism into painting. One of the cardinal tenets [of nominalism] is that outline does not exist in nature.... If form does not exist prior to things, naturally it is realism to paint things."[91] In giving birth to relativism and hence egotism, nominalism produced a decline in art where the goal was no longer the depiction of transcendent and integrating ideals; rather, the concern was with the subjective and sensate, with the expression of ego through technique—and all perpetrated in the name of "realism."

"The degenerative influences" of nominalism in music commenced with the departure from "the traditional forms...of freedom and restraint, of balance and resiliency" furnished by Mozart.[92] "The portents of change came with Beethoven," Weaver wrote, whose emphasis upon "dynamism and of strains of individualism pointed the way which the succeeding century was to take."[93] Ultimately, Weaver observed, "Music had its Impressionist movement. With Liszt and Debussy, especially, it turned to the exploitation of color and atmosphere.... This phase was technically a flight from the construction and balance of classical form, in effect it was a concentration upon "emotive fragments."[94] As the ego was driven ever inward in search of meaning and solace, it turned to jazz (and later "rock") which was "the clearest of all signs of our age's deep-seated predilection for barbarism."[95] Jazz, Weaver argued, "[Was] a triumph of grotesque, even hysterical, emotion over propriety and reasonableness." Indeed, he wondered, "Jazz often sounds as if in a rage to divest itself of anything that suggests structure or confinement."[96] Jazz reflects a mood "impatient for titillation," and it reflects the desire of the performer for "fullest liberty to express himself as an egotist."[97] Weaver contended, "By dissolving forms, it [jazz] has left man free to move without reference, expressing dithyrambically whatever surges up from below. It is a music not of dreams—certainly not of our metaphysical dream—but of drunkenness."[98] In short, jazz "shows how the soul of modern man craves orgiastic disorder."[99] Even more tragically, "[o]ne can detect signs of suicidal impulse; one feels at times that the modern world is calling for madder music and for stronger wine, is craving some delirium which will take it completely away from reality."[100]

Finally, and most critically, rhetoric had succumbed to nominalism. What is rhetoric? "Rhetoric is anciently and properly defined as the art of persuasion."[101] Weaver wrote, "[Man is] born into history, with an endowment of passion and a sense of the ought.... His life is therefore characterized by movement toward goals. It is largely the power of rhetoric which influences and governs that movement."[102] More simply, rhetoric is "the attempt through language to make one's point of view."[103] Rhetoric then is concerned with words, written and spoken, and their use in the pursuit of values and goals. Depending upon the values served, rhetoric is good or bad. As the Platonic-Christian tradition had taught since antiquity, it was imperative to discern the "nature of things," to perceive the transcendent ideals, to comprehend the proper hierarchy of values, to eschew relativism, and to construct and preserve that language which rendered service to the ultimate good: "So rhetoric at its truest seeks to perfect men by showing them better versions of themselves, links in that chain, extending up toward the ideal, which only the intellect can apprehend and only the soul have affection for."[104]

Rhetoric is the key to a culture; it is the tie that binds and affords cohesion; it expresses the soul and essence of a people—it tells of their "being." If rhetoric is corrupt, this is a symptom that society is corrupt; conversely, a society of integrity will have a rhetoric of integrity. By denying that ultimate essences and values were knowable, nominalism had grievously afflicted rhetoric.

In erecting the new idol of relativism, nominalism had left us with "exactly the same atomization which we have deplored in other fields."[105] At best, language had become banal and frivolous—note the world of journalism and advertising; too often, even in supposedly serious literary forms, language reflected an ethic with an insatiable appetite for titillation through descriptions of the brutal, obscene, and debased. Indeed, it was a measure of the scandal of the new ethic of relativism that it could not even define "brutality," "obscenity," and kindred debasements—after all, "all is relative," and evaluations are dependent solely upon the subjective eye of the individual beholder.

By inducing the modern mind to repudiate the notion of integrating ideals at the center, nominalism had undercut the entire Platonic-Christian position. The effect was to set in motion a theoretical and cultural unraveling of far-reaching consequences: not only was there rejection of the concept of enduring essences at the center, there followed logically a denial of any discernible "structure of reality"; a denial that things had essential natures which were knowable; a denial of the dualism of the transcendent and material and the superiority of the transcendent; and a denial that hierarchy was inherent in the nature of being and that the development of standards and values consistent with this hierarchy was of the highest priority in a purportedly civilized culture. In addition, there was a complete turning away from certain theoretical essentials of the biblical view; namely, original sin, evil, and tragedy. Sin and evil were beyond the comprehension of the modern mind, for out of the relativism generated by nominalism there was no conception of right versus wrong, there were no standards by which to evaluate and judge. The position of the modern mind was either to ignore tragedy, as there were no philosophical resources to cope with it, or to pretend that, as man had only a material dimension, a perfected science would eventually eradicate it. Science then would redeem mankind—this was the final effrontery of the modern mind: there was an absence of piety, an absence of that "protective virtue of humility." Unrestrained and shameless egotism was the basic symbol of the modern age; and it stood as the stark antithesis to the Platonic-Christian heritage.

IV.

In the American experience, the heritage of the Old South, Weaver contended, offered the intellectual base for overcoming the debilitating effects of nominalism: "The South which has spent so many years as America's stepchild, is proving to have the gift which may save the household from destruction."[106] Lest the shallow romanticists should misunderstand, Weaver cautioned that he was not speaking of the South of "the moonlight and magnolia tradition," nor of "the old rebel yell." Likewise, he noted that the South was a land of "anomalies" and "contradictions," and there was "the danger of taking hold of the South by a simple handle."

Weaver admonished against accepting uncritically the ways of the old South. He warned that things had to be looked at "in the round" and that the Old South had its deficiencies: on occasion it had worshiped status at the expense of warranted change; it had too frequently contributed to the "depreciation of the intellectual"; and thus it "needed a Burke or a Hegel," but it "produced lawyers and journalists."[107] Yet, in spite of these limitations, when compared with the New South model, which was merely a call for the contemporary South to conform to the national standard of nominalism, "The Old South may indeed be a hall hung with splendid tapestries in which no one would care to live; but from them we can learn something of how to live."[108] More than any other section of the country, the Old South afforded the philosophical material essential for reversing the momentum of nominalism and rekindling the Platonic Christian heritage. Although he was not prone to dwell extensively upon the particulars of the influence, clearly Southern Agrarianism in general, and that "subtle doctor" John Crowe Ransom in particular, had made an indelible mark on Weaver's thinking.

It appears paradoxical that Weaver should turn to that section of the country which is by conventional wisdom the most provincial in order to direct society from the fragmented world of nominalism to a restoration of faith in universals. But upon reflection there is no contradiction: the South is provincial in the American context precisely because it is that section with roots most deeply in the Platonic-Christian heritage. "Even in the South today," Weaver observed, "one can find surviving large segments of the classical Christian-medieval synthesis."[109] In contrast to the nation as a whole, the South had over the years nurtured its European roots, and this gave its thinking and way of life a degree of maturity not found in the more secular, optimistic, pragmatic, and progress oriented ethic of the broader national experience.

In keeping with the Platonic tradition, Weaver noted that the South was "based upon a paradigmatic ideal," meaning that Southern culture showed "a degree of centripetalism or orientation toward a center, which was characteristic of all high cultures."[110] As evidence of this "orientation toward a center," one could speak of "the South," "Southernness" and be understood as indicating a way of life; there was no other region of the country where that was so, for the other regions, under the fragmenting impact of nominalism, lacked "a center." Concerning this pull to the center as uniquely characteristic of the South, Weaver wrote, "An

American reared as a Southerner is in a sense like a man born into the Church of Rome; it is questionable whether he ever finds it possible to repudiate the South entirely."[111]

Consistent with the Platonic view, the traditional Southern mind had accepted the notion that there was a "structure of reality," that things had essential natures. More particularly, the South had kept "at the heart of its faith and belief in the dual nature of man."[112] The components of this dualism are the material and transcendent, and "the basis of [Southern] culture, like that of all true cultures, is transcendental."[113] Indeed, it was in the Old South that one found "the last nonmaterialistic civilization in the Western World."[114] Finally, the traditional South reflected the Platonic interest in standards, evaluation, hierarchy, and antiegalitarianism:

> The South has never lost sight of the fact that society means structuring and differentiation and that "society" and "mass" are antithetical terms. It has never fallen for a simple equalitarianism, nor has it embraced the sentimentalism that anyone on the bottom *ipso facto* belongs on top.[115]

In addition, Weaver reasoned, the South was the best equipped to serve as the "flywheel" of the American nation and to lead the forces of restoration because of its traditional religious fundamentalism: "More conservative than America as a whole, the South shows an almost unanimous opposition to those tendencies which would destroy the poetic-religious myths and create the mass state."[116] Weaver added, "The South remains the stronghold of religious and perhaps also of ethical fundamentalism":

> The typical Southerner is an authentically religious being if one means by religion not a neat set of moralities but a deep and even frightening intuition of man's radical dependence in this world...I suggest that the Southerner's practice of viewing the world in this way is the postulate of all his thinking.[117]

Historically, the Old South put its confidence—its faith—in "the older religious" rather than in "psychiatry and socialism." The Southerner implicitly understood the wisdom of former North Carolina Governor Charles Aycock's statement: "Nowhere within [North Carolina's] borders [is there] a man ignorant enough to join the fool in saying 'There is no God.'"[118] The traditional Southerner was religious in the deepest sense, for he comprehended the crucial meaning of the words "inscrutable" and "mystery": the Southerner "has a sense of the inscrutable, which leaves man convinced of the existence of supernatural intelligence and power, and leads him to the acceptance of life as mystery."[119] The South's religious patrimony was decidedly Christian and orthodox: the concepts of original sin, evil, and tragedy had unquestioned meaning to the Southerner. Concerning original sin and evil, the Southerner was "opposed to the chimerical notion that man is by nature good. He argued that on the contrary no government can hope to survive which does not proceed on the assumption that man is a fallen being."[120] To the orthodox religious mind of the South it was cardinal error and heresy "to substitute a sentimental optimism and humanitarianism for the old and proved doctrine of man's natural depravity."[121] Above all else, the Southerner understood the reality of tragedy. As had no other section of the country, the South had tasted the bitter "cup of defeat." Yet out of this defeat did not emerge despair or bitterness; as one Southerner observed shortly after the close of the Civil War, "It is only the atheist who adopts success as a criterion of right. It is not a new thing in the history of men that God appoints to the brave and the true the stern task of contending and falling, in a righteous quarrel."[122] As the Southern mind viewed it, Weaver explained: "God had foreseen all, and our suffering and our defeats in this world were part of a discipline whose final fruit it was not given to mortal minds to perceive.... Great calamities had to be regarded as part of the design of inscrutable Providence."[123]

Defeat and suffering were looked upon not as evidence of repudiation; rather, they were considered as parts of God's mysterious plan— the book of Job had artfully instructed men in this most fundamental of lessons. In Southern religious thought, there was no basis for questioning or despair in defeat, for even defeat was God's will and therefore good, and out of God's plan ultimately came hope and affirmation. In orthodox Southern religiousness it was "God who wielded the thunder," and there was no such thing as "the lost cause."

As a result of the Platonic-Christian heritage, the "ancient virtue of pietas" dominated the thinking of the older South. There existed veneration for the transcendent and the order of things; there was reverence for nature, tradition, history, and status. Man was the creature, not the Creator, and it was that most ancient vice, hubris, that contended man was self-produced and thus entitled to war on creation and the nature of things; there was, then, a spirit of restraint and sensitivity, of chivalry and humaneness. Although man was finite and existed as a "mist" or "shadow," the ultimate forms and essences endured. In view of man's position in this scheme of things, the traditional Southern mind, in keeping with the

Platonic-Christian tradition, had understood the meaning of piety. It was Robert E. Lee, the quintessence of Southernness, whom Weaver quoted to show the deep sense of piety present in the Old South. Lee wrote:

> Nor...do I despair of the future. The march of Providence is so slow, and our desires so impatient, the work of progress is so immense, and our means of aiding it so feeble, the life of humanity is so long, and that of the individual so brief, that we often see only the ebb of the advancing wave and are thus discouraged. It is history that teaches us to hope.[124]

Weaver was profoundly moved by this assessment. He exclaimed:

> It is a rare distillation. If Lee had been a member of that archetypal republic which a great philosopher imagined, with its orders of valor and wisdom, is it not likely that he would have been promoted a grade? I think that he would have risen from warrior to philosopher king.[125]

"I see no way," Weaver concluded, "to sum up the offense of modern man except to say that he is impious."[126] As piety had historically existed in the South, more than in any other area of the country, it was understandable why Weaver looked to this region to commence the search for the philosophical resources to reverse "the fearful descent" of the modern age.

V.

Weaver accepted the label "conservative" as accurately describing his philosophical position; nevertheless he was sympathetic to the libertarian spirit: "My instincts are libertarian, and I am sure that I would never have joined effort with the conservatives if I had not been convinced that they are the defenders of freedom today."[127] In fact, Weaver observed, "I think conservatives and libertarians stand together.... Both of them believe that there is an order of things, which will largely take care of itself if you leave it alone."[128] A crucial question emerges: was Weaver saying libertarianism and conservatism are identical perspectives? Weaver never expressly elaborated on this question; however, a reading of his works does suggest he saw an important difference and that he preferred the conservative view.

From Weaver's perspective, libertarianism was eminently correct in its concern for individual liberty; yet it unduly limited itself by offering only "freedom from" and not confronting the deeper question, "freedom from what?" In fact, a narrowly conceived philosophy emphasizing only freedom for the individual to do as he chooses, depending upon the whim of the subjective inner self, is perilously close to the crude and undeserved egotism of nominalism—impiety lies close at hand. The concept of freedom alone is not sufficient to sustain that undeniable and irrepressible longing of man, reflected in philosophers and theologians, to know of the nature and order of things, to know of the meaning and purpose of man's being—in a word, to know of Truth. Libertarianism does not purport to answer those questions; still they persist, they do not melt away. In Weaver's thinking, it is American conservatism which, although sharing the libertarian's concern for human freedom, develops a more mature philosophy dealing with the ultimate questions, a philosophy which does seek to pursue and discern, however dimly and imperfectly, meaning, purpose, and truth in the human experience. More specifically, conservatism is a philosophy of affirmation:

> The conservative I therefore see as standing on *terra firma* of antecedent reality; having accepted some things as given, lasting and good, he is in a position to use his effort where effort will produce solid results.... The conservative wants to conserve the great structural reality which has been given us and which is on the whole beneficial.[129]

"There is," argued Weaver, "iron in our nature sufficient to withstand any fact that is present in a context of affirmation."[130] Poignantly reflecting his conservatism of affirmation, Weaver concluded:

> We are eager to know whether, on the broad issues of this life, [a man stands] with the pessimists or the optimists. This is putting the matter in simple terms, of course; but humanity has a clear mind on this issue; it will not have for its great teachers those who despair of the condition of man. It will read them for excitement; it will utilize them as a corrective, but it will not cherish them as its final oracles. It prefers Aristotle to Diogense and Augustine to Schopenhauer. It does not wish to hear said, however brilliantly, that life is a tale told by an idiot; it wants an unmistakable, if chastened, recommendation of life.[131]

In seeking a philosophy sustaining a recommendation of life, Weaver turned to those venerable traditions of Western thought that spoke in terms of meaning, purpose and truth—in terms of affirmation: He turned to the Platonic-Christian heritage and its manifestation in the American South. In response to this modern age that had denied categorically—and often perversely and gleefully—notions of meaning, purpose, truth and that had succumbed to nominalism and its progeny of fanaticism and nihilism, Weaver declined to posit a conservatism of despair and negation. He responded by articulating a conservatism of hope and affirmation—a firm foundation for a founding father to have laid.

Notes

1. Richard Weaver, *Life without Prejudice and Other Essays* (Chicago, 1965), 132.
2. Richard M. Weaver, "Agrarianism in Exile," *Sewanee Review* 58 (Autumn 1950): 592.
3. Wilma R. Ebbitt, "Richard M. Weaver: An Appreciation," *Modern Age* 17 (Winter 1963): 416.
4. Frank S. Meyer, "Richard M. Weaver: An Appreciation," *Modern Age*, XIV (Summer-Fall, 1970): 243-44.
5. Willmoore Kendall, "How to Read Richard Weaver: Philosopher of 'We the (Virtuous) People'," in Nellie D. Kendall, ed., *Willmoore Kendall Contra Mundum* (New Rochelle, N.Y., 1971), 393.
6. Russell Kirk, Foreword, in Richard M. Weaver, *Visions of Order: The Cultural Crisis of Our Time* (Baton Rouge, 1964), ix.
7. Weaver, *Life without Prejudice*, 157.
8. Richard M. Weaver, Letter to the Editor, *New York Times Book Review* (21 March 1948): 29.
9. Richard M. Weaver, *The Ethics of Rhetoric* (Chicago, 1953), 4.
10. Richard M. Weaver, *Academic Freedom: The Principle and the Problems* (Bryn Mawr, Penn., 1963), 3.
11. Weaver, *Life without Prejudice*, 158-59.
12. Weaver, "Liberalism with a Ballast," *Sewanee Review*, 62 (April-June 1954): 341.
13. Weaver, *Ideas Have Consequences* (Chicago, 1948), 130-31.
14. Ibid., 59.
15. Ibid., 23.
16. Weaver, *Ethics of Rhetoric*, 112.
17. Weaver, "Illusions of Illusion," *Modern Age* 4 (Summer 1960): 319.
18. Weaver, *Relativism and the Crisis of Our Times* (Bryn Mawr, Penn., 1961), 3.
19. Weaver, "Humanism in an Age of Science," *Intercollegiate Review* 7 (Fall 1970): 16.
20. Weaver, *Life without Prejudice*, 17.
21. Weaver, *Visions of Order*, 13.
22. Ibid.
23. Weaver, "Illusions of Illusion," 318.
24. Weaver, *Ideas Have Consequences*, 19.
25. Ibid, 17.
26. Weaver, "Illusions of Illusion," 318.
27. Ibid.
28. Richard M. Weaver, *The Southern Tradition at Bay: A History of Postbellum Thought*, ed. George Core and M. E. Bradford (New Rochelle, N.Y., 1968), 36.
29. Weaver, *Ideas Have Consequences*, 40.
30. Weaver, *Visions of Order*, 16.
31. Weaver, "The Humanities in the Century of the Common Man," *New Individualist Review* 3, no. 3 (1964): 21.

32. Weaver, *Life without Prejudice*, 45, 15.
33. Weaver, *Visions of Order*, 140; Weaver, *Life without Prejudice*, 141.
34. Weaver, *Visions of Order*, 143.
35. Weaver, *Life without Prejudice*, 155.
36. Weaver, *Visions of Order*, 91.
37. Weaver, *Southern Tradition*, 43.
38. Weaver, *Visions of Order*.
39. Ibid., 88.
40. Richard M. Weaver, "Christian Letters," *Modern Age* 3 (Fall 1959): 420.
41. Weaver, "Lord Acton: The Historian as Thinker," *Modern Age* 5 (Winter 1960-61): 15.
42. Weaver, "Impact of Society on Mr. Russell," *Commonweal* (20 February 1953): 504.
43. Weaver, *Visions of Order*, 67.
44. Weaver, *Life without Prejudice*, 146.
45. Weaver, "Contemporary Southern Literature," *Texas Quarterly Review* 2 (Summer 1959): 139-40.
46. Ibid., 127.
47. Weaver, *Ideas Have Consequences*, 11.
48. Weaver, "Humanities," 11-12.
49. Weaver, "Contemporary Southern Literature," 137.
50. Weaver, "Humanities," 11-12.
51. Ibid., 12.
52. Ibid., 21.
53. Weaver, *Ideas Have Consequences*, 187.
54. Weaver, *Life without Prejudice*, 143.
55. Weaver, "Aspects of the Southern Philosophy," in Louis D. Rubin, Jr., and Robert D. Jacobs, eds., *Southern Renascence: The Literature of the Modern South* (Baltimore, Md., 1953), 20.
56. Weaver, *Southern Tradition*, 32.
57. Weaver, *Life without Prejudice*, 141.
58. Weaver, *Ideas Have Consequences*, 184.
59. Ibid., 170.
60. Ibid., 170-71 (italics added).
61. Ibid., 185; Weaver, *Southern Tradition*, 33.
62. Weaver, *Life without Prejudice*, 144.
63. Weaver, *Ideas Have Consequences*, 3, 2.
64. Ibid., 21.
65. Ibid., 52-53.
66. Weaver, *Visions of Order*, 38.
67. Weaver, "Illusions of Illusion," 320.
68. Weaver, *Ideas Have Consequences*, 57.
69. Ibid., 65.
70. Weaver, *Relativism and the Crisis of Our Times*, 4.
71. Ibid., 5-7.
72. Ibid., 7.
73. Weaver, *Ideas Have Consequences*, 130.
74. Weaver, *Life without Prejudice*, 153.
75. Weaver, *Visions of Order*, 125; Weaver, *Relativism and the Crisis of Our Times*, 12.

76. Weaver, *Visions of Order*, 126.
77. Richard M. Weaver, "From Poetry to Bitter Fruit," *National Review* (25 January 1956): 27; Weaver, *Life without Prejudice*, 63.
78. Weaver, *Visions of Order*, 115.
79. Ibid., 128.
80. Weaver, "Humanities," 20.
81. Weaver, *Ideas Have Consequences*, 48; Weaver, *Visions of Order*, 115.
82. Weaver, *Ideas Have Consequences*, 104.
83. Ibid., 108.
84. Ibid., chap. 5.
85. Ibid., 93.
86. Ibid., 28.
87. Ibid., 98; Weaver, *Visions of Order*, 53.
88. Weaver, *Ideas Have Consequences*, 112.
89. Richard M. Weaver, "Realism and the Local Color Interlude," *Georgia Review* 22 (Fall 1968): 302.
90. Weaver, *Ideas Have Consequences*, 88.
91. Ibid., 89.
92. Ibid., 83.
93. Ibid.
94. Ibid., 84.
95. Ibid., 85.
96. Ibid.
97. Ibid., 86.
98. Ibid., 87.
99. Ibid.
100. Ibid., 185.
101. Richard M. Weaver, *Language is Sermonic: Richard M. Weaver on the Nature of Rhetoric*, ed. Richard L. Johanessen, Rennard Strickland, and Ralph T. Eubanks (Baton Rouge, 1970), 140.
102. Ibid., 221.
103. Ibid., 220.
104. Weaver, *Ethics of Rhetoric*, 25.
105. Weaver, *Ideas Have Consequences*, 152.
106. Weaver, "Contemporary Southern Literature," 144.
107. Weaver, *The Southern Tradition*, 389.
108. Ibid., 396.
109. Weaver, "The South and the American Union," in Louis D. Rubin, Jr., and James Jackson Kilpatrick, eds., *The Lasting South: Fourteen Southerners Look at Their Home* (Chicago, 1957), 50.
110. Weaver, "An Altered Stand," *National Review* (17 June 1961): 389; Weaver, "Humanities," 8.
111. Weaver, *Southern Tradition*, 330.
112. Weaver, "Contemporary Southern Literature," 126.
113. Ibid., 133.
114. Weaver, *The Southern Tradition*, 391.
115. Weaver, "The South and the American Union," in Rubin and Kilpatrick, eds. *The Lasting South*, 126.
116. Weaver, "The South and the Revolution of Nihilism," *South Atlantic Quarterly* 43 (April 1944): 196.

117. Weaver, "Aspects of the Southern Renascence," in Rubin and Jacobs, eds., *Southern Renascence,* 19, 15.
118. Weaver, *Southern Tradition,* 376.
119. Ibid., 48.
120. Ibid., 143.
121. Ibid.
122. Ibid., 147.
123. Ibid., 209.
124. Weaver, "Lee the Philosopher," *Georgia Review* 2 (Fall 1948): 303; also quoted in Weaver, *The Southern Tradition at Bay,* 209-10.
125. Weaver, "Lee the Philosopher," 303.
126. Weaver, *Ideas Have Consequences,* 170.
127. Weaver, *Life without Prejudice,* 164.
128. Ibid., 163.
129. Ibid., 159.
130. Weaver, *Ideas Have Consequences,* 104.
131. Weaver, "Lee the Philosopher," 302.

IV

Final Thoughts: Weaver in Our Time

12

Stranger in Paradise

Chilton Williamson, Jr.

Glancing through the manuscripts for this testimonial back-of-the book section, I am struck by the number of contributors who were personally acquainted with their subject.[1] I never knew Richard Weaver—had in fact never heard of him until perhaps a dozen years ago—and even today cannot claim to regret the fact. (How many modern authors would one actually *care* to know? I can think of maybe three: William Faulkner, Flannery O'Connor, and H. L. Mencken. The rest I am perfectly content to meet only in their shelf lives.) While Weaver's writings suggest a strong vein of affability and even sweetness of spirit, nevertheless crankiness keeps breaking in: the special brand of cantankerousness that hangs like stale tobacco smell about middle-aged bachelors who work and live out of residential hotel rooms, taking their meals at restaurants around the corner or reheating them in Pullman kitchens shared with roaches and illuminated by the neon bar signs across the street. It is, partly, the irritability of a man who has made his choice between writing and living, and stuck with it; also, I suspect, it represents the tempered disgruntlement of one who, while deploring the tendencies of a wayward world, remains wise enough to comprehend that everything has a part and a place in God's creation.

The truth is that Richard Weaver appears—at least to this reader—to have been one of those men for whom that modicum of balance called Happiness is to be found, intellectually speaking, neither in temperament nor in activity, but in the philosophical and moral process of reconciliation. He considered negativism and despair pusillanimous, yet his fundamental incapacity for worldly optimism would, I imagine, have made Weaver a marginally dour and sharp-elbowed presence in the 1980s.

Two decades of continued Yankeefication in the Sunbelt South would be more than sufficient to stir something not unlike misery in the soul of this native son of North Carolina, who argued—in *The Southern Tradition at Bay* and other places—that the Old South represented the last feudal society in the Western world; a society fundamentally conservative in thought and habit that would—as the nation in large aged and in aging grew more susceptible to the frailties and woes that beset societies as well as men in their maturity—teach patience and fortitude in adversity, even perhaps tragedy, to its less-experienced brethren in the North and West. That the facts of recent history show the influence to have flowed in the opposite direction—with the Southerner partaking of the crassest materialism of the Yankee while inculcating, apparently, nothing in return—would inevitably have come as a dreadful disappointment, which many casual readers of Weaver might be tempted to ascribe to his "agrarianism": meaning, his well-known preference for the feudal over the industrial, the rural over the urban milieu, the rustic over the city man.

That Weaver entertained such preferences—or, as he would say, "prejudices"—is indisputable. Over and over again—particularly in *Ideas Have Consequences* and *The Southern Tradition* but elsewhere as well—he uses "urban" as a synonym for "mass" and "Mass man" for "contemporary society" or "modern man" upon whom "all higher values are as good as lost" (Rauschning as quoted by Weaver, *Ideas*). There is, therefore, an easy tendency to see Weaver as a dyed-in-the-wool back-to-the-land agrarian (he studied for a year under John Crowe Ransom at Vanderbilt) more than eager to take his stand with the yeoman farmer, sharecropper, and perhaps (as critics have darkly muttered) the slaveholder himself. Support for this reading is to be found in many passages from his work, such as this (from *Ideas Have Consequences*):

> What humane spirit after reading a newspaper or attending a popular motion picture or listening to the farrago of nonsense on a radio program has not found relief in fixing his gaze upon some characteristic bit of nature? It is escape from the sickly metaphysical dream. Out of the surfeit of falsity born of technology and commercialism we rejoice in returning to primary data and to assurance that the world is a world of enduring forms which in themselves are neither brutal or sentimental.

Or this (from the same source): "No one can be excused for moral degradation, but we are tempted to say of the urban dweller, as of the heathen, that he never had an opportunity for salvation."

Now that sounds like a hopelessly archaic mode of speech in many conservative—as well as most Republican—circles in the 1980s, a period of conservative ascendancy unfortunately infected at the national level by a boisterous right-wing optimism, entirely devoid of the tragic sense, by which America in the late twentieth century is made to appear as a sort of historical Nirvana owing to its potentially fecund economy, its enormous technological ingenuity and its alleged rediscovery of "basic values" (which upon inspection too often reveals itself to be an illusion created by populist fundamentalism employing all the dishonest and manipulative practices learned from its sworn enemies, the mass media). According to new "conservative" (and particularly "neoconservative") creeds, the sky is the clear, clear limit, with no cloud to be seen threatening disaster from resource depletion, environmental depredation, crowd culture, uncontrolled immigration from Third World countries, the dehumanizing effects of technology, or metaphysical materialism—so long, of course, as all the proper prescriptions, as handed down by Republican politicians and "conservative" think-tanks are conscientiously applied.

Richard Weaver could not be comfortable in company with this new breed of conservative. I will insist, though, that his reply to it would have nothing in common, either, with that of the "New" Left, or of the Sierra Club—or, for that matter, of many of the contributors to the volume *I'll Take My Stand*. Perhaps he might not have any reply—in the sense of an "answer"—at all; though I believe he would certainly have a word of caution, amounting to a reminder of what conservatism *is* and to what it attempts to point.

Writing in 1953, Weaver complained that the Republicanism of the 1920s had taken the promotion of prosperity to be the chief end of government and that, as of the 1950s, it still did. Seeing more deeply than do the GOP boosters of the 1980s into the socially and morally destructive aspects of that form of industrial capitalism we call the West and by extension, Freedom, he would doubtless have been horrified by the extent to which the Right has purloined with adaptation the economic argument from the Left, so as to exchange the Great Society of Lyndon Johnson for the Cornucopic Society of George Gilder. Doubtless too the author of *The Ethics of Rhetoric* would have understood how this came about. How Burke, in preferring the liberal mode of argument "from circumstance" to the conservative one a *priori* with which to condemn the French Revolution, foreshadowed the position of today's commonsensical "conservatives" in opposition to the "idealists" of the Left. Understood and probably sympathized, too, as he sympathized with

Burke while himself preferring Abraham Lincoln's unfaltering instinct for the argument "from definition." Sympathized while never losing sight of the truth that what is really of value in industrial-capitalistic democracy is the independent freedom of self-realization, the freedom to translate the ideal into the actual whether by drilling oil wells or manufacturing micro-chips, rather than the good actually produced or the comforts secured those goods and that comfort being in the long run, subversive of freedom and self-realization. Because when all is said, there remains a sense in which an obsession with trickle-down is superogatory. "As far as I'm concerned," Flannery O'Connor observed, "we are all The Poor."

What Weaver took the West to task for was what, finally, he reproached the Old South with as well: the failure to "define its way of life." In the case of the former, he located the fault in diffidence and unconcern; in the case of the latter, in negligence. And yet the antebellum South *did* possess a moral sense of itself that, lingering on almost to the present day, held out a glimmering hope that it might finally—either with its last breath or in the gathering force of a longed-for convalescence—transmit it to the North, to the nation, to modernity. That sense did not, definitionally, proceed from what Weaver called "total immersion in nature" (leaving man "sentient but unreflective") but spiritual (God, tradition) reality. Properly addressed, it might indeed have impinged upon the consciousness of the land of "total abstraction" where all roads "[lead] philosophically to denial of substance ([which] may be symbolized by flight to the city)."

There was, of course, no proper address, and the flight to the city continues, to the point where the South now contains many megalopolises itself. Perhaps the life of man is not so arbitrarily fixed as it might seem at three score and ten (and Richard Weaver's was nearly a third less); perhaps it is simply that, in seventy years, a man can see too much. Perhaps too, from where this wise and unassuming man stands now, Atlanta, Georgia, *looks better* (if, in fact, it "looks" at all).

Note

1. The December 31, 1985 issue of *National Review* was that periodical's thirtieth anniversary issue. It contained essays on ten of its original contributing editors. In addition to this essay, Frank Meyer, Russell Kirk, Whittaker Chambers, John Dos Passos, James Burnham, Willmoore Kendall, Will Herberg, and Henry Hazlitt were also profiled.

13

Looking Before and After

Marion Montgomery

> *Personality is that little private area of selfhood in which the person is at once conscious of his relationship to the transcendental and the living community.*
>
> *A creature designed to look before and after finds that to do the latter has gone out of fashion and that to do the former is becoming impossible.*
> —Richard Weaver, *Ideas Have Consequences*

When *Modern Age* was very young [the winter of 1958-1959], Richard Weaver (who was a founding editor) wrote in its pages about his resolute struggle "Up from Liberalism." He was looking back on twenty-five years of his own intellectual history, as I have been doing in recovering these essays of mine. He recalls that in the autumn of 1939 he found himself driving west across Texas prairie toward a teaching post "in a large technical college," returning to a position that had become increasingly intolerable to him: "It came to me like a revelation that I did not have to go back to this job...and that I did not have to go on professing the clichés of liberalism, which were becoming meaningless to me." It is one of the signs of the newfound freedom of spirit he was discovering that he did finish his contract at the outpost of technology and liberalism in the Texas prairie, though he stopped professing liberal clichés; his sense of responsibility to that new freedom would not allow him to chuck the job for which he had contracted without due notice in order to go home to North Carolina mountains. (A different sense of freedom from Weaver's was to sweep the academic world in the years just ahead. "Freedom" in the realm of idea, divorced from responsibility, was to be used to justify "ripping off" that conveniently vague monster, "The System," whether freedom was twisted to mean abandoning a personal commitment or perverting a public trust.) In due time Weaver began a recovery of mind, an education denied him by the institutions he had attended, the result of which reeducation was his posthumous *The Southern Tradition at Bay*. (A memoir in *Modern Age* in the spring of 1987, by an undergraduate friend at the University of Kentucky, gives an account of Weaver as "liberal" thirty years before the essay.)

In "Up from Liberalism" Weaver very nearly touches upon the private, as opposed to the personal; upon an open moment of soul-searching as he recounts his journey to a position whose conclusions are at least firmly personal. The distinction between private and personal is not easily made in our world, though one may immediately recognize a difference between the ghosted Hollywood memoir on the best-seller list and Weaver's essay. As a people (a community of persons) the Greeks understood the distinction well at one period; they ceased to do so as their civilization decayed. One could, I believe, trace the symptoms of that decay from the plays of Aeschylus through Euripides and discover valuable lessons for our own age.

It will have to be, increasingly, a private attempt to do so. That is, in the academic current of the moment, a student is swept along by the latest fad in "thinkers" and except by fortunate accident is not likely to encounter and consider with his teachers and peers either Aeschylus or Euripides, or most of the great minds in the Western intellectual tradition. Those minds will continue for a while, a fading influence on our thought, a residual and vague presence at best, but the deliberate deconstruction of mind, justified by vague social concerns if justified at all, or by exigencies of production that demand stylized production of specialized minds, is so largely institutional policy now that it will dominate for some time yet. Recently at Stanford University, for instance, faculty and students in concert—by all account a minority of the affected—engineered a violent rejection of Western culture from their undergraduate study. The term violent applies, not only to argument as noise to drown out counterargument, but to actual threats of physical violence of such a sufficient likelihood apparently as to intimidate the administrative authority of that institution. The result has been to replace Homer and Dante in the undergraduate Western culture course with the latest radical thinkers on pop social concerns, those whom the particular instructor happens to be "into" at the moment. A scattering of the older minds are still named, but with texts unspecified, so that there can be no assurance that two students from Stanford, certified as Bachelors of Arts, will have read the same works.

What happened at Stanford has been happening, usually with less spectacle and so with less media notice, throughout the American academy, in witness of which is the surprising attention paid to Allan Bloom's scathing indictment of higher education, *The Closing of the American Mind* (1987). Secretary of Education William Bennett visited Stanford to defend Western civilization, a strange necessity but clearly a necessity. At Stanford on April 18, 1988, he gave a clear and effective defense, at the level of vital intellect, of "Why the West?" (published in *National Review,* 27 May 1988), and he has been increasingly under attack by vested interests of the academy since. Professor Sidney Hook analyzes the consequences of the Stanford event in *Measure* (April 1988) as an "Educational Disaster at Stanford University." But such is the impetus of intellectual decline in the academy that I do not believe their cogent arguments, nor Bloom's, will have the effect we should desire. At most I fear the effect will be that the entrenched deconstructors of mind will be more cautious about stirring a public interest in what is happening to our young minds, "our hope of the future," as they will be told by some visiting name on their graduation day. Too much public interest might prove dangerous, for common sense is still potentially viable in the public mind. It would be very dangerous to stir it too much.

The present educational establishment would have to be "born again" intellectually if we were to recover mind in its proper relation to the realities of the world. That is not a prospect which would lead Jimmy the Greek to give encouraging odds. Certainly the signs of a return to clear-mindedness about the common good are not propitious in the academy. For such has been the accelerating trend of public education, higher and lower, that touchstones to the common good, bequeathed us by Western civilization, are ghostly at best in our curricula. A more certain knowledge of our cultural heritage is needed than we possess as a society, even to reenlist common sense in its defense.

But for our present purposes, perhaps we may still recall the personal witness Sophocles's Oedipus bears in addressing the citizens of Thebes, in sharp contrast to the moment of private agony when he recognizes and accepts his failure as king (however much "fated" that failure). The playwright knew it would be a spiritual violation of the audience itself to present the open spectacle of Oedipus' blinding himself at that moment. For our part, we have become inured to the public display of the properly private, to obscenities treated with sentimentality. A mother crouches grieving near a twisted bike, clutching her dead child on a public street; a picture of her affronts us from the front page of our evening paper. A television reporter thrusts his microphone at the mother of an Atlanta black child whose body has just been discovered in underbrush and asks in tenderized tones how she feels on hearing the news; the camera zooms in on her tearful face while block letters give her name. The extreme naturalism of fact and image is assumed sufficient justification for such violence as if an extreme naturalism were the whole of reality and thus sufficient justification for transgressions upon human nature. Thus the victim is further victimized, though that victim will know instinctively that he is violated. Idle curiosity and a fascination with the sensational are thus pandered to at the expense of the unfortunate. Such violations of persons as we have illustrated are a consequence of what Weaver calls "the repudiation of sentiment for immediacy."

Moments of revelation touch us at the deepest, most private seat of our being, whether they are visions such as the mystic guardedly reports or invasions such as affront us daily in the press and on television. And thus affected, we bear ourselves as changed in the community of persons, either enlarged or reduced in our capacities as humans. But it is a dangerous intrusion to open the private to sentimental curiosity. Nor is the object of that curiosity, the distraught mother, the only victim. The intrusion erodes the curious person from within. The manipulators of power recognize the advantage of such erosion, as the history of the public trials in the Soviet Union between the two world wars will remind us. Public drama of this nature intends to drug community, not purge it, the litany of confessions dulling a person's response into bland conformity. Our current inclination in the same dire action is signaled by the increasing pressure to televise courtroom trials, thus providing a new species of docudrama which purports to make us better citizens. When the private becomes steady fare like Saturday cartoons for the children, when person is reduced to individual in public spectacle, justice as a virtue will suffer the same fate that violence as a reality does when the cartoon character, smashed by a stone or riddled by bullets, appears undiminished in the next frame. The individual of today's show returns on trial tomorrow in a new frame of references to the idea of justice, an idea increasingly removed from concrete reality as the televised individual is removed from his personhood. Ideas will seem inconsequential to reality when they will have become in fact subversive of reality.

Richard Weaver, recognizing the complex relation of the personal and private and the danger to public health when the distinction is lost, revisits his own moment of revelation in "Up from Liberalism," but with a proper discretion. He does so to explain his new conviction that "somehow our education will have to recover the lost vision of the person as a creature of both intellect and will." For it is the person of intellect and will who must establish a public presence in any community that is truly free. Such distinctions are well-nigh lost beyond recovery when the private is deliberately turned into public spectacle, into such obscenities as I have mentioned as our daily fare. We find a range of violations, from intrusions upon obscure citizens in their moments of private grief to elaborate "happenings" calculated to affront community by personal self-destructions in X-rated movies and plays. The pietistic defenses of the media for presenting this range of violations, always in the name of freedom, are so shrill that the tone of that defense ought to alert us. And we were alerted by *Ideas Have Consequences* to "the extremes of passion and suffering...served up to enliven the breakfast table or to lighten the boredom of an evening at home. The area of privacy has been abandoned because the definition of person has been lost; there is no longer a standard by which to judge what belongs to the individual man. Behind the offense lies the repudiation of sentiment in favor of immediacy."

Weaver saw our world fragmenting in consequence of the manipulations of personal freedom, the person thus forced or tricked into abandoning community responsibility, till he is left at last merely an individual summed by statistics, whether through Nielsen ratings or five-year plans. In the isolation of his individuality, he becomes easy victim of ideology, from the right or left. For, while the person alone may be sustained in solitude by his sense of encompassing community, the individual discovers not solitude but merely loneliness. He is the more easily driven since his community hunger is reduced to herd instinct, to ideological shelters out of the terrors of alienation, little noticing the keepers who drive him to the pen. Through the 1950s, 1960s, and 1970s there occurs an acceleration of the individual's concern for what was camouflaged to resemble personal well-being by ideologues but which turned out to be a discomforting randomness in nature and community. Violating the springs of their own selfhood, of the person, individuals struggled to put on "life-styles" bought of the nearest purveyor in the exhilaration of a panic vision. Bought from cut rate haberdashers who clip and stitch the latest ideas, insisting them the only suitable cover for one's personal and private intellectual nakedness.

What cause has legitimate call upon us as persons? What idea is capable of restoring us to our personhood? In a confused moment of history, Weaver steadies us. He knew, early enough to help us, that violence of language and to language speaks a person or a people dislocated from the surest grounds of ideas, from an old faith in being that is necessary to community vision and vitality. It is the loss of that ground that he explores in *Ideas Have Consequences,* especially as that loss is reflected in our shifting from a primary concern with being to the chimera of becoming divorced from reality. The limits of one's becoming, he reminds us, are already in our limited being; our potential is implicit. But when our language shows us committed to "life-styles" (as if one might out of desire alone purchase a cloak of being, the new purchase detachable at will), we are already well on the way to self and community destructions, destructions that are dangerous at every level of our encounter with reality.

My appreciation of Richard Weaver's contribution to conserving thought is not of his originality, of course. (Originality is an idea that we easily transform into a personal idol.) Weaver's concern with "the person as a creature of both intellect and will" finds its roots in ancient minds; it is a concern common to many of those whom I have chosen as fathers, some of whom I have intended to celebrate in these pages. He and they intend to recall us to common principles of mind as mind engages the world with deliberate will. What he and Flannery O'Connor and Eric Voegelin and the Fugitive-Agrarians speak for in common is a sacrificial openness, a suspension of that self-interest that cultures our pride as a raw egg cultures the hidden violence of bacteria. This openness of mind to reality we sometimes call love (a root meaning in *philosophy*). Its general presence among men in community we speak of as piety, and it includes a discriminating as well as a sacrificial openness—a balance of will and intellect that allows and governs sentiment, lest sentiment decay into sentimentality. Within the common bond of such piety, one recognizes originality when it occurs as a gift of grace, welcomed and valued, but not idolized either for itself or in that medium to community, the person, through whom it is given in the common good. (With rare exception, genius shines through humility.)

In our company of like-minded wayfarers, one is thankful that the personal limits of our several callings complement each other. Some, failing to recognize that blessing, might find Richard Weaver alone somewhat thin. The leaven in his logic is wit and irony. In him one might miss the deeper resonances of a poet's words, or that humor one finds in Weaver's fellow Southerners William Faulkner or Flannery O'Connor. But by such variety of persons the largeness of humanity is enriched; by discriminating piety we share in a largesse of humanity beyond our personal limits. Richard Weaver in our pilgrim company bears himself with the steady resoluteness of the prophet, showing with devastating incisiveness where and how we have lost the vision of the person as creature, as Faulkner dramatizes it with poignant humor. Weaver's manner as prophet is very much the one we know in those persons who are our companions of mind descended to us through the Old Testament.

The poet's way and the rhetor's way are not the same. The poet has a different freedom—to range among human sentiments acting out a moment of soul in words; the rhetor's is to examine and maintain the intellect's responsibility to words as words touch reality. A rhetor like Weaver tests the poet's imaginative visions with and against the limits of mind, lest soul be seduced by masked illusion—especially through the nominalistic temptation to the poet as he loses his ground in reality. (*The Ethics of Rhetoric* is concerned with a false poetry, with constructions of words that do not establish a true relation of mind to reality.) The tensions between poet and rhetor since Plato reveal their symbiotic dependence, despite their populized wars. Thus T. S. Eliot speaks for both poet and rhetor when he says of a common concern, having practiced both callings himself: "Speech impelled us/ To purify the dialect of the Tribe/ And urge the mind to aftersight and foresight." Mind thus engaged becomes one in a community of minds no longer restricted to a time or a place, becomes member in that body of a timeless community whether it finds itself in a London publishing house or a Chicago university. Still, home "is where one starts from," as Eliot reminds us in a serenity of conviction. We return to that home at the end of all our exploring and at last "know the place for the first time," grace permitting. Russell Kirk tells us, soon after Richard Weaver's death, that Weaver expected to go back home to Weaverville, there to spend his full years "writing and meditating in the place where his ancestors have lived and died." But that would have to be after his battles in the outer jungles of modernism, and he never came to that earned retreat.

There appeared in the *Southern Partisan* in fall 1981 a memorial Weaver gave of his Uncle Doug, dead at ninety-seven. "The Pattern of Life" is poignant, hovering very near the private, as was proper enough since it was a eulogy within the bosom of the family, given at a reunion at Weaverville in August 1954. Uncle Doug's life was one denied Weaver himself, not because he died young but because of the responsibility he felt to stay abroad. He chose to wage words with and for those of us who have lost the good of the intellect, have lost the old vision of order made possible through will and intellect joined in a service to the fullness of person and thereby to the good of community. "What an extraordinary thing it is in this age," he says in the eulogy to Uncle Doug, "and what a fine thing in any age for a man to sit on his porch and watch the shade tree he planted with his own hands grow for sixty years!...In a world where so much is superficial, aimless, and even hysterical, he kept a grasp upon those values which are neither old-fashioned nor new-fashioned, but are central, permanent, and certain in their reward." And what a valuable gift is left us, we say in turn, in *Ideas Have Consequences, The Ethics of Rhetoric, Visions of Order,* and *The Southern Tradition at Bay*. What a lasting help toward our recovering abiding values. Weaver's words clear away wild random inclinations of the will and intellect so that we may the more certainly watch the steady presence of the permanent at the center of any home we return to, eyes opened. A shade in a weary land of words.

And so this tribute to Weaver, Cleanth Brooks, and Flannery O'Connor, and Alexander Solzhenitsyn and all the others I have been privileged to praise in words. Now is a moment of winter sun. I sit on my front porch in Crawford and look at trees I did not plant, able to value the planting and accept my continuing responsibility to the life dormant in them. Able to do so in part because of these and other companionable minds who are with me in very real ways in this very real place. They remind me that my intellectual and spiritual state is affected by my consent to their wisdom, though I am responsible not to accept as wise all that they may have bequeathed me. But such is the clarity of their vision of man and his nature that they insist I must choose to will, in either accepting or rejecting. I know from them that my willing is consequential to my being.

In neither realm, spiritual or intellectual, can I plead the determinist's escape. We are deeply affected by ideas only through our ratification of them by intellect and will—deeply meaning to the good of our being. Recognizing the point, we join them in the struggle to recover the piety Weaver discusses in closing his argument about the consequences of ideas, "the belief that personality, like the earth we tread on, is something given us." He adds, "The plea for piety asks only that we admit the right to self-ordering of the substance of other beings." Sitting on my front porch in Crawford, in the middle of a winter day, I recognize in those words a depth beyond the early shibboleths of freedom and personality that assail us from every quarter from the parasites of being. The oaks look dead now, and certainly they appear threatened by heavy tangles of ivy and knots of mistletoe. But that is only an illusion in a leafless season, as we each realize when we are moved to aftersight and foresight.

14

Is the Battle Over...Or Has It Just Begun? The Southern Tradition Twenty Years After Richard Weaver

Thomas Landess

The image of Richard Weaver that sticks in my memory is a disturbing one. He is standing before an audience in a conference room at Vanderbilt University, his gnome-like features barely rising above the tall, polished oak podium that holds his manuscript. He wears a brown, wrinkled suit, shiny at the elbows, and at midmorning he is already in need of a second shave.

Slightly nervous, he reads in an accent that is decidedly East Tennessee or Western North Carolina; for despite his education and his years at The University of Chicago, he is still a mountain man, with a nasal twang and hard R's that sometimes sound more Midwestern than deep South. Because he is straining, his voice becomes almost shrill against a background of nearby crashing and shouting. The audience leans forward, cupping their ears, trying to make out his words above the racket.

For outside a wrecking crew is demolishing a neighboring building, and it is with this terrible confusion that Weaver is attempting to compete. He is trying to tell his listeners that the South, more than any other region, honors and preserves its past, that for this reason its poets and novelists have been able to draw on a tradition that is still vital and whole, despite the march of modernism with its idolatry of science and its commitment to the idea of progress.

But no one can hear him. The walls are trembling. The ground is shaking. The workmen are shouting. They are tearing down Kissam Hall, where all the Fugitive-Agrarians lived during their formative years, as did many generations of other Vanderbilt alumni. But the building is old, its architecture offensive to modern sensibilities; and Chancellor Harvie Branscomb—a great believer in progress—has commissioned the university architects to design a quadrangle of cracker box dormitories to replace Kissam Hall. The quadrangle, according to the Chancellor, will be "approximately the dimensions of Harvard Yard."

Weaver, realizing that he is fighting a losing battle with the wrecking crew, begins to shuffle through the pages of his talk, skipping huge sections in order to bring the ordeal to a speedy conclusion. Someone from the Vanderbilt English Department rises and slips quietly out of the door, determined to stop the noise. After a couple of minutes he returns and shakes his head. The workmen have to follow a rigid schedule. They have their orders. The roaring and crashing continue. Finally, in a clatter of crumbling bricks, Weaver finishes his paper and the audience gives him a great burst of applause that for a moment drowns out the noise of the wrecking crew. When the crowd files out the door they see that Kissam Hall is now nothing more than a heap of dust-cloud bricks with a few sections from a marble archway jutting out above the rubble.

As I say, this is a disturbing memory, partially because Weaver, a shy and modest man, found the chore of a public performance even more difficult than usual, but mostly because of the eerie symbolism of the occasion. The events outside the window mocked everything that Weaver was saying that day and they did so at the direction of a man who opposed most of what Weaver and the Agrarians stood for, only the latest in a succession of chancellors who believed in modernism and the sanctity of scientific progress.

That was twenty-five years ago, however, and while the campus of Vanderbilt University has grown more unsightly with the years, the intellectual landscape has altered ever so slightly in Weaver's favor. The critics who scoffed at the dire predictions in *I'll Take My Stand* have grown silent as one by one the prophecies have been fulfilled. Fewer and fewer Americans trust the efficacy of science today, and if you ask young people if they believe the world is getting better and better they will tell you they don't think so.

Yet the larger battle that Richard Weaver was waging is by no means won. Indeed I would suggest that the outcome is still very much in the balance, with no clear sign that truth will win in the near future. For

Weaver, more than any other twentieth century Southerner, saw the struggle as a clash between right reason on the one hand and non-reason or ideology on the other. He saw the breakdown of Western civilization not as the consequence of industrialism and technology (these too are consequences) but rather as the result of faulty thinking—not the absence of thought altogether; and in the course of exploring this conviction Weaver wrote a number of important books and essays, three of which, it seems to me, are seminal studies.

These three works—*Ideas Have Consequences*, *The Ethics of Rhetoric* and *The Southern Tradition at Bay*—lay important groundwork, awaiting the hand of a master builder, someone with philosophic insights commensurate with Weaver's to come along and pull the parts together, to oversee the Restoration. These books, I hasten to say, are not Kantian in their depth and complexity. To the contrary, they are deceptively simple, available to any intelligent reader who is willing to devote time and thought to their arguments. Together they tell us precisely who we are at a moment in our history when most of us have forgotten and for this reason alone they require close and respectful reading.

II.

The first of these, *Ideas Have Consequences,* was published in 1948, at a time when Americans were in no mood for jeremiads. In the aftermath of a military victory over European fascism they were pleased with what they had become. Yet Weaver was saying that this nation in particular stood on the edge of the abyss.

As a consequence his study went unnoticed in the academy because it did not fit easily into the dialectic of the times and therefore did not lend itself to glib paraphrase. Thirty-five years later *Ideas Have Consequences* still demands a fuller discussion than anyone would stand still for, but its meaning is probably clearer now than in 1948 since the problems Weaver was addressing are more apparent and more crucial. Also, a number of important voices have been heard from since that time, voices that echo Weaver's language and ideas, giving them a new currency in the intellectual marketplace, rendering them ever more intelligible to the average reader.

Of course his initial premise still proves a formidable obstacle to most. He wants to argue that the structure and texture of twentieth-century life can be traced to a philosophical controversy in the fourteenth century, and most people who read, yes, even the *New York Times,* have difficulty thinking about any time so remote as the administration of Calvin Coolidge. Yet Weaver asks them to believe that the nominalism of William of Occam contained the seeds of modern chaos. The proposition called "Occam's Razor" (entities are not to be multiplied except as may be necessary) attacks the idea that an absolute universal truth exists against which all our experience must be measured. Thus for Occam and for all his descendants such categories as "tree" and "human being" and "evil" are merely convenient ways of talking about the world, but they don't correspond to anything that is real or ultimately true. As Weaver puts its, "The practical result of nominalist philosophy is to banish the reality that which is perceived by the senses." The result is a gradual decline of belief in the transcendent and the emergence of modern materialism and moral relativism.

At first, Weaver doesn't really attempt to prove this proposition as a philosopher would, at least not through the rigid application of logic to a well-developed abstract argument. He simply states his convictions in the introductory chapter and then glosses them in enough detail throughout the book so that the reader will know finally with what he is being asked to agree; so the "proof" comes in the body of this beautifully structured book and is cumulative in its rhetorical force. Read to its conclusion, *Ideas Have Consequences* is a devastating polemic, irresistible in its flashes of pure logic and its precise use of evidence.

Although the work is a defense of right reason, Weaver is no narrow rationalist. He makes it clear from the outset that reason itself is not the ultimate source of wisdom but rather sentiment, "an intuitive feeling about the imminent nature of reality." Reason, he points out, is not self-justifying. If one affirms its validity one does so acknowledging a prior commitment to the reasonable nature of reality, to what he calls "the metaphysical dream."

It is this "dream," a belief in transcendence, which has always characterized Western thought and informed its communities, a commitment to the dominion of an ultimate truth under which all other truths are organized and from which they take their meaning. Assuming the existence of those "things unseen" which give form and validity to "things seen," Weaver goes on to draw a conclusion that is unsettling to most twentieth-century sensibilities. He says that a belief in transcendence implies a commitment to political and social hierarchy and a consequent rejection of the egalitarianism that has more and more become the shibboleth of our age. If knowledge and virtue are attributes of the transcendent, he argues, then in choosing their leaders the electorate should seek out these qualities, which all men do not possess equally. The only purely democratic process, he suggests, would be government by lot, since any elective system is based on the implicit but logical idea that some people are better qualified to rule than others.

In discussing this point he has a few words to say about socialism, a tag he uses without apology. Here he shows his rhetorical teeth by terming the Marxist an outgrowth of what they most despise—the middle class, which Weaver describes as "risking little, terrified by change, its aim...to establish a materialistic civilization which will banish threats to its complacency." "The goal of social democracy," he says scornfully, "is scientific feeding."

Though Weaver makes it quite clear that he believes in the idea of equality under the law, he says that other kind of egalitarianism which attempts to subvert natural authority merely wants to substitute a bureaucratic hierarchy for the government that Jefferson envisioned, a hierarchy of "gifts and attainments." This segment of Weaver's essay probably seemed more outrageous and less credible three decades ago than it does today, when the tyranny of a federal bureaucracy is beginning to intimidate even those who formerly urged its omnipotence (writers for the *New Republic* now openly complain about the U.S. Postal Service). Still even in the 1980s Weaver's attack on egalitarianism constitutes an implicit scandal to Americans as a whole, who have almost forgotten the formidable limitations the Founding Fathers placed on the conduct of American democracy.

Another dire consequence of egalitarianism, says Weaver, is the fragmentation of modern society into specialists who revere their own isolated rules in a world they regard as economic but who have no understanding of the community as a whole, much less the truths that once undergirded it. Knowledge of the whole of Creation was the aspiration of the medieval "philosophic doctor" and his successor the renaissance gentleman; but in more recent times, the so-called expert is so obsessed with his own fragment of the puzzle that he stands on the borderline of psychosis. Or so Weaver argues, echoing the sentiments of T. S. Eliot, Allen Tate, John Crowe Ransom and a number of other literary critics who took up this problem in an effort to explain the plight of the modern poet in a technocratic society that no longer has use for his wisdom.

Weaver also considers the situation of modern artists and artisans, demonstrating that labor of any sort in contemporary society is regarded as a necessary evil, whereas in earlier times, with some transcendent idea of what work should accomplish, people took pride in their craftsmanship; for, as he puts it, "to labor is to pray, for conscientious effort to realize an ideal is a kind of fidelity." Again it is the ideal, the transcendent, that gives meaning and dignity to everyday life. Thus, with the modern rejection of universal truth, even the daily activity of life-sustaining labor is rendered dull and meaningless merely a means to material self-gratification. The result: built-in obsolescence and undisciplined art.

Turning to the popular press, Weaver argues that the counterfeit vision of the "media" (not his word) is distorted and simplistic in order to bring the public into easy conformity with current orthodoxy. Summarizing his opinion Weaver writes, "How...can one hesitate to conclude that we would live in greater peace and enjoy sounder moral health if the institution of the newspaper were abolished entirely?" His only optimistic observation is that despite persistent and dishonest opposition from the press, right-minded politicians are still elected to public office and skepticism is widening, even among educated people, as to the credibility of the media.

And what kind of society do the falsifiers of truth depict for Americans to admire? Weaver concludes that we are urged to be spoiled children, addicted to comfort and incapable of any heroic sacrifice, a generation of undisciplined egotists who are less and less willing to work for the plethora of material goods our leaders tell us we deserve. In addition, he points out that, driven by envy and bewildered by the presence of unequal wealth when he cannot admit unequal merit, modern man moves to take away the property of others with the fallacious argument that "property rights should not be allowed to stand in the way of human rights."

It is important to note here that Weaver considers property to be "the last metaphysical right" upon which other rights depend, and he does so not out of any deep-seated conviction that the free-market economy is superior to collectivism or that capitalism is the salvation of the West, but out of a reasonable assumption about the essential nature of freedom and man's capacity to act morally when he is owned outright by some impersonal social institution, however benevolently conceived. Here and only here does Weaver's traditionalism strike a sort of accommodation with the economic conservatives of the Northeast. The rest of the time they stand beyond the pale of his philosophy and are often the enemy, particularly when they smack of social Darwinism.

In the final analysis, what Weaver defends in his brilliant study is something as simple and elusive as truth, the kind of truth that men once believed in as a matter of course, even when they disagreed about its nature. But truth requires property to defend it; piety towards nature, neighbors, the past to nurture it; and a renewed respect for language to reveal it and to render it compelling. This truth is the tenuous thread he offers as a means to escape from the labyrinthine modernity that he has defined for us all too well.

III.

Like *Ideas Have Consequences, The Ethics of Rhetoric* is one of those small books that has the power to alter the thinking of an entire generation. Unfortunately, it hasn't done so, largely, I suspect, because too many people believe it is for specialists in linguistic studies. And indeed two or three chapters are so restricted in their focus that they may be of no more than passing interest to the general reader. But the book as a whole is not about language alone but about social and political truths, about the ultimate realities which stand behind words and inform the structure of Being itself. In fact, of all Weaver's works I find this one the most original and incisive. Here he is on his own, no longer apprentice to the Agrarians, an accomplished master ready to do things that Ransom, Davidson and Tate could not do well, if at all.

The book begins with a commentary on Plato's *Phaedrus* that serves as a framework for the essays that follow, defining for the reader the way in which the persuasive user of language, the rhetor, must approach words in order to be morally worthy of his task. I am not thoroughly familiar with the scholarship, but I suspect that this interpretation of Plato's famous dialogue (which is ostensibly about love rather than language) is one of the most original essays ever written on the Greek philosopher. Yet Weaver is surely right when he argues that Plato's two kinds of lovers—the selfish lover and the unselfish lover—are intended to be seen as rhetors who approach language, the object of their affection, with a desire either to exploit it for their own ends or else to serve the ultimate truth that language, at its best, reveals.

The false lover (rhetor) is the Sophist, who still uses any means to achieve his ends. He does not believe that the truth exists, so the manner in which he manipulates grammar, logic, and rhetoric is subject to no external restrictions, such as those of moral conscience. He therefore feels free to say anything that will help him possess what he most yearns after. He strives to use the beloved for his own gratification rather than to love for the beloved's sake. The Greek word for such love is "eros"; the English word is "lust." And such love is radically self-centered and finally immoral, since it grows out of a total disregard for the sanctity of the beloved, which, in Weaver's argument, is ultimate truth.

The true lover (rhetor) on the other hand, believes in the infinite worth of the beloved and will therefore use language in such a way as to reveal this worth rather than to distort or abuse it. This lover will not violate the sanctity of the beloved, will not falsify logic and language in order to achieve his ends; for he wants to be servant rather than master. Such love in the Greek is called "agape" and in older English usage was "charity," though significantly the distinction between "eros" and "agape" is impossible to make in our contemporary diction.

What Weaver is attacking in this essay is the loose morality that lies behind such modern rhetors as advertising copy writers and ambitious politicians, who will say anything in order to sell their product or to be elected to office. If such people know about logic at all they use their knowledge to deceive members of their audience rather than to enlighten them. In fact, the advertisements in magazines and on television offer prime classroom examples of fallacious reasoning to the few college professors who still teach courses in formal logic, and the next best source for such negative examples is political discourse, not excluding the rhetoric found on the front pages of newspapers and on the CBS evening news, Dan Rather reporting.

If this essay is the most original and broad-ranging in the collection, Weaver's discussion of the Scopes trial is perhaps the most dramatic. Anyone who has seen *Inherit the Wind* or read retrospective accounts of the famous showdown at Dayton must think that Clarence Darrow was a quiet defender of justice while Williams Jennings Bryan was a blustering fool. They must also have concluded that Scope's conviction was one of those mean and arbitrary judgements that are sometimes handed down in rural courts when simple people get their backs up and refuse out of prejudice to do what the law prescribes. To everyone who has accepted this interpretation of the events at Dayton, Weaver offers a devastating rebuttal, one that no honest observer could seriously quarrel with, so carefully mustered is his evidence.

In the first place, it seems that Bryan was by no means a fool in the conduct of the trial—at least not *all* the time. His famous attempt to defend Biblical literalism was, of course, ludicrous, even to those intelligent men who agreed with him on the subject. But, as Weaver points out, the question of Biblical or scientific truth should never have been at issue in the first place, that Bryan understood this point, and that he eloquently argued as much to the judge, who erred in failing to restrict the testimony to matters of legal relevance. In quoting extensively from the transcript of the trial, Weaver demonstrates beyond reasonable doubt that at one stage of the proceedings it was Bryan rather than Darrow who was the masterful logician and that he all but won the legal case before he ever took the stand to talk about Adam and Noah and the Whale.

In the first place, as Bryan argued (and as Weaver affirms), the wisdom of the Tennessee law forbidding the teaching of any creation theory (whether scientific or Biblical) was not an issue to bring before the court. It was, instead, a matter properly addressed in the legislature, where such law, according to the federal and state constitutions, are to be debated and either passed or rejected. If the law is unwise, Bryan argued, then it should be repealed. But once passed, it has to be obeyed unless one wants to argue that the people of a state, who pay for the establishment of public schools through their taxes, have no right to say what subjects are to be taught there—a proposition patently absurd. You couldn't simply claim that because a few self-appointed experts say that the theory of evolution should be taught, the courts can presume to set aside the judgment of the people of the state.

Darrow, of course, called to his aid a number of expert witnesses who argued the truth of evolution as an "accepted fact." Bryan, however, countered by saying that the truth or falsity of evolution was finally irrelevant, since a number of truths and facts were not taught in the public schools for one reason or another.

In discussing this exchange Weaver points out that the truth of evolution was by no means a "fact," as Darrow and his experts argued, but something two times removed from fact. A fact, he says, is a verifiable entity in time and space. To suggest that facts have a relationship to one another, as Darwin does, is to express an opinion about fact. To say that this opinion is true is to express an opinion about an opinion about a fact, a distinction that Bryan seemed better able to make than Darrow, who wanted to argue that the state of Tennessee had no right to suppress "truth," whatever the social consequences.

At this point, Bryan delivered what should have been the *coupe de grace* in an exchange you can bet Mencken never reported. He pointed out that Darrow—who now maintained that the state had no right to omit the theory of evolution from its curriculum—had only recently defended Leopold and Loeb on precisely the opposite grounds. The community, Darrow had argued in Illinois, was partially to blame for the "thrill murder" of a young boy by two college students. And why? Because these killers had been inspired to commit their cold-blooded act by the writings of Nietzsche, *which they found in the public library*. If the public allows such dangerous ideas to be broadcast, Darrow had thundered, then how can they hold these young impressionable students entirely to blame for what they did.

Bryan quickly pointed out the horrid inconsistency of Darrow's argument in Illinois; and his argument in Tennessee; and he was not too foolish or too senile to note that Nietzsche's theory was based in some measure on the theory of evolution, which Darrow now wanted to say was undeniably true and therefore could not be banned from the curriculum of Tennessee schools.

In Weaver's account, we see a Bryan and a Darrow hithertofore hidden from the public eye. Instead of the doddering old bigot we find the aging orator who still has a few arrows left in his quiver, the great champion of the people who makes one last stand for their rights, this time in the face of a new breed of technocrats who want to control education without any interference from those who establish and pay for it. Darrow, on the other hand, is no longer quite the doughty defender of truth but rather a seedy sentimentalist who uses his rhetorical powers first on one side and then the other, wherever whim or fame or the Almighty Dollar beckons. And the contrast between the two illustrates precisely the thesis that Weaver explores in *Ideas Have Consequences*: that those who believe in truth are better able to make distinctions than those who argue from the gut of their own egos.

Turning from Bryan and Darrow, he takes up Abraham Lincoln and Edmund Burke, and here I have a problem with his perspective. If he errs at all in this volume it is in his love for what he calls "the argument from definition," a deductive approach that deals in abstract principles rather than in particulars of the concrete world. In contrast to the argument from definition he cites the "argument from circumstance," an inductive approach that draws on the particularities surrounding an issue without significant reference to abstract truth. I will say more about this blind spot later, though I don't believe it is crucial to an understanding of Weaver's thought as a whole. At this point suffice it to say that he chooses Lincoln to illustrate the argument from definition and Burke for the argument from circumstance, questionable choices, I think, though Weaver's illustrative passages are convincing enough.

Since Weaver himself is a believer in the validity of ultimate definitions, why should he choose Abraham Lincoln for his model of this method? Lincoln was among the most pragmatic abusers of legal definition in his unrestrained efforts to save the Union. On the other hand, why should Weaver—a traditionalist by temperament—choose a like-minded thinker, Edmund Burke, to illustrate what he considers the "lower road" in formal argument (though a permissible one)?

I don't know the answers to these questions, but I suspect that he adopted this strategy because he knew his audience and concluded that if he hoped to make any impact on their modern, secular sensibilities he would have to do so by shocking them into some new understanding of the nature of rhetoric. "To those of you who want to argue pragmatically," he may have been saying, "look to your greatest hero, Lincoln, who at his best argues from immutable principle. On the other hand, look at Burke, whose philosophy you despise, and see how often he argues the way you do. Which would you rather emulate? And are you not now ready to reconsider your rejection of the idea of higher truth?"

At worst, this strategy makes a few of us uncomfortable, though we cannot deny the persuasive selection of examples that he places before us. We can only say in reply that Lincoln often argued from circumstance and that Burke argued from definition, though never without some reference to the real world in which all human action takes place. (If I had to choose between the two, I would take Burke and the argument from circumstance; but such a choice would surely be a false dilemma, and Weaver is by no means suggesting that we must be impaled on its horns.)

The other essays in this volume are almost as rewarding as those I have singled out, though perhaps a little less innovative and profound. But all are directly relevant to the idea that rhetoric and thought go hand in hand and that together they constitute the most vital informing force in the political order. To many of us who have made a career of studying language this book is awesome and moving, the only one of Weaver's studies, it seems to me, that gives us the full measure of his quiet and impregnable genius. Alone it could stand as the achievement of a lifetime—and one that would bid to have a perennial and curative effect on the scholarly community.

IV.

The Southern Tradition at Bay, though published posthumously in 1968, was written over twenty-five years earlier as a doctoral dissertation and then revised later for publication. Significantly Cleanth Brooks was "Chairman of the Examining Committee" and both Robert Penn Warren and John Crowe Ransom receive thanks in Weaver's original preface. But written acknowledgement of his debt is unnecessary, because the text itself amply reveals the degree to which his thought is an extension of Agrarianism. Indeed the published version of this study could be regarded as a formal and scholarly presentation of the arguments made in *I'll Take My Stand* and in other diverse essays of that group during the 1930s.

For one thing, Weaver begins where they began—with an attack on science and technology as "the most powerful force of corruption in our age." Such a statement seems almost commonplace in the 1980s, because what Weaver and the Agrarians were saying a half century ago has now become part of a new and confused leftist orthodoxy so mindless and militant that if one didn't know better, one might be tempted to feel sorry for the military-industrial complex.

Of course the young street politicians of our day have yet to see the connection between a sinister technology and the ills of widespread urbanization, something that Weaver makes explicit in this volume when he writes, "Man has lost piety toward Nature in proportion as he has left her and shut himself up in cities with rationalism for his philosophy." Against this trend in the nation as a whole, Weaver juxtaposes the South, which, he says, is "alone among the sections...in regarding science as a false messiah." Why this statement is true really constitutes the subject of his study as a whole, and he explains in fine and abundant detail the several important characteristics of the modern Southerner's heritage which have fortified him against the assault of modernity.

First, he says, the region from its earliest times subscribed to a "feudal system" patterned after a declining European order. Agricultural in its economic bias, Southern society was hierarchial in structure, with the plantation as the model of the community and each member of the plantation household assuming a definite station and task in the scheme of things. "In the social order which was overthrown by the Civil War," Weaver writes, "there existed a feature of feudalism incomprehensible to the modern mind with its egotism and enlightened selfishness, subordination without envy, and superiority without fear."

Even the Agrarians had not been willing to go so far, and in essay after essay they deny that the South was aristocratic (Weaver says that in some respects it was), and they point most often to the yeoman farmer as a normative figure rather than to the plantation owner. In fact, Weaver does in his study what the Agrarians have been mistakenly accused of doing—offering a militant defense of the Old Regime. And while Weaver is careful to include careful qualifications, in a sense he is the most unreconstructed of them all.

He exhibits this quality most clearly in his brief discussion of the code of chivalry, an important element in the temperament of the Old South, which he feels has affected the evolving nature of the region, even into modern times. Without pursuing the matter too vigorously, he calls Southern chivalric notions "a romantic idealism, closely related to Christianity, which makes honor the guiding principle of conduct," and he argues that "it was an institution of strong and, on the whole, good influence," though at least one observer has blamed it for the loss of the War.

His explanation for the appearance of such a tradition is altogether different from that of Mark Twain and a host of latter-day critics who have said that Southerners took too seriously the spirit of what they read in the romances of Sir Walter Scott. The Scott theory is widely accepted, but Weaver's account is down-to-earth, historical, and less archly literary: "Since chivalry has been one of the main traditions of European civilization," he says, "it was not strange that a chivalric code should develop in the South, which was disposed to accept rather than reject European traditions." Simple enough, and more credible than Twain and his followers who have never bothered to explain why Southerners would have been attracted to Scott's works in the first place if they had not been *predisposed* to admire the chivalric.

Weaver's discussion of the gentleman and his education is much fuller and considerably more rewarding than his treatment of chivalry, though here again he is cutting against the grain of current mythology. Much has been written in refutation of the idea that Southerners were educated at all, much less that they were given the "humanistic" preparation that Weaver supposes, an education that emphasized "the classic qualities of magnificence, magnanimity, and liberality." Yet Weaver offers numerous examples and convincing glosses; his treatment is more than merely sentimental opinion, which is all the negative side in this debate can muster.

His treatment of Southern religion, like that of the Agrarians, suggests that the region's piety is constant but compromised by "doctrinal innocence"; for, as he says, "the average Southerner knew little and appeared to care less about casuistical theology or the metaphysical underlying all religion—what he recognized was the acknowledgement, the submissiveness of the will, and that general respect for order, natural and institutional, which is piety. A religious solid South preceded the political solid South"

The benefits of such theological laxity, according to Weaver, were a high degree of religious quiescence and a belief among neighbors of various sects that "a certain portion of life must remain inscrutable." He admits, however, that the shortcomings of this attitude are more far-reaching.

For in an epilogue to *The Southern Tradition at Bay* he says that one of the great errors of the South has been "a failure to study its position until it arrived at metaphysical foundations." No Southerner, he argues, "could say why the South was right finally," and as a consequence, when the region was attacked by its Puritan enemies, Southerners had nothing to offer in response but impotent and uncontrollable anger. What has always been needed, he says, is a *Summa Theologica,* a comprehensive study of the Southern mind written by a Burke or a Hegel instead of random essays by lawyers and journalists.

On such a magnum opus, he says, a new and successful initiative might still be mounted, "one which would give the common man a world view completely different from that which he has constructed out of his random knowledge of science." Such a counteroffensive—which he feels must be carried to the enemy by poets, artists, and intellectuals—would involve remanning "the barricades of revealed Christianity, of humanism, of sentiment," though not, he says, in the name of the Lost Cause, whose final offensive failed in the 1890s with the organization of the United Confederate Veterans and their subsequent failure to attract new recruits from the young. An effective movement, he concludes, must subtly incorporate the values of the past while exploiting the rhetoric of progress and the future.

It is impossible with justice to gloss and praise this substantial volume, which is richer and more complicated than Weaver's other works, though perhaps not so original. As Donald Davidson points out in his introduction to the published edition, Weaver uses every conceivable type of source in examining his subject—political, literary, personal, public—and he does so with careful attention to dissenting opinion and to embarrassing exceptions. He is neither unequivocally positive about its future. But he does offer something more than tenuous apologies or outright apostasy. He has written a call to battle that we can ignore only at our peril, and he may have written the very work he calls for at the end of his long and rewarding study. Not to consider that possibility is to pay him less homage than he clearly deserves.

V.

Weaver has been dead twenty years now, and he has been missed every single day; but the same old wrecking crew is with us still, tearing down what is old and well-built in order to throw up something modern and transient, their mouths pursed, their worried little eyes blinking nervously. They constantly consult their watches, new ones which they have to press in order to see. They are behind schedule. American society should have been torn down long before now. The foundation for an entirely new economic system was to have been poured last Thursday. And now Reagan is in the White House, which means further delays (though not as many as they once feared). They shout to one another. The bulldozers roar into action. The driver sets down the grade. And they're off in a flurry of endless activity, for they know that you can't destroy a world if you don't keep moving.

At the same time, somewhere in a classroom or library, Richard Weaver through the printed word continues to explain where we have gone wrong and how we can correct our error. He insists that we have time if we will only proceed with reason and prudence. No one has won or lost anything—at least, not yet.

Indeed, Weaver and his mentors the Agrarians, speak more forcefully in the year 1983 than they did in the 1930s and 1940s. Yet some of us who admire and believe them are not sure if they are prophets of a genuine cultural renaissance or the last survivors of an order that has, like all its predecessors, doomed itself to final destruction. It depends on how our day has gone, doesn't it? Or what we read in the morning newspapers. None of us is as certain about things as Weaver was, though he never held out false hopes or underestimated the difficulty of a Restoration.

But of course he brought some strengths to the battle that most of us lack, and I would like to say just a word about them. First, however, in deference to his own argumentative practice, I feel obliged to mention what I consider to be his shortcomings, which are so inconsequential as to warrant no more than a sentence or two.

First, it seems to me that he is occasionally just a bit too Platonic to credit the full complexity of human beings and their corporate behavior. He has God the Father (the Mind) well in hand, but from time to time he has a little trouble with the Son and the Holy Spirit. You don't always have a problem solved when you explain it in reasonable terms, and there is a case to be made for a folk wisdom that contributes as much to political understanding as do the Philosopher Kings; Weaver didn't often forget how wise his own uneducated mountain neighbors could be, but he sometimes did. And they would never have been caught using anything but an argument from circumstance, believing, as they did, in the absolute truth of the Incarnation.

Second, like Davidson, Ransom and the early Tate, Weaver thinks and says too little about the Church's role in the definition of western culture—past, present and future. (Only Cleanth Brooks and Andrew Lytle are sound here.) The medieval certitude he admired was, after all, a characteristic of Christendom, only Platonic by way of St. Augustine and, to a far lesser degree, St. Thomas Aquinas. But it was the body and soul of the Church as much as its mind that gave order and meaning to the medieval world, and I could not imagine a Restoration of the sort for which Weaver worked that would not have a revitalized Christianity at its center.

Weaver knew these things most of the time and took them into account. In addition, he brought some extraordinary virtues into the great struggles of our age, virtues which the rest of us lack. First, he had a genuinely philosophic mind rather then a merely a polemical one. Davidson, the best polemicist in the group, was content to muster his rhetoric for The Cause without probing too deeply into the substratum of meaning that would engage a disinterested student of Western thought. Tate and Lytle delved more profoundly beneath the surface as they ground their axes, polemicists with definite philosophical import. Weaver, however, is always the philosopher first, though he never hesitates to fly his colors and do battle with the enemy. *Ideas Have Consequences,* therefore, has a logical rigor and a formal structure which give the work an air of authority that it would lack as a mere essay of opinion.

Then, too, Weaver had a rugged honesty about him that made his writings both ingenuous and intimidating. At times he was almost blunt in his statements about such controversial issues as equality, freedom and the press. Where his logic led him he followed, and when he came to an unpopular conclusion he was not afraid to state it plainly, the way mountain people generally do. He could muster rhetoric for every legitimate purpose, but he never used it to mitigate or conceal truth in order to placate the spirit of the age. The rest of us, for the most part, lack his courage, and as a consequence fall short of his strength and power.

Finally, he generated an aura of absolute faith in all that he wrote and said. By the time he finished *The Southern Tradition at Bay* he had put socialism behind him, reordered his thinking, and come to a final accommodation with the world. And while he changed his mind about some matters in later years, he never gave an inch on the fundamentals. For this reason you can read his works—each quite different in concept and focus—and know that he was the same man at the end that he was when late in life, he came over to the losing side and took his station, beside a ragged and beleaguered band of defenders. Before Ransom, Davidson and the rest he was taken; and we are left with his indispensable legacy of thought and with the challenge of a life lived in service to a splendid vision of order that no crew of sleek upstarts can ever tear down.

Selected Bibliography

Books by Richard M. Weaver

Ideas Have Consequences. Chicago: The University of Chicago Press, 1948. (Reprinted in paperback, 1950.)
The Ethics of Rhetoric. Chicago: Henry Regnery Co., 1953. (Published in 1985 in the United States by Hermagoras Press, Davis, Calif.)
Composition: A Course in Reading and Writing. New York: Holt, Rinehart, and Winston, 1957. (Revised with the assistance of Richard S. Beal and reprinted as *Rhetoric and Composition,* 2d ed., 1967.)
Visions of Order: The Cultural Crisis of Our Time. Baton Rouge: Louisiana State University Press, 1964.
Life without Prejudice and Other Essays. Chicago: Henry Regnery Co., 1965.
The Southern Tradition at Bay: A History of Postbellum Thought, edited by George Core and M. E. Bradford. New Rochelle, N.Y.: Arlington House, 1968. (Published in 1989 by Regnery Gateway, Washington, D.C.).
Language is Sermonic: Richard M. Weaver on the Nature of Rhetoric. edited by Richard L. Johannesen, Rennard Strickland, and Ralph T. Eubanks. Baton Rouge: Louisiana State University Press, 1970. (Reprinted in paperback, 1985.)
The Southern Essays of Richard M. Weaver, edited by George M. Curtis III and James J. Thompson, Jr. Indianapolis: Liberty Press, 1987.

Selected Essays and Other Publications by Richard M. Weaver

"The Best of Everything." *National Review* 1 (1 February 1956): 21-22.
"The Middle of The Road: Where It Leads." *Human Events* (24 March 1956).
"The Middle Way: A Political Meditation." *National Review* 3 (20 January 1957), 63-64.
"The Roots of Liberal Complacency." *National Review* 3 (8 June 1957): 541-43.
"Life without Prejudice." *Modern Age* 1 (Summer 1957): 4-8.
"On Setting the Clock Right." *National Review* 4 (13 October 1957): 321-23.
"Individuality and Modernity," in Felix Morley, ed., *Essays on Individuality,* 63-81. Princeton, 1958.

Education and the Individual. Philadelphia: Intercollegiate Society of Individualists, 1959.
"Up from Liberalism." *Modern Age* 2 (Winter 1958-59): 21-32.
"The Regime of the South," *National Review* 6 (14 March 1959): 587-89.
"Conservatism and Libertarianism: The Common Ground." *The Individualist* 4 (old series, May 1960): 4-8.
"Mass Plutocracy." *National Review* 9 (5 November 1960): 273-75, 290. (Reprinted in *The Individualist* 5 [October 1960]: 5-8.)
Relativism and the Crisis of Our Time. Philadelphia: The Intercollegiate Society of Individualists. 1961.
"The Importance of Cultural Freedom." *Modern Age* 5 (Winter 1961-1962): 21-34.
Academic Freedom: The Principle and the Problems. Philadelphia: Intercollegiate Society of Individualists, 1963.
"Two Types of American Individualism." *Modern Age* 7 (Spring 1963): 119-34.
"The Humanities in the Century of the Common Man." *New Individualist Review* 2, no. 3 (1964): 17-24.
"The American as a Regenerate Being," edited by George Core and M. E. Bradford. *Southern Review* 4, n.s. (Summer 1968): 633-46.
"Realism and the Local Color Interlude," edited by George Core. *Georgia Review* 22 (Fall 1968): 300-305.

Essays and Articles About Richard M. Weaver

Amyx, Clifford. "Weaver the Liberal: A Memoir." *Modern Age* (Spring 1987): 101-106.
Ancil, Ralph T. "Richard Weaver and the Metaphysics of Property." *Intercollegiate Review* (Spring 1992): 33-43.
Bliese, John. "Rhetoric and the Tyrannizing Image." *Modern Age* (Spring/Summer 1984): 208-14.
Bradford, M. E. "The Agrarianism of Richard Weaver: Beginnings and Completions." *Modern Age* (Summer/Fall 1970): 249-56.
―――. Review of *Language is Sermonic*. In *National Review* (17 November 1970).
Bradford, M. E., and George Core. Introduction to *The Southern Tradition at Bay.*
Brown, Calvin S. "Southern Thought and National Materialism." *The Southern Literary Journal* 1, no. 2 (Fall 1969). (Review of *The Southern Tradition at Bay.*)
Brownfeld, Allan. "The South Wisely Perceived." *University Bookman* (Fall 1989): 17-22. (Review of *The Southern Essays of Richard Weaver.*)

Core, George. Review of *Life without Prejudice and Other Essays*. *Georgia Review* (Fall 1967): 416.

———. "One View of the Castle: Richard Weaver and the Incarnate World of the South." In *The Poetry of Community: Essays on the Southern Sensibility of History and Literature*, edited by Lewis P. Simpson. Atlanta: Georgia State University, 1972.

———. Foreword to *The Southern Essays of Richard Weaver*, xi–xiii.

Core, George, and M. E. Bradford. Introduction to *The Southern Tradition at Bay*.

Davidson, Donald. "The Vision of Richard Weaver." Foreword to *The Southern Tradition at Bay*, 13–25.

———. "The Inspired Amateur." *Modern Age* (Spring 1966): 206–207. (Review of *Life without Prejudice and Other Essays*.)

Davidson, Eugene. "Richard Malcolm Weaver—Conservative." *Modern Age* (Summer 1963): 226–30.

East, John P. "The Conservatism of Affirmation." *Modern Age* (Fall 1975): 338–54. (Also in *The American Conservative Movement: The Philosophical Founders*. Washington, D.C.: Regnery/Gateway, 1986.)

Ebbit, Wilma R. "Richard M. Weaver, Teacher of Rhetoric." *Georgia Review* (Winter 1963): 415–18.

Eubanks, Ralph T. "Richard M. Weaver: In Memoriam." *Georgia Review* (Winter 1963): 412–15.

Fermatt, John. Review of *Ideas Have Consequences*. *Catholic World* (June 1948): 278–79.

Frankel, Charles. "Property, Language, and Piety." *The Nation* (29 May 1948): 609–10. (Review of *Ideas Have Consequences*.)

Garrison, W. E. "Unraveling Mr. Weaver." *The Christian Century* (5 May 1948): 415–16. (Review of *Ideas Have Consequences*.)

Geiger, George R. "We Note...the Consequences of Some Ideas." *Antioch Review* (June 1948): 251–54.

Havard, William C. "Richard Weaver: The Rhetor as Philosopher," in *The Vanderbilt Tradition: Essays in Honor of Thomas Daniel Young*, 163–174. Baton Rouge: Louisiana State University Press, 1991.

Hobson, Fred. "Richard Weaver." In *Tell About the South: The Southern Rage to Explain*, 323–35. Baton Rouge: Louisiana State University Press, 1983.

Johannesen, Richard L., Rennard Strickland, and Ralph T. Eubanks. "Richard M. Weaver on the Nature of Rhetoric." Introduction to *Language is Sermonic*, 7–30.

Jordan, Michael. "Richard Weaver and the True Southern Spirit." *Southern Partisan* (Spring 1988): 34–36. (Review of *The Southern Essays of Richard Weaver*.)

Kendall, Willmoore. "How to Read Richard Weaver: Philosopher of We the [Virtuous] People." *Intercollegiate Review* (September 1965): 77-86.

―――. Review of *Ideas Have Consequences*, in *The Conservative Affirmation*, 184-87. Chicago: Henry Regnery Company, 1963.

Kirk, Russell. "Ethical Labor." *Sewanee Review* (July 1954): 485-503. (Review of *The Ethics of Rhetoric* and *The Quest for Community* by Robert Nisbet.)

―――. "Richard M. Weaver, R.I.P." *National Review* 14 (23 April 1963), 308. (Reprinted in *Confessions of a Bohemian Tory*. New York: Fleet Publishing Corporation, 1963; and *The Individualist* [September 1963]: 2.)

―――. Introduction to *Visions of Order*. Baton Rouge: Louisiana State Press, 1964.

Landess, Thomas. "Is the Battle Over...Or Has It Just Begun? The Southern Tradition Twenty Years After Richard Weaver." *Southern Partisan* (Spring 1983): 11-19.

Meyer, Frank S. "Richard M. Weaver: An Appreciation." *Modern Age* (Fall 1970): 243-48.

Milone, Victor, E. "The Uniqueness of Richard M. Weaver." *The Intercollegiate Review* 2 (September 1965): 67.

Montgomery, Marion. "Richard M. Weaver, 1948." *Modern Age* (Summer/Fall 1982): 252-55. Reprinted in a different form as "Afterword: Looking Before and After," in *The Men I Have Chosen for Fathers*, 232-38. Columbia: University of Missouri Press, 1991.

―――. "Richard Weaver against the Establishment: The Southern Tradition at Bay," in *The Men I Have Chosen for Fathers*, 103-27. Columbia: University of Missouri Press, 1991.

Muller, Herbert J. "The Revival of the Absolute." *Antioch Review* (March 1949): 99-110. (Review of *Ideas Have Consequences*.)

Orton, W. A. Review of *Ideas Have Consequences*. *Commonweal* (14 May 1948): 119-20.

Perry, Charner. Review of *Ideas Have Consequences*. *Ethics* (June 1948): 227-28.

Powell, James. "The Foundations of Weaver's Traditionalism." *New Individualist Review* 2, no. 3 (1964): 3-6.

Regnery, Henry. "A Southern Agrarian at the University of Chicago." *Modern Age* (Spring 1988): 102-12.

Sullivan, Walter. "Richard Weaver and the Bishop's Widow." *Southern Literary Journal* (Spring 1988). Reprinted in a different form in *In Praise of Blood Sports and Other Essays*, 26-38. Baton Rouge: Louisiana State Press, 1990.

Talley, J. M. "The Last Fortress." *Modern Age* (Summer 1964): 305-307. (Review of *The Southern Tradition at Bay*.)

Vivas, Eliseo. "Historian and Moralist." *Kenyon Review* (Spring 1948): 346-49. (Review of *Ideas Have Consequences* and *The Misinterpretation of Man* by Paul Roubiczek.)

———. "The Mind of Richard Weaver." *Modern Age* (Summer 1964): 307-10. (Review of *Visions of Order*.)

———. Introduction to *Life without Prejudice and Other Essays*. Chicago: Henry Regnery, 1965.

Walraff, Charles F. Review of *The Ethics of Rhetoric*. *Arizona Quarterly* (Summer 1954): 183-85.

White, Bruce, A. "Dialectic Rhetorician." *Modern Age* (Summer/Fall 1982): 256-59.

Williamson, Jr., Chilton. "Stranger in Paradise." *National Review* (31 December 1985): 96-98.

About the Contributors

Ralph T. Ancil is president of the Wilhelm Roepke Institute in Kensington, Maryland. He formerly served as an economist in the Office of Program Analysis with the Department of the Interior in Washington, D.C.

John Bliese has served as professor of speech communications and director of forensics at Iowa State University.

M. E. Bradford was a Professor of English at the University of Dallas and a long time contributor to *Sewanee Review, National Review, Modern Age, Chronicles* and *The Southern Partisan*. His many books of social, political and literary criticism include *Generations of a Faithful Heart, A Better Guide Than Reason, Remembering Who We Are, The Reactionary Imperative*, and most recently, *Against the Barbarians*. He also wrote an introduction to the works of Allen Tate and edited a collection of essays on Andrew Lytle. At the time of his death in 1993, Mr. Bradford was editor of *The Southern Classics Series* (published by J.S. Sanders & Company) and at work on a biography of Donald Davidson.

Calvin S. Brown taught English for many years at the University of Georgia where he founded that institution's Department of Comparative Literature. He was a frequent contributor to *Sewanee Review*, writing on such subjects as *Beowulf*, Richard Wagner, and translations of Rilke. His books include *A Glossary of Faulkner's South, Music and Literature: A Comparison of the Arts*, and *Repetition in Zola's Novels*.

Allan Brownfeld is a syndicated columnist and the author of five books, the latest of which is titled *The Revolution Lobby*. He is also associate editor of *The Lincoln Review* and a contributing editor of *America's Future* and *Human Events*.

Donald Davidson was a charter member of both the Fugitive and Agrarian literary movements. For over forty years, he was a member of the English Department at Vanderbilt University. Mr. Davidson was the author of numerous books of poetry, social and literary criticism including *The Long Street, The Tall Men, Lee in the Mountains, The Attack on Leviathan, Still Rebels, Still Yankees,* and *The Tennessee,* the latter a two-volume history of the Tennessee River. He also was the author of a popular textbook, *American Composition and Rhetoric* and a libretto for a folk opera, *Singin' Billy.*

John P. East served as North Carolina's junior United States senator from 1981 until his death in 1986. From 1964 to 1980, he was professor of political science at East Carolina University, Greenville, N.C. Mr. East was the author of *The American Conservative Movement: The Philosophical Founders.* He was a member of the editorial advisory boards of *Modern Age* and *The Political Science Reviewer.*

Ralph T. Eubanks is professor emeritus of communication arts at the University of West Florida.

Richard L. Johannesen is chairman of the Department of Communication Studies at Northern Illinois University.

Thomas Landess was formerly a professor of English at Converse University in South Carolina and at the University of Dallas. He has published a study of Julia Peterkin for the Twayne United States Author Series, a monography on the novelist Larry McMurty, and numerous articles and poems in *Sewanee Review, Southern Review,* and *Mississippi Review.* He is a senior editor at *Southern Partisan* and also works for the U.S. Department of Education in Washington, D.C.

Marion Montgomery is Professor Emeritus of English at the University of Georgia where he had taught writing and literature for more than thirty years. He has published three collections of poems, three novels, a novella, and several volumes of criticism, most recently *Liberal Arts and Community: The Feeding of the Larger Body* and *The Men I Have Chosen for Fathers.*

Henry Regnery is the founder of the Henry Regnery Company, widely recognized as one of the nation's premier publishing companies specializing in conservative literature. In 1977, he founded Gateway Editions, Ltd., Book Publishers, now Regnery/Gateway. He is the author of *Memoirs of a Dissident Publisher.*

Rennard Strickland is John W. Shleppey Research Professor of Law and History at the University of Tulsa.

Eliseo Vivas was a professor of philosophy at many places, including the University of Wisconsin, the University of Chicago, Ohio State University, Northwestern University, and Rockford College. His books include *The Moral Life and the Ethical Life, Creation and Discovery,* and *D.H. Lawrence: The Failure and Triumph of Art.* For over fifty years, he contributed reviews and essays to various scholarly journals.

Bruce A. White has been a writer-in-residence at the University of Maryland.

Chilton Williamson, Jr., is senior book editor for *Chronicles*. He served for a number of years in the same capacity at *National Review*. He is the author of several novels, including *The Homestead*.

Index

Adams, Henry, 25, 47
Adler, Mortimer, 95
Agape, 214
Agrarianism, 10-14, 86-87, 133-41, 159, 218-21
"The Agrarianism of Richard M. Weaver" (Bradford), 11
American Civil War, 23-25, 46-47, 88, 148
American Socialist Party, 20-21, 163
Amyx, Clifford, 3
Ancil, Ralph T., 61-72
Annals of the American Academy, 152
Antioch Review, 152
Aquinas, Thomas (Saint), 222
Arguments, rhetorical, 100-105, 122, 217
Aristotle, 104, 113, 178
Art, modern, 177-78
"Aspects of the Southern Philosophy" (Weaver), 42, 89
Auburn University, 5
Augustine (Saint), 170, 222
Aycock, Charles, 182

Barlowe, Raleigh, 69
Beaton, Kendall, 2
Beethoven, Ludwig van, 178
Bennett, William, 199
Bledsoe, Albert Taylor, 50
Bliese, John, 119-28
Bloom, Allan, 199
Bradford, M.E., 6, 10-11, 112, 119, 133-41, 159
Brooks, Cleanth, 5, 43, 53, 218
Brown, Calvin S., 53-59
Brownfeld, Allan C., 85-90
Bryan, William Jennings, 153, 214-16
Buchanan, Patrick J., 15

Burke, Edmund, 102-3, 113-14, 153-54, 195, 217
Burke, Kenneth, 97, 103
Burnham, James, 14
Bush, George, 15

Carlyle, Thomas, 57, 112, 154
Caruthers, William A., 49
Caste and Class in a Southern Town (Dollard), 42
Cavalier and Yankee (Taylor), 48-50
Charles II, 89
Chivalry, code of, 32-36, 55-57, 219-20
Chodorov, Frank, 12
The Christian Century, 152
Christianity, 30, 115, 124, 168-76, 222-23
The City of God (St. Augustine), 170
Civil War. *See* American Civil War
Classless society, 56-57
The Closing of the American Mind (Bloom), 199
College English, 104
Commonweal, 152
Composition (Weaver), 9, 93-94, 104
Confederacy, 54
"The Confederate South, 1865-1910" (Weaver dissertation), 6
Conservatism, 10-14, 96-97, 163-64
   Christian roots of, 168-74
   Platonic roots of, 164-68
The Conservative Mind (Kirk), 160
The Conservative Movement (Fleming & Gottfried), 15
Cooper, James Fenimore, 49
Corbett, Edward P.J., 104
Core, George, 6, 159
Couch, William T., 8-9, 149, 161
Cratylus (Plato), 67

Culture, 78
  nature of, 80-81, 114-15
  and rhetoric, 119-28

Darrow, Clarence, 153, 214-16
Darwin, Charles, 80, 157, 213, 216
Davidson, Donald, 16, 41-51, 53-54, 94, 117, 139, 159-60, 221, 223
Davidson, Eugene, 115
Davis, Jefferson, 50
Dawson, Christopher, 127
Democracy, 30
Depression. *See* Great Depression
Destruction and Reconstruction (Taylor), 50
Dewey, John, 176
Dialectic, 99, 111-17, 124, 156
Dixon, Thomas, 50
Donnelly, Francis P., 104
Duhmeal, Albert, 7

East, John P., 119, 163-86
Ebbitt, Wilma, 7-8
Education, 115-16
  traditional vs. progressive, 176
Egalitarianism, 211-12
Eliot, T.S., 120, 203-4
Embry, Carrie. *See* Weaver, Carrie Embry
Eros, 214
Ethics, 152
The Ethics of Rhetoric (Weaver), 9, 79, 93, 113-14, 121, 137, 152-55, 164, 213-18
Eubanks, Ralph T., 86, 93-105
Euthyphro (Plato), 173
Evil, existence of, 29-31, 171
Evolution, 153, 157, 214-16

Faulkner, William, 57-59, 87, 203
Fermatt, John, 111-12
Finland, 31
Fleming, Thomas, 15
Ford, Gerald, 15
Fourteenth Amendment, 51
Frankel, Charles, 152
Freedmen, 51
Fugitive-Agrarians, 202, 208

Geiger, George R., 152

Glasgow, Ellen, 50
God without Thunder (Ransom), 5, 22, 46, 113, 136, 163
Goldwater, Barry, 15
Good, idea of, 95
Gottfried, Paul, 15
Great Depression, 3, 20
Greeks, 124, 169, 198

Hale, Sarah Josepha, 49
Hartz, Louis, 48
Hastings, Warren, 103
Havard, William, 6
Hayakawa, S.I., 95
Hayek, Frederich, 12, 160
Herskovits, Melville, 81
Hertz, Richard, 12
Hertzler, J.O., 112
Hobson, Fred, 9
Hook, Sidney, 199
Hooker, Thomas, 172
Hopkins Review, 42
Hundley, Daniel, 49

Ideas Have Consequences (Weaver), 8-9, 11-14, 16-17, 44-45, 61-71, 111-13, 160-61, 164-66, 172-73, 209-13
I'll Take My Stand, 4, 86-87, 89, 133-34, 147, 195, 208, 218
The Impact of Science on Society (Russell), 170
Impressionism, 178
Industrialism, 135
Intercollegiate Studies Institute, 16
Is Davis a Traitor? (Bledsoe), 50

James, Henry, 154
Jazz, 178-79
Jefferson, Thomas, 211
Johannesen, Richard L., 93-105, 119
Johnson, Lyndon, 15
Jones, Howard Mumford, 112, 152
Journalism, 177, 212

Kendall, Willmoore, 94, 119, 164
Kennedy, John Pendleton, 49
Kirk, Russell, 7, 11, 15, 28, 94-95, 102-3, 158, 160, 164, 204
Knowledge, nature of, 95

Landess, Thomas, 207-23
Language, 151
"Language is Sermonic" (Weaver), 9, 86, 94, 116-17, 164
Lee, Robert E., 56, 184
"Lee the Philosopher" (Weaver), 8
Liberalism, 34-35, 113
Libertarianism, 184-85
Life without Prejudice and Other Essays (Weaver), 9, 94, 117, 138-39, 158-59, 164
Lincoln, Abraham, 101, 113-14, 122, 154, 196, 217
Linton, Ralph, 78
Louisiana State University, 5-6
Lytle, Andrew, 139, 223

Man, essential nature of, 96
Maritain, Jacques, 68
Marx, Karl, 69-70
Mass media, 112, 177, 212
Measure, 199
Meyer, Frank S., 11-12, 14, 111, 119, 164
Middle Ages, 172
Milone, E. Victor, 16
Milton, John, 89
The Mind of the South (Cash), 42
Modern Age, 9, 45, 94, 116, 157, 164, 197
Molnar, Thomas, 68
Montgomery, Marion, 10, 197-205
Mozart, Wolfgang, 178
Music, 178-79

NAFTA, 15
The Nation, 20, 152
National Review, 9, 94
New Deal, 7-8, 11-12, 15
New York Times, 152
Niebuhr, Reinhold, 152
Nixon, Richard, 15
Nock, Albert Jay, 12
Nominalism, 112, 120, 150, 174-80, 210

O'Connor, Flannery, 196, 202-3
"The Older Religiousness of the South" (Weaver), 8, 25
One World (Wilkee), 11
Original sin, 150

Origins of the New South (Woodward), 43
Orton, William A., 152
Orwell, George, 114
Owsley, Frank, 139

Page, Thomas Nelson, 50
Page, Walter Hines, 50
Painting, modern, 177-78
Pascal, Blaise, 79
Patriarchy, 70-71
Paulding, James Kirke, 49
Paul (Saint), 172
Peguy, Charles, 19
Perry, Charner, 152
Persian Gulf War, 15
Personality, 63-65
Phaedrus (Plato), 113, 152-53, 213-14
Piety, 64, 172-74
Plato, 13, 67, 94-95, 97-98, 101, 112-13, 151, 164-77, 203, 213-14
Political freedom, 61-62
Property, 61-72, 151, 212-13

Quantrell Prize, 16, 146

Randolph, John, 116, 158
Ransom, John Crowe, 5, 22, 44-45, 94, 113, 136, 139, 147, 163, 181, 218
Reagan, Ronald, 15
Reconstruction, 54
Regnery, Henry, 10, 12, 145-61
Republican Party, 122-23, 195
Rhetoric, 97-105
  and culture, 115, 119-28
Rilke, Rainer Maria, 41
The Road to Serfdom (Hayek), 12, 160
Rockford Institute, 16
Roosevelt, Franklin D., 11-12, 155
Russell, Bertrand, 170

Samuel, Maurice, 34
Schopenhauer, Arthur, 26
Scopes, John T., 153, 215
Scopes trial, 153, 214-16
Scotchie, Joseph, 1-17
Scott, Sir Walter, 219
Sherman, William T., 56
Shils, Edward, 7
Simms, William Gilmore, 49

Socialism, 20-21, 45, 147, 163
Socrates, 115-16, 156
Sophocles, 199-200
The Sound and the Fury (Faulkner), 57-59
South, 28-29
  agrarian tradition of, 4, 10-14, 86-87, 94, 133-41, 159, 218-21
  chivalric code of, 32-36, 55-57, 219-20
  heritage of, 6
  literary renascence in, 136
  and national materialism, 53-59
  Old, 180-84
  perception of, 85-90
  postbellum, 47-51
  religiousness of, 25
"A Southern Agrarian at the University of Chicago" (Regnery), 10
The Southern Essays of Richard M. Weaver, 9, 157-59
Southern Partisan, 204
Southern Regions (Odum), 42
Southern Review, 5
The Southern Tradition at Bay (Weaver), 6, 8, 41-51, 53-59, 153, 159-60, 164, 194, 198, 218-21
Stanford University, 198-99
"Stranger in Paradise" (Williamson), 15-16
Streeter, Robert E., 161
Strickland, Rennard, 93-105
Sutherland, William R., 3

Tate, Allen, 23-24, 94, 139, 223
Taylor, Richard, 50
Taylor, William R., 48-50
Texas, 46
Texas A & M University, 5, 23
Thoreau, Henry, 29, 112, 114-16, 158
Thucydides, 126
Tillich, Paul, 93, 152
Transcendentalism, 115-16
Turner, Arlin, 44
Twain, Mark (Samuel Clemens), 219

United Confederate Veterans, 221
University of Chicago, 6-10, 145-61
University of Kentucky, 2-4, 19-20, 147-49

"Up from Liberalism" (Weaver), 4, 19-36, 45, 111, 113, 133, 147, 171, 197-99

Vanderbilt University, 5, 21-22, 94, 146-47, 208
Virtue, 62
Visions of Order (Weaver), 6, 9, 45, 77-82, 93-94, 97, 114-15, 127, 137, 155-57, 164
Vivas, Eliseo, 3, 9-10, 42, 77-82, 93, 115, 117, 127, 146, 152, 157-59
Voegelin, Eric, 202
Von Mises, Ludwig, 12

Wade, John Donald, 139
War, 32-36, 141, 149
Warren, Robert Penn, 5, 43, 94, 139, 218
Washington, Booker T., 113
Washington, George, 13
Weaver, Carrie Embry, 1
Weaver, Ethan Douglas, 145-46
Weaver, John, 1
Weaver, Montraville, 1
Weaver, Richard Malcolm
  agrarianism of, 133-41
  childhood of, 1
  on chivalry, war, and technology, 32-36
  chronological life events of, 37-38
  conservatism of, 10-14, 96-97, 163-86
  education of, 2-6
  on evil, 29-31
  on history, 23-26
  influence of, 14-16
  on metaphysics of property, 61-72, 151, 212-13
  mind of, 77-82
  as rhetorical scholar, 93-105, 151
  at Texas A & M University, 5
  at University of Chicago, 6-10, 145-61
  "Up from Liberalism," 19-36, 111, 113, 133, 147, 171, 197-99
Weaver, Richard Malcolm, Sr., 1
"Weaver the Liberal: A Memoir" (Amyx), 3
Western Civilization (college course), 198-99

White, Bruce A., 111-17, 119-20
Whitman, Walt, 27, 168
Wilkee, Wendell, 11
William of Occam, 68, 112, 120, 150, 174, 210
Williamson, Chilton, Jr., 15-16, 193-96
Wirt, William, 49

Women, 70-71, 152
World War II, 5-6, 31-32, 111, 114-15, 136, 150

Yalta Conference, 31
Yeats, William Butler, 19, 48